Modern Judgements

MARVELL

MODERN JUDGEMENTS

General Editor: P. N. FURBANK

Dickens   A. E. Dyson
Henry James   Tony Tanner
Marvell   Michael Wilding
Milton   Alan Rudrum
O'Casey   Ronald Ayling
Pasternak   Donald Davie and Angela Livingstone
Racine   R. C. Knight
Walter Scott   D. D. Devlin
Shelley   Robert Woodings
Swift   A. Norman Jeffares

IN PREPARATION

Matthew Arnold   P. A. W. Collins
Ford Madox Ford   Richard A. Cassell
Freud   F. Cioffi
Pope   Graham Martin

Marvell

MODERN JUDGEMENTS

edited by

MICHAEL WILDING

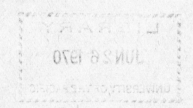
MACMILLAN

Selection and editorial matter © Michael Wilding 1969

First published in 1969 by
MACMILLAN AND CO LTD
Little Essex Street London WC2
and also at Bombay Calcutta and Madras
Macmillan South Africa (Publishers) Pty Ltd Johannesburg
The Macmillan Company of Australia Pty Ltd Melbourne
The Macmillan Company of Canada Ltd Toronto
Gill and Macmillan Ltd Dublin

Printed in Great Britain by
WESTERN PRINTING SERVICES LTD
Bristol

TO EDGAR BILLINGHAM

Contents

Acknowledgements	7
General Editor's Preface	9
Introduction	10
Editor's Note	39
Chronology	41

T. S. ELIOT Andrew Marvell I — 45

T. S. ELIOT Andrew Marvell II — 57

WILLIAM EMPSON Marvell's 'Garden' — 60

CHRISTOPHER HILL Society and Andrew Marvell — 65

CLEANTH BROOKS Marvell's 'Horatian Ode' — 93

DOUGLAS BUSH Marvell's 'Horatian Ode' — 114

FRANK KERMODE The Argument of Marvell's 'Garden' — 125

JOSEPH H. SUMMERS Marvell's 'Nature' — 141

J. V. CUNNINGHAM Logic and Lyric: 'To his Coy Mistress' — 155

F. W. BATESON and F. R. LEAVIS 'A Dialogue between the Soul and Body': a debate — 165

A. ALVAREZ Marvell and the Poetry of Judgement — 182

J. B. LEISHMAN Some Themes and Variations in the Poetry of Andrew Marvell — 194

MAREN-SOFIE RØSTVIG 'Upon Appleton House' — 215

JOHN E. HARDY   Andrew Marvell's 'The
   Coronet': the frame of curiosity   233

E. W. TAYLER   Marvell's Garden of the Mind   249

EARL MINER   The Death of Innocence in
   Marvell's 'Nymph complaining for the death
   of her Faun'   273

Select Bibliography   285
Notes on Contributors   289
Index   293

Acknowledgements

T. S. Eliot, 'Andrew Marvell I', from *Selected Essays*, 1932 (Faber & Faber Ltd) and 'Andrew Marvell II', from *Nation and Athenaeum*, 29 September 1923 (Mrs V. Eliot); William Empson, 'Marvell's "Garden" ', from *Determinations*, ed. F. R. Leavis, 1934 (Chatto & Windus Ltd); Christopher Hill, 'Society and Andrew Marvell', from *Puritanism and Revolution* (Secker & Warburg Ltd and Schocken Books Inc.; © Christopher Hill); Cleanth Brooks, 'Marvell's "Horatian Ode" ', from *English Institute Essays 1946* (Columbia University Press); Douglas Bush, 'Marvell's "Horation Ode" ', from *Sewanee Review*, LX (1952) (Douglas Bush and the University of the South); Frank Kermode, 'The Argument of Marvell's "Garden" ', from *Essays in Criticism II*, 1952 (Professor Frank Kermode and F. W. Bateson); Joseph H. Summers, 'Marvell's "Nature" ', from *Journal of English Literary History*, XX no. 2 (1953) (The Johns Hopkins Press); J. V. Cunningham, 'Logic and Lyric: "To his Coy Mistress" ', from *Modern Philology*, LI (August 1953) 33–8 (University of Chicago Press and the Swallow Press Inc.); F. W. Bateson and F. R. Leavis, ' "A Dialogue between the Soul and the Body": a debate', from 'The Function of Criticism at the Present Time' in *English Poetry: a critical introduction*, by F. W. Bateson, 2nd ed. (1966) (Longmans, Green & Co. Ltd and Barnes & Noble Inc.) and extracts from 'The Responsible Critic: or the function of criticism at any time', by F. R. Leavis (pp. 162–70), F. W. Bateson's reply (pp. 317–19) and F. R. Leavis's reply (p. 322) from *Scrutiny*, XIX (1953) (Cambridge University Press); A. Alvarez, 'Marvell and the Poetry of Judgement', from *The School of Donne* (Chatto & Windus Ltd and the American Library Inc., New York; © A. Alvarez, 1961, 1967); J. B. Leishman, 'Some Themes and Variations in the Poetry of Andrew Marvell', from *Proceedings of the British Academy*, XLVII (1961) (Oxford University Press); Maren-Sofie

Røstvig, 'Upon Appleton House', from *The Happy Man*, 2nd ed. (1962) (Professor Røstvig and Norwegian Universities Press); John E. Hardy, 'Andrew Marvell's "The Coronet": the frame of curiosity', from *The Curious Frame* (© 1962 by University of Notre Dame Press, U.S.A.); E. W. Tayler, 'Marvell's Garden of the Mind', from *Nature and Art in Renaissance Literature* (1964) pp. 142–68 (Professor Edward W. Tayler and Columbia University Press); Earl Miner, 'The Death of Innocence in Marvell's "Nymph complaining for the death of her Faun" ', from *Modern Philology*, LXV (1967) (Professor Earl Miner and the University of Chicago Press).

General Editor's Preface

LITERARY criticism has only recently come of age as an academic discipline, and the intellectual activity that, a hundred years ago, went into theological discussion, now finds its most natural outlet in the critical essay. Amid a good deal that is dull or silly or pretentious, every year now produces a crop of critical essays that are brilliant and profound, not only as contributions to the understanding of a particular author, but as statements of an original way of looking at literature and the world. Hence it often seems that the most useful undertaking for an academic publisher might be, not so much to commission new books of literary criticism or scholarship, as to make the best of what exists easily available. This at least is the purpose of the present series of anthologies, each of which is devoted to a single major writer.

The guiding principle of selection is to assemble the best *modern* criticism – broadly speaking, that of the last twenty or thirty years – and to include historic and classic essays, however famous, only when they are still influential and represent the best statements of their particular point of view. It will, however, be one of the functions of each editor's Introduction to sketch in the earlier history of criticism in regard to the author concerned.

Each volume will attempt to strike a balance between general essays and ones on specialised aspects, or particular works, of the writer in question. And though in many instances the bulk of the articles will come from British and American sources, certain of the volumes will draw heavily on material in other European languages – most of it being translated for the first time.

P. N. FURBANK

Introduction

FOR nearly three centuries the problem facing writers on Andrew Marvell has been how to take into account the different facets of their subject. He was lyric poet, verse satirist, prose controversialist, conscientious Member of Parliament, defender of religious liberty, patriot. These different aspects have all at different times been emphasised, and in the critical and biographical accounts of him we see continually shifting emphases, rather than the achievement of any integrated or balanced assessment of his variety. For the twentieth century he is primarily a lyric poet, and it is something of a shock to realise that for his contemporaries, and for the century and a half following his death, this was the least significant of his roles.

A few of his non-satirical poems are known to have been published or circulated in his lifetime, but they seem to have attracted little comment. John Aubrey, who knew Marvell, remarked briefly that 'he was a great master of the Latin tongue; an excellent poet in Latin or English; for Latin verse there was no man could come into competition with him'.[1] But the hostile author of *A Letter from Amsterdam to a Friend in England* (1678) commented 'it is well he is now transposed into politicks; they say he had much ado to live upon poetry'. Samuel Parker, whom Marvell had attacked in *The Rehearsal Transpros'd*, referred in his *Reproof* (1673) to the attack, to Marvell's 'having profess'd wit and rithm these fifty years' and mentioned his 'juvenile Essays of Ballads, Poesies, Anagrams, and Acrosticks'. Parker returned to Marvell in his *History of His Own Time*, which appeared in an English translation by Thomas Newlin in 1727. Two index entries set the tone: 'Marvel, a scurrilous slanderer, publishes infamous libels', and 'Libels (infamous). See Marvel.' Parker records:

[1] *Aubrey's Brief Lives*, ed. A. Clark (1898) II 53.

As he had liv'd in all manner of wickedness from his youth, so being of a singular impudence and petulancy of nature, he exercised the province of a Satyrist, for the use of the Faction, being not so much a Satyrist thro' quickness of wit, as sowerness of temper; of but indifferent parts, except it were in the talent of railing and malignity. . . . A vagabond, ragged, hungry Poetaster, being beaten at every tavern, he daily receiv'd the rewards of his sawciness in kicks and blows. At length, by the interest of *Milton*, to whom he was somewhat agreeable for his ill-natur'd wit, he was made Under-secretary to *Cromwell*'s Secretary. Pleas'd with which honour, he publish'd a congratulatory poem in praise of the Tyrant; but when he had a long time labour'd to squeeze out a panegyrick, he brought forth a satyr upon all rightful Kings.

And Parker goes on to give a lengthy paraphrase of the 'First Anniversary'. Parker had no doubts about its authorship, although it had first appeared anonymously and had later been attributed to Waller.

In 1681 a posthumous collection of *Miscellaneous Poems* 'By Andrew Marvell, Esq; Late Member of the Honourable House of Commons', was issued. Probably to capitalise on his reputation for political satire, readers were reminded that he was an M.P. Anthony à Wood recorded that upon publication the poems 'were then taken into the hands of many persons of his persuasion, and by them cried up as excellent'.[1] But no record of such praise is known, and any possible political controversy the volume might have provoked was prevented by the removal of the three Cromwell poems during production of the book. Only two copies of the edition are known to contain them.

Marvell was remembered not as a poet, but as a politician of incorruptible integrity, and as a satirist and controversialist. 'This island's watchful sentinel' he is called in the anonymous poem 'On His Excellent Friend, Mr Andrew Marvell' (1678). His name was frequently used in the eighteenth century as an exemplum of loyalty and probity. William Mason made Marvell hero of his 'Ode to Independence' (1756), and Charles Churchill commemorated Marvell's 'spotless virtues' in a sonnet, and in six lines of 'The Author' (1763). To his contemporaries and immediate successors, he was best known for his controversial prose writings. *The Rehearsal Transpros'd* provoked the admiration of Anthony à Wood in *Athenae Oxonienses*, Rochester in 'Tunbridge Wells', Bishop Burnet in his *History of My Own Time* and Swift in the *Tale of a Tub;* Swift, indeed, shows the influence of

[1] Wood, *Athenae Oxonienses*, ed. P. Bliss (1819) IV 232.

Marvell's prose style. And as well as such distinguished praise, Marvell provoked attacks from Dryden in his 'Epistle to the Whigs' and the preface to *Religio Laici*. The verse satires circulated mainly in manuscript during Marvell's lifetime, but they became known to a wider readership after his death, when they were collected in the *Poems on Affairs of State*. Two of those collections announced on their title-page that they were by 'A—— M——l Esq; and other Eminent Wits'. His name, distinctively, was the name to sell a collection of political satires, and this reputation survived into the eighteenth century. Daniel Defoe, writing in his *Review* on 28 March 1713, recorded that the 'Dialogue between the two Horses' 'so pleas'd the king, that tho' it was the bitterest Satyr, *upon him and his Father*, that ever was made, the king would often repeat them [the verses] with a great deal of Pleasure . . .' Having quoted from the satire, Defoe commented:

> Let us see anything so sprightly now from the Wits of this Age, and something may be said for them: A Pasquinade ought to be pointing like a Dart, that should wound Mortally at every cast; the sting should be so very sharp, that it should kill even all the Resentment of the Persons Satyriz'd: so that the Person pointed at should be asham'd to be Angry . . . we pretend much to have a degree of Polite Wit beyond those Days; yet nothing of that keenness of Satyr, the happy turns and brightness of Fancy appears in the Lampoons of this Age, that were seen in *Andr. Marvell*, *Sir John Denham*, *Rochester*, *Buckingham*, *Sidley*, and others . . .

Defoe's comments are as close as we get to analytic criticism; though Joseph Spence in his *Observations, Anecdotes and Characters of Books and Men* assembled from Pope and his circle recorded the defining comment of a Mr Scott saying in 1730 that Marvell's satires were 'rough like Oldham'. No remark of Pope himself is known, though he had certainly read some of the satires.

Enthusiasm for the satires was not, however, universal, and though Marvell has been summoned up as a patriot in John Ayloffe's *Marvell's Ghost* (1689), the patriotism was not always recognised or admired. Thomas Newcomb, in *Bibliotheca . . . a Modern Library* (1712), groaned:

> Nay, to augment my last despair
> Place Ayloffe's self and Marvell there
> (A fam'd dull pair, that purely wrote
> To raise our spleen, and die forgot).

When Nicholls included *Bibliotheca* in his *Select Collection of Poems* (1780) he added the note, 'the satire on Marvell is wonderfully misplaced', but though he included Ayloffe's poem in his collection, Marvell found no place.

II

When we turn from the satires and controversial prose, when we turn from Marvell the public figure to Marvell the lyric poet, however, there is a sudden absence of comment. His *Miscellaneous Poems* seem to have attracted no attention. The explanation must be that, although poems were still being written in a metaphysical style in the 1680s, the taste for the metaphysical conceit was rapidly passing, while a widespread enthusiasm for Marvell's nature reveries had yet to develop. Dryden remarked in the preface to his *Fables* (1700), probably referring to Cowley, 'one of our late great Poets is sunk in his Reputation, because he could never forgive any Conceit which came his way; but swept like a Drag-net, great and small . . .'[1]

For nearly two centuries this distaste for the conceit persisted. Addison's *Spectator* essays on false wit were directed largely against the metaphysical poets, though he never alludes to Marvell. He was, however, familiar with 'To his Coy Mistress'. *Spectator* 89 (12 June 1711), dedicated to 'those that have to do with Women of Dilatory Tempers', contained some striking reminiscences.

> First of all I would have them seriously think on the Shortness of their Time. Life is not long enough for a Coquet to play all her Tricks in. A timorous Woman drops into the Grave before she has done deliberating. Were the Age of Man the same that it was before the Flood, a Lady might sacrifice half a century to a Scruple, and be two or three Ages in demurring. Had she Nine Hundred years good, she might hold out to the Conversion of the *Jews*, before she thought fit to be prevailed upon. . . . The finest Skin wrinkles in a few Years, and loses the Strength of its Colouring so soon, that we have scarce time to admire it.

Though the reminiscence shows clearly that Marvell's poem was known, it shows equally that it was not known well. If Addison plagiarised,

[1] Cited in A. H. Nethercot, 'The Reputation of the "Metaphysical Poets" during the seventeenth century', in *Journal of English and Germanic Philology*, XXIII (April 1924) 196. See also R. L. Sharp, *From Donne to Dryden: the revolt against metaphysical poetry* (Chapel Hill, 1940).

he must have felt confident none of his readers would recognise the original. If, as is usually supposed, the echo was unconscious, it shows he had no cause to be aware of or to make a conscious record of what Marvell wrote.

There was scarcely any critical comment on Marvell's poetry in the eighteenth century, although the poems themselves were far from totally lost to view. Of the non-satirical verse, 'Thyrsis and Dorinda', 'To his Coy Mistress', 'Bellipotens Virgo', 'Eyes and Tears', 'The First Anniversary', 'On Blake's Victory' and 'Climb at Court' were printed in late-seventeenth- and early-eighteenth-century collections, though not always over Marvell's name. But his authorship was clearly ascribed when Tonson included nine poems in both his fourth and fifth editions of Dryden's *Miscellany Poems* in 1716 and 1727: the poems were 'Climb at Court', 'The Nymph', 'Young Love', 'Daphnis and Chloe', 'Damon the Mower', 'Ametas and Thestylis', 'Musicks Empire', 'The Garden' and 'On Paradise Lost'.[1]

Thomas Cooke's two-volume edition of Marvell's works, containing lyrics, satires and some prose, appeared in 1726. 'I make no Doubt, but the Works of a Man, who has every Way deserved so well of his country, as Mr Marvell has, will meet with the Success they deserve', Cooke remarked in his dedication to the Duke of Devonshire. The poems were hung on the peg of Marvell's political reputation, and Cooke had little to say about them.

> There are few of his Poems which have not Something pleasing in them, and some he must be allowed to have excelled in. Most of them seem to be the Effect of a lively Genius, and manly Sense, but at the same Time seem to want that Correctness he was capable of making. If we have any which may be properly said to come finished from his Hands, they are these, *On Milton's Paradise Lost*, *On Blood's stealing the Crown*, and *A Dialogue between two Horses*. The last of which is a Satire good as it is severe...

The lyrics conspicuously failed to arouse Cooke's interest. His concern in his introductory Life was with Marvell's political reputation and writings. The most enthusiastic response to one of Marvell's lyrics in

---

[1] Douglas Bush, *English Literature in the Earlier Seventeenth Century* (Oxford, 1945) p. 103; H. M. Margoliouth, in *Times Literary Supplement*, 19 May 1950, p. 309; T. T. Dombras, ''Poetical Miscellanies 1684–1716' (unpublished D.Phil thesis, Oxford, 1951); E. F. Hart, 'Caroline Lyrics and Contemporary Song-books', in *Library*, VIII 5th series (June 1953) 98, 108–9.

the century occurs in *Human Physiognomy Explained* (1747), a series of lectures to the Royal Society by James Parsons, a doctor of wide reading. Discussing tears, and having quoted from Juvenal, he remarked on 'Eyes and Tears':

> But, besides these, I find an *English* Poet singing their other Uses in the most pathetic and engaging manner; whose charming Song it would be unpardonable to conceal, since no Language can boast of one more expressive upon the Subject, and wherein he has shewn, that Tears are a Blessing peculiar only to human Nature.

He quotes the first twelve stanzas, and appends Marvell's name. Parson's praise is high, and we find nothing similar until the next century. Though he was still remembered as a poet at Cambridge: Edmund Carler in his *History of the University of Cambridge* (1753) recorded amongst the other poets from Trinity, 'Andrew Marvell Esq: the Poet Laureat of the Dissenters; famed for his Wit, but foiled in his own Weapon by Divine Herbert . . .'

Cooke's biography served as the basis for the account of Marvell in volume IV of the *The Lives of the Poets* 'By Mr Cibber and other hands' – in fact by Robert Shiels – (1753). Shiels repeated Cooke's comments and added a further paragraph of his own criticism:

> In order to shew the versification of Mr Marvel, we shall add a beautiful dialogue between the resolved soul, and created pleasure. It is written with a true spirit of poetry, the numbers are various, and harmonious, and is one of the best pieces, in the serious way, of which he is author.

The 'Dialogue' and 'On Blood's Stealing the Crown' are printed in full. Cooke's edition was sufficiently in demand to be reprinted in 1772, and this was followed in 1776 by Captain Edward Thompson's edition of Marvell's works, which for the first time printed all the Cromwell poems – Thompson remarked that 'the English language does not boast a more elegant elegiack poem' than that on the death of Cromwell – as well as work by Addison, Watts and Mallett, which he ascribed to Marvell. 'Poor Mallett!' Gibbon commented, 'his only good piece of poetry . . . turns out to be the work of the celebrated Andrew Marvell.'[1] The poems are relegated to volume III, following the letters to the Hull corporation and the prose. Thompson's comments show perhaps a

---

[1] *Letters of Edward Gibbon*, ed. J. E. Norton (1956) II 110.

little more appreciation of the poetry than Cooke's, but he habitually
drifts into biographical fantasy.

> The compositions of our author are of various sorts, and not less excellent
> in verse than prose; especially any of those pieces with which he has taken
> pains: but in general they appear to be the warm effusions of a lively fancy,
> and are very often thrown off in the extempore moment of their conception
> and birth, whether begotten in satire or humour . . . The poem to his *coy
> mistress* is sweet, natural and easy, and bespeaks his heart to be high in love;
> and perhaps his not being married might arise from her coldness . . . His
> little poem of the *Gallery* loosely and pleasingly depicts this beloved fair one,
> whom he follows through all his pastoral dialogues, and in a most pleasing
> and epigrammatical manner in that of *Thyrsis and Dorinda* . . . The satires
> and state poems are not more severe than humorous; and indeed, when
> satire is conveyed in risible terms, so as to raise the laugh against the object,
> it is the most poignant of any . . .
>
> His poem *Flecknoe*, though in a slovenly metre, contains much humour and
> satire upon that incorrigible poetaster, Richard Flecknoe; which was the
> happy means of giving title, and perhaps birth to the best satyrical poem in
> the English language, I mean *McFlecknoe*, written by the first poet of this
> country . . .

Thompson's choice of Dryden as his 'first poet' explains his lack of
enthusiasm for the 'slovenly metre', and his assumption that Marvell
did not always take pains to perfect his verses.

There were 146 subscribers to Thompson's edition: Gray's edition of
Hudibras in 1745 had 1553 subscribers. Amongst this modest number
were the naturalist Gilbert White and the statesman Edmund Burke.
Burke once quotes from 'On Paradise Lost' (a poem Thompson found
'elegant') in his correspondence,[1] but there is no record of what either
of these writers thought of Marvell. Christopher Smart is one of the
few eighteenth-century poets who shows any familiarity with his
works.[2] Despite Thompson's and Cooke's editions, Marvell was not
thought to be a significant or representative poet in the eighteenth
century. Dr Johnson quoted from 'Ametas and Thestylis' and 'On
Blood's Stealing the Crown' in his *Dictionary* (1755) and from 'On
Paradise Lost' in his life of Dryden twenty-five years later, but, although
the sale catalogue of his library (1785) shows that he possessed a copy

---

[1] *The Correspondence of Edmund Burke*, ed. Alfred Cobban and Robert A. Smith (1967)
VI 23.

[2] See E. E. Duncan-Jones, in *Notes and Queries*, XIV (May 1967) 182.

of Thompson's edition, he did not give Marvell a mention in his onslaught on the metaphysicals in his life of Cowley, though the criticism of the metaphysicals expressed there so classically explains much of Marvell's unpopularity. Anderson in the Preface to his *Poets of Great Britain*, complained at the omission of Marvell (among others) from Johnson's selection, but did not include him in his own, either.

III

With the nineteenth century, interest in Marvell slowly developed. His lyrics were more congenial to Romantic taste than they had been to that of the eighteenth century. Joseph Ritson had included 'The Nymph complaining' in *The English Anthology* (1793), and the second edition of George Ellis's *Specimens of English Poetry* (1801) contained abridgements of 'Daphnis and Chloe' and 'Young Love'. In 1816 the Rev. Francis Wrangham included a life of Marvell in volume IV of *The British Plutarch*, which, though almost totally political in concern, included the verses to Joseph Maniban, 'Bellipotens Virgo', 'The Coronet', 'On Paradise Lost' and 'Britannia and Rawleigh'. The *Quarterly Review* complained in July 1814 of Marvell's omission from Alexander Chalmers's English Poets, but in 1819 Thomas Campbell included in his *Specimens of the British Poets* 'Bermudas', 'Young Love' and part of 'The Nymph'. 'His few poetical pieces betray some adherence to the school of conceit, but there is much in it that comes from the heart warm, pure, and affectionate', Campbell commented, provoking Francis Jeffrey to remark in the *Edinburgh Review* in March 1819 that 'Mr Campbell does not do justice to the sweetness and tenderness which characterize the poetry, as it did the private life, of this inflexible patriot'. In 1824 Marvell was represented in Hazlitt's *Select British Poets*, in 1827 in Montgomery's *The Christian Poet* (Glasgow) and in 1837 in *Passages from the Poets* (Derby).

References to Marvell, though more frequent, remained marginal observations. No sustained critical essay was yet devoted to him. But the observations show a new appreciation of the poet. In his edition of *Pope* (1806) the Rev. William Lisle Bowles, in a note to 'Windsor Forest' remarked on 'Appleton House' and 'Billborow':

Marvel abounds with conceits and false thoughts, but some of his descriptive touches are picturesque and beautiful. His description of a gently rising

eminence is more picturesque, although not so elegantly and justly expressed.
... Sometimes Marvel observes little circumstances of rural nature with the
eye and feeling of a true Poet:

> Then as I careless on the bed
> Of *gelid strawberries* do tread,
> And thro' the hazles thick, espy
> The *hatching thrustle's shining eye*.

The last circumstance is new, highly poetical, and could only have been
described by one who was a real lover of nature, and a witness of her beauties
in her most solitary retirements. It is the observation of such *circumstances*,
which can alone form an accurate descriptive rural Poet.

The characterisation as nature poet was strengthened in John Aikin's
General Biography (1807) the following year, in a description also
placing him firmly amongst the metaphysicals: 'His early poems express
a fondness for the charm of rural nature, and much delicacy of sentiment; they are ingenious and full of fancy, after the manner of Cowley
and his contemporaries.'

The major breakthrough in establishing Marvell's reputation as a
lyric poet was the work of three critics, close acquaintances of each
other, Lamb, Hazlitt and Leigh Hunt. None of them wrote an essay
devoted to Marvell, yet all continually returned to him. Hazlitt, often
quoting from Marvell, was the poet's constant advocate. His first
critical comment dates from 1818 when, discussing the seventeenth
century in his *Lectures on the English Poets*, he wrote:

Marvell is a writer of nearly the same period, and worthy of a better age.
Some of his verses are harsh, as the words of Mercury; others musical, as is
Apollo's lute. Of the latter kind are his boat-song, his description of a fawn,
and his lines to Lady Vere. His lines prefixed to *Paradise Lost* are by no means
the most favourable specimen of his powers.

In his lectures on *The English Comic Writers* (1818–19) he wrote:

Marvel (on whom I have already bestowed such praise as I could, for elegance
and tenderness in his descriptive poems) in his satires and witty pieces was
addicted to the affected and involved style here reprobated, as in his Flecknoe
... and in his satire on the Dutch. As an instance of this forced, far-fetched
method of treating his subject, he says, in ridicule of the Hollanders, that
when their dykes overflowed, the fish used to come to table with them, 'And

sat not as a meat, but as a guest'. There is a poem of Marvel's on the death of
King Charles I which I have not seen, but which I have heard praised by one
whose praise is never high but of the highest things, for the beauty and pathos,
as well as generous frankness of the sentiments, coming, as they did, from a
determined and incorruptible political foe.

Hazlitt praised the 'true poet' Marvell again, bringing him into one of
his *Lectures on the Age of Elizabeth* (1819) and quoting 'To his Coy
Mistress' in full as evidence of his 'sweetness and power'. Including
Marvell in his *Select British Poets* (1824) he remarked: 'His satires were
coarse, quaint and virulent; but his other productions are full of a
lively, tender, and elegant fancy. His verses leave an echo on the ear,
and find one in the heart.'[1]
    Lamb as early as 1800 quoted, in a letter, from 'Appleton House'
'two honest lines by Marvel, (whose poems by the way I am just
going to possess)'.[2] It is possible that he was responsible for introducing
the poet to Hazlitt and Hunt, but his first published comment, later
than either of them, was not until 1820, when he referred to 'his fine
poem' 'Bermudas' – though linking it with a poem on a Kangaroo by
Barron Field would scarcely have ensured it popularity.[3] The following year in an Elia essay he quoted five stanzas of 'The Garden',
remarking, 'they are full, as all his serious poetry was, of a witty
delicacy', and it was as 'that garden-loving poet' he referred to him in
1824, quoting from 'Appleton House'.[4]
    Leigh Hunt recorded in *Wit and Humour* (1846) how he and Lamb
had failed to make Hazlitt see the humour of the 'Character of Holland'.
Hunt himself wrote about its humour in 1819, comparing it with
Samuel Butler's poem on Holland: 'Marvell's wit has the advantage
of Butler's, not in learning or multiplicity of contrasts (for nobody
ever beat him there), but in a greater variety of them, and in being
able, from the more poetical turn of his mind, to bring graver and more
imaginative things to wait upon his levity.' Marvell 'rivalled him in
wit, and excelled him in poetry', Hunt remarked. And Hunt deals
with the non-satirical poetry in later essays. In 1820, praising 'On

[1] Hazlitt, *Complete Works*, ed. P. P. Howe (1930–4) V 83, VI 54, 311–13, IX 238.
[2] *The Letters of Charles Lamb . . . and Mary Lamb*, ed. E. V. Lucas (1935) I 234, 335.
[3] 'First Fruits of Australian Poetry', in *Examiner* (16 Jan 1820), reprinted in *The Works
of Charles and Mary Lamb*, ed. E. V. Lucas (1912) I *Miscellaneous Prose*, pp. 232–4.
[4] 'The Old Benchers of the Inner Temple', in *London Magazine* IV (Sept 1821) 279–80
and 'Blakesmore in H—shire', in *London Magazine*, X (Sept 1824) 226, reprinted in
Works, II *Essays of Elia*, pp. 96, 176.

Paradise Lost' as 'spirited and worthy', he went on to write 'We
remember how delighted we were to find who Andrew Marvell was,
and that he could be so pleasant and lively as well as grave', and in
1823 he remarked on Marvell's 'strong and grave talent for poetry'.
In 1837 he wrote, quoting from 'An Horatian Ode', that 'Marvell
unites wit with earnestness and depth of sentiment, beyond any
miscellaneous writer in the language'.[1]

Lamb, Hazlitt and Hunt mention only nine poems of Marvell's
between them, and their comments are not always such as to assure us
of their close familiarity with the texts. And yet, because of the popularity of their essays, much reprinted and anthologised, their exhorta-
tions that Marvell should be read reached a wide public and did much
to establish the poet's reputation.

'Marvell is a writer almost forgotten', Hazlitt remarked in 1824, and
the *Retrospective Review* the same year remarked that 'his *poems*, little
read, are by no means so generally known or so critically admired as
they richly deserve to be'. The *Review* offered, in the first essay devoted
to Marvell, some critical admiration. It found the 'Nymph complaining' 'the most interesting poetical piece in the whole collection'
(of 1681); 'To the Glow-worms' 'pretty and fanciful, and more in the
taste of the times than Marvell's verse in general'; the 'Dialogue between the Soul and Body' 'fanciful and ingenious'; and the 'Character
of Holland' 'one of the pleasantest of Marvell's poems . . . pregnant
with wit'. Also quoted or mentioned were 'Appleton House', 'Eyes
and Tears', 'The Garden', 'Flecknoe', 'On Paradise Lost' and 'Climb
at Court'.

> As a poet, Marvel was certainly unequal; and some of his most beautiful
> passages are alloyed with vulgarism and common-place similes. His poem of
> the Nymph lamenting the Death of her Fawn is, perhaps, the most finished,
> and, on the whole, the best of the collection. All the poems, however, con-
> tain more or less of poetic beauty; some, great tenderness of feeling and
> expression; and other, successful descriptions of nature and pastoral scenes.[2]

Though the criticisms were not extended, they were of the sort to

---

[1] *Indicator*, VII (24 Nov 1819) 51, LI (27 Sept 1820) 406, LXXXIII (in *Literary Examiner*,
6 Sept 1823, p. 148); *Monthly Repository* II (i) NS (Dec 1837) 413–14. Reprinted in *Leigh
Hunt as Poet and Essayist*, ed. Charles Kent (1889) pp. 114–16, 239, 401, and *Leigh Hunt's
Literary Criticism*, ed. C. H. and C. W. Houtchens (New York, 1956) pp. 194–5.
[2] *Retrospective Review*, X ii (1824) 328–43; XI i (1825) 174–95.

entice readers – and they show the widest familiarity with Marvell's poetry hitherto.

The changes of taste of the Romantic movement had produced a sort of acceptance of Marvell's non-satirical verse. The eighteenth century's dislike of his 'slovenly metre', want of 'correctness', and qualified enthusiasm for his 'extempore effects' and the 'warm effusion of a lively fancy' are gradually left behind. There is less apparent difficulty in finding anything to say, and a new readiness to discover qualities similar to those of Romantic poetry: feeling 'that comes from the heart warm, pure and affectionate', 'sweetness and tenderness', the 'picturesque', 'successful descriptions of nature and pastoral scenes', the detailed recording of 'little circumstances of rural nature', 'delicacy', 'beauty and pathos'. Conceits and remote images were coldly passed by, as in the eighteenth century, and Lamb alone remarked on the 'witty delicacy'. Only the persistent memory of the patriot and champion of liberty, existing as strongly as ever, guarded Marvell from becoming an embodiment of the sentimental. He was the poet of nature, sweetness, tenderness. Oddly, however, his poetry seems to have had little influence on the verse of the Romantics; possibly the last couplet of 'Bermudas' led to the first couplet of Tom Moore's 'Canadian Boat Song', and cases have been made for the influence of 'On Paradise Lost' on Shelley's 'To a Skylark',[1] and 'On a Drop of Dew' on Wordsworth's 'Intimations of Immortality'.[2] Certainly Wordsworth admired 'On a Drop of Dew' and included it (all but the last four lines) in a Christmas album he presented to Lady Mary Lowther in 1819. Wordsworth also knew of Marvell as a political figure of integrity,[3] one of those 'who called Milton friend' he calls him in his 'Great Men' sonnet of 1802, and he had some familiarity, like Coleridge,[4] with the satires. Indeed the patriot and controversialist image persisted, often overshadowing the lyric poet. Isaac D'Israeli in his *Quarrels of Authors* (1814) discussed the Parker–Marvell exchange and made some percipient remarks on Marvell's style as a controversialist. Landor put Marvell in five *Imaginary Conversations*, but though two of those with Milton discuss poetry, Marvell's lyrics are

[1] Irving T. Richards, in *PMLA* L (June 1935) 565–7.
[2] A. F. Potts, *The Elegiac Mode* (Ithaca, N.Y., 1967) p. 91.
[3] Una Venable Tuckerman, 'Wordsworth's Plan for his Imitation of Juvenal', in *Modern Language Notes*, XLV (April 1930) 209–15, and *The Early Letters of William and Dorothy Wordsworth*, ed. E. de Selincourt (1935) p. 541.
[4] *The Notebooks of S. T. Coleridge*, ed. Kathleen Coburn (1957) items 702–8.

ignored. For D'Israeli and Landor, Marvell was not primarily a poet, but, as he was for John Clare (who wrote a poem in his name), 'a great advocate for liberty'.[1]

IV

The first book-length study was John Dove's *The Life of Andrew Marvell, the Celebrated Patriot* (1832). Its title indicates the emphasis on political biography, but sixteen poems are appended. The critical observations are eclectically plagiarised from Aikin, Thompson, D'Israeli and the *Retrospective Review*, but at least Dove gave them currency, like a Modern Judgements volume. The following year appeared *Biographia Borealis or lives of Distinguished Northerns* by Hartley Coleridge, son of the poet. This contained a life of Marvell differing in only the slightest verbal details from Dove's, though without the appendix of poems and their accompanying critical comments. But a paragraph of original comment was added, presumably Coleridge's own:

> The poems of Marvell are, for the most part, productions of his early youth. They have much of that over-activity of fancy, that remoteness of allusion, which distinguishes the school of Cowley; but they have also a heartfelt tenderness, a childish simplicity of feeling, among all their complication of thought, which would atone for all their conceits, if conceit were indeed as great an offence against poetic nature as Addison and other critics of the French school pretend. But though there are cold conceits, a conceit is not necessarily cold. The mind, in certain states of passion, finds comfort in playing with occult or casual resemblances, and dallies with the echo of a sound.

But he exempted the poems to Fairfax and Cromwell from this praise as being 'dull'. Coleridge's collection of lives was reprinted under different titles in 1835, 1836 and 1852, and the *Life of Marvell* was reissued separately (by two different Hull publishers) in 1835. The *Life* lacked the paragraph of criticism quoted above and contained part of 'An Horatian Ode' instead, together with an appendix of eight poems, though without Dove's comments.

The various printings of the *Life* gave Marvell's name currency, and reviewers (they all reviewed Dove's volume and hence encountered

[1] John and Anne Tibble, *John Clare: his life and poetry* (1946) pp. 128, 176.

the poems) further extended – though coolly – his reputation. The
Eclectic Review remarked in November 1832, with truth, that 'his
name has preserved his writings, rather than his writings his name' and
felt that his works 'are not worth republishing' in entirety any more
than Swift's or Defoe's.

It must surely have been in his juvenile days, if the poem be really his, that
Marvell addressed 'to his coy mistress', the quaint and unequal lines, not
quite unworthy of Cowley, in which we are surprised with the following
striking thought:

> But at my back I alwaies hear
> Times winged Charriot hurrying near:
> And yonder all before us lye
> Desarts of vast Eternity.

And the reviewer doubted that the 'Resolved Soul and Created Pleasure'
was Marvell's since 'the versification seems much too polished, the
turns of thought too delicate, and the whole is in too pure a taste for
Marvell's day: it must we think, be of later date . . . It is by far the most
beautiful . . . ' His final evaluation was that though 'Marvell might
occasionally trifle in poetry' his prose showed him the 'intrepid
advocate of freedom'. Similarly the *Westminster Review*, in January
1833, though finding that 'Appleton House' 'displays an intense
feeling for the beauties of nature, expressed with a felicity which not
unfrequently recalls L'Allegro and Il Penseroso', concluded that 'The
admiration of Marvell is to be based, not on his intellectual, but his
moral qualities. Neither as a philosopher nor as a poet, does Marvell
belong to the first order of great minds.' Likewise Henry Rogers in
the *Edinburgh Review* in January 1844, in a long account of Marvell
(belatedly reviewing Dove), dealt primarily with the politician and
patriot. He offered some critical observations on the satirical and controversial writings, but the lyrics failed to interest him: those he thought
best were the non-Marvellian inclusions in Thompson's edition.
'Still, there are unquestionably many of his genuine poems which
indicate a rich, though ill-cultivated fancy; and in some few stanzas
there is no little grace of expression.'

The reviewers of Dove's *Life*, even more than Dove himself, treated
the poems as marginalia to the political and patriotic figure. But
slowly this view was dying. In 1836 S. C. Hall had included 'Bermudas',

'Little T.C.', 'To his Coy Mistress' and the 'Nymph complaining' in his *Book of Gems*, commenting,

> He was not of the highest order, nor perhaps in even a high order, but what he did was genuine. It is sweetness speaking out in sweetness. In the language there is nothing more exquisitely tender than the 'Nymph Complaining for the loss of her Fawn'. Such poems as this and 'the Bermudas' may live, and deserve to live, as long as the longest and the mightiest. Of as real a quality are the majority of the poems of Marvell. In a playful and fantastic expression of tender and voluptuous beauty, they are well nigh unrivalled. His fancy indeed sometimes overmasters him, but it is always a sweet and pleasant mastery. His strong love of the actual at times bursts forth, but his poetry still survives it, and will not be fairly clogged and over-laden with the body corporate.

And ten years later Leigh Hunt, in his anthology *Wit and Humour* (1846), in which he represented Marvell's humour, referred also to the 'devout and beautiful' 'Bermudas' and 'the sweet overflowing fancies' of the 'Nymph'.

Criticism did not get clogged down, fortunately, in this early Victorian sweetness and exclusion of the 'actual'. G. L. Craik, in his *Sketches of the History of Literature and Learning in England* (1844) finely caught the tonal shifts, the levity and seriousness of Marvell. He was one of the first critics to recognise the sophistication and complexity of Marvell's technique, an important advance on the earlier impressions of 'spontaneity', naturalness, 'childish simplicity of feeling'. The lyrics, he wrote, are

> eminent both for the delicate bloom of the sentiment and for grace of form. ['Bermudas'] is a gem of melody, picturesqueness, and sentiment, nearly without a flaw, and is familiar to every lover of poetry. Not of such purity of execution throughout are the lines entitled 'To His Coy Mistress,' but still there are few short poems in the language so remarkable for the union of grace and force, and the easy and flowing transition from a light and playful tone to solemnity, passion, and grandeur. How elegant, and even deferential, is the gay extravagance of the commencement [lines 1–20 quoted]. And then how skillfully managed is the rise from this badinage of courtesy and compliment to the strain almost of the ode or the hymn; and how harmonious, notwithstanding its suddenness, is the contrast between the sparkling levity of the prelude and the solemn pathos that follows [lines 21–6]. Till, at the end, the pent-up accumulation of passion bursts its floodgates in the noble lines [lines 41–4].

He found 'Little T.C.' 'exquisitely elegant and tuneful': 'certainly neither Carew, nor Waller, nor any other court poet of that day, has produced anything in the same style finer than these lines'. And the lines on *Paradise Lost* 'have throughout almost the dignity, and in parts more than the strength, of Waller'. Craik's perceptive observations were reprinted in the numerous editions (in various forms and under various titles) of his book, a book that became the standard handbook for Civil Service and other examinees through the century. In his allocation of space to Marvell (in comment and excerpt, more than to Butler, Cowley, Dryden or Waller) and in his commentary he did much to establish him in the canon of English literature. Though a comparable survey, Henry Hallam's *Introduction to the Literature of Europe* (1839, and often reprinted) remarked simply: 'Marvell wrote sometimes with more taste and feeling than was usual, but his satires are gross and stupid.' Throughout the century, histories of English literature appeared that either ignored Marvell completely, or treated him, usually contemptuously, solely as a satirist.

v

Yet slowly Marvell gathered admirers. Mary Russell Mitford in *Recollections of a Literary Life* (1852), remarked on his 'rich profusion of fancy which almost dazzles the mind', his 'earnestness and heartiness', and 'a frequent felicity of phrase, which when once read, fixes itself in the memory and *will* not be forgotten'. In the following year E. P. Hood, in *Andrew Marvell, the Wit, Statesman and Poet*, described him as 'a very sweet' poet, 'not in the first class', though 'had Marvell dedicated his powers to poetry, he must have stood very high'. 'His verses mostly originate in the spontaneous flow of gentle thought and sweet indulgence, and dallying with nature', Hood wrote, and found them to 'breathe the tranquillity of grove and field'. And a new article in the eighth edition of the *Encyclopaedia Britannica* (1857) (by R. C.-S.) remarked, 'besides his controversial and political services, Marvell had written some minor poems of great tenderness, fancy, and beauty, which were deservedly popular. His lyrical stanzas on the sailing of the emigrants for Bermudas . . . form one of the finest strains of the Puritan muse'.

Both Miss Mitford and E. P. Hood noted with regret Marvell's sharing the vice of the age – conceits. They noted also how little known his poetry was. But in the 1860s he was included in a number of anthologies, pre-eminent among which was F, T. Palgrave's *Golden Treasury* (1861). By inclusion in this phenomenally popular volume, Marvell was set firmly before the Victorian reading poetry. In his notes Palgrave offered high praise, finding in Marvell and Milton 'the first noble attempts at pure description of nature, destined in our own age to be continued and equalled'. On 'The Garden' he remarked: 'these truly wonderful verses, which, like "Lycidas", may be regarded as a test of any readers' insight into the most poetical aspects of Poetry. The general differences between them are vast: but in imaginative intensity Marvell and Shelley are closely related.' He also included 'An Horatian Ode', remarking that it was 'beyond doubt one of the finest in our language', and 'Bermudas'. Tennyson pressed him to include more and 'greatly pleaded' for 'To his Coy Mistress', but, conscious of Victorian prudishness, Palgrave refused: 'I thought one or two lines too *strong* for this age.'[1] In 1883 he added part of the 'Nymph complaining', commenting in the notes, 'perhaps no poem in this collection is more delicately fancied, more exquisitely finished', and in 1891 'Little T.C.'. Palgrave returned to Marvell in his Oxford lectures, *Landscape in Poetry* (1897), calling him 'one of the most original poets of the Stuart period'.

Palgrave's use of 'The Garden' in *The Golden Treasury* looked forward to Matthew Arnold's touchstones of poetry; but Marvell was not amongst them, nor did Arnold ever discuss him critically. However, in 1861 Arnold sent the French critic Sainte-Beuve a copy of *The Golden Treasury*, and in a covering letter drew attention enthusiastically to 'An Horatian Ode'. 'Il [Palgrave] a aussi déterré des vrais trésors qui restaient enfouis, et inconnus à presque tout le monde; remarquez surtout une Ode à Andrew Marvell à p. 50. Tout le monde l'ignorait; et cependant qu'elle est belle et forte, cette Ode!' Three years later, reviewing Taine's history of English literature (which ignored Marvell), Sainte-Beuve himself drew attention to the Ode and remarked:

Jamais le feu de l'enthousiasme pour la chose publique, jamais la grandeur et la terreur qu'inspirent ces grands sauveurs révolutionnaires, hommes de glaive et d'épée, ne trouvèrent de plus vibrants at de plus vrais accents s'échappant à flots pressés d'une poitrine sincère [lines 25–36 translated].

[1] C. J. Horne, 'Palgrave's "Golden Treasury" ', in *English Studies*, II NS (1949) 60; K. Tillotson, 'Donne's Poetry in the Nineteenth Century', in *Elizabethan and Jacobean Studies Presented to Frank Percy Wilson* (1959) p. 322.

On sent ici comme la réalité anglaise et la franchise du ton se contiennent mal sous l'imitation classique, comme elles percent et crèvent en quelque sorte l'enveloppe d'Horace.[1]

In fact, 'An Horatian Ode' was not as unknown as Arnold believed: since its publication by Thompson, it had been praised by Hazlitt, Hunt in 1837, Mary Russell Mitford, E. P. Hood, the *Biographical Magazine* (1853) and the *Eclectic Magazine* (August 1853) and Henry Reed in his *Lectures on the British Poets* (1857) given in 1841. Reviewing W. W. Wilkins' *Political Ballads of the 17th and 18th Centuries* (1860), Herman Merivale remarked in the *Edinburgh Review* for January 1861 of 'that magnificent ode of Andrew Marvell's':

This style of political poetry, manly and forcible in a high degree, but often hard, and deficient in natural flow as well as in polish, with a strong tendency to the epigrammatic, continued in fashion while men were much in earnest; but it lost its power when political life became itself commonplace; political verse then became stilted whenever it endeavoured the heroic.

In 1868 two further anthologies represented Marvell. George Macdonald, in *England's Antiphon*, remarked of Marvell, 'any one of some half dozen of his few poems is to my mind worth all the verse that Cowley ever made. It is a pity he wrote so little.' He included 'On a Drop of Dew' – 'surely a lovely fancy of resemblance, exquisitely wrought out; an instance of the lighter play of the mystical mind, which yet shadows forth truth' – and 'The Coronet' – a much smaller selection than he gave to Crashaw, Donne, Herbert or Vaughan. R. C. Trench, in his *Household Book of English Poetry*, included the Ode, 'On a Drop of Dew' and 'Eyes and Tears', advising readers to read the latter two or three times to discover 'the depth and riches of meaning which under their unpretending form lie concealed'. In their brief comments, Macdonald and Trench show for the first time in the nineteenth century an awareness that the simplicity of Marvell's expression and treatment covers a depth of subtlety and significance. E. P. Hood had remarked, 'the lines on Appleton House are as simple as verses penned in the golden, or mythic age; and rural sounds fall upon our ear, and rural sights move before our eye, awakening only the impression they are disposed to give'. And John Dennis wrote as late as

---

[1] Arnold's letter is printed by T. B. Smart in the *Athenaeum*, part DCCCXLIX (3 Sept 1898) 325; Sainte-Beuve's review appeared in *Constitutionnel* (6 June 1864), reprinted *Nouveaux Lundis*, 3rd ed. rev. (Paris, 1879) VIII 100–1.

1872 that Marvell was author of 'a few beautiful poems, which are
impregnated with a fine rural flavour'.[1] The rural flavour, the rural
sounds are certainly there: but they are only part of the poems. Macdonald and Trench mark the new realisation of the allegoric and symbolic nature of Marvell's poetry.

These popular anthologies had put Marvell firmly – though in-
completely – before the Victorian public, and in July 1869 John
Ormsby contributed to the *Cornhill Magazine* an article on Marvell
that can be taken as a convenient expression of the current evaluation
of Marvell's poetry by the intelligent reader. The satire on Flecknoe,
he found,

> might easily pass for one of Donne's, so thoroughly has he caught not only
> the manner and rugged vigorous versification of Donne's satires, but also
> his very turns of thought, and the passion for elaborate conceits, recondite
> analogies, and out-of-the-way similitudes ... His 'Nymph complaining ... '
> graceful, simple, and tender as the lines are, is not free from these *tours de
> force* of fancy which disfigure so much of the poetry of that day. Even the
> lowest, the most verbal form of this forced wit, breaks out ... 'Left me his
> *fawn,*/But took his heart.' ... On the other hand ... 'Bermudas' ... is as
> direct, natural and unaffected as a poem of Wordsworth's could be ... In
> 'To His Coy Mistress', the extravagant fancy, that in the graver sort of
> poetry is a blemish, becomes an ornament, employed as it is to push a kind
> of *argumentum ad absurdum* to the farthest possible limits, and its effect is
> heightened by the exquisite assumption of gravity in the opening lines ...
> [The poem is] characteristic of Marvell in many ways, but more especially
> of that peculiarity of his ... his trick – if anything so obviously natural and
> spontaneous can be called a trick – of passing suddenly from a light, bantering,
> trivial tone, to one of deep feeling, and even ... of solemnity. ... Lightly and
> playfully as the subject is treated, it suggests thoughts that lead to a graver and
> more impassioned strain. A few pages further on we find a poem which is in
> truth only a conceit expanded into a poem, but which in its very flimsiness
> shows a rare lightness of hand, and neatness of execution. It is a sort of
> miniature idyll cast in the amoeban form, and entitled 'Ametas and Thestylis
> ... ' Nothing could be more designedly trifling than this, and yet what a
> finished elegance there is about it. It is not the highest art, perhaps, but there
> is a certain antique grace in the workmanship that reminds one somehow, of
> a cameo or an old engraved gem.

[1] 'English Rural Poetry', in *Cornhill*, xxv (Feb 1872) 164–76, reprinted in Dennis,
Studies in English Literature (1876). Dennis discusses Marvell again in his *Heroes of Literature*
(1883) pp. 150–2.

Despite the sensitivity of his analysis – or perhaps because of it – Ormsby could not rank Marvell's poetry 'with the very highest', 'but it unquestionably has high and varied qualities. It makes little pretension to depth or stability, but it abounds in wit and humour, true feeling, melody, and a certain scholarly elegance and delicate fancy.'

<h2 style="text-align:center">VI</h2>

Marvell's poetry was now sufficiently well known and appreciated to produce a demand for new editions. Thompson's had appeared practically a hundred years earlier, and most nineteenth-century readers could read Marvell only in anthologies. In 1857 there had been an American edition of his poems, and this was now reprinted in London in 1870 and 1881. In 1872 the first of Alexander Grosart's four volumes of Marvell's works appeared. Although a limited edition – the reprinted American edition did far more to make the poems accessible for the general reader – it was a major factor in establishing Marvell. At last there was a full text available for scholars, critics, collectors and students. Grosart ventured few critical comments, but his perceptive remark on conceits is a relief from the pages of routine denunciation by his contemporaries.

> And yet beneath the conceit, when you come to look lovingly and lingeringly, you find that it is sprung out of a vital thought or emotion or fancy, precisely as the chipped and shapen (misshapen) yews were really rooted in the rich mould, and really nurtured by celestial influences.

The recognition of the conceit's truth to thought or emotion, its psychological realism, was one of those recognitions allowing for the fuller understanding of the metaphysicals (whom Grosart was now editing), which led to their eventual acceptance.

But widespread acceptance still came slowly. W. D. Christie in the *Saturday Review* (26 April 1873) had scarcely a word for the lyrics in Grosart, but delivered a lengthy attack on the 'loathsome obscenity and virulent malice', the 'extreme grossness and unmitigated filth' of the satires. Naturally he did not quote the offending lines, but he gave the line numbers 'for proof of our assertion of the filthy indecency'. Goldwin Smith, in a note to the Marvell selection in volume II of T. H. Ward's *English Poets* (1880), also objected to 'the dirtiness

of Restoration thought' and found the lyrics 'often slovenly, sometimes
intolerably diffuse . . . eminently afflicted with the gift of "wit" or
ingenuity' and Marvell only a part-time poet. He was not even a part-
time poet for Osmund Airy, whose article in the ninth edition of the
Encyclopaedia Britannica (1883) treated him solely as politician and
controversialist. Edmund Gosse, in *From Shakespeare to Pope* (1885),
was cool, though, importantly, for him Marvell is essentially 'seriously-
minded' and the 'childish' is an aberrance in him, rather than, as it was
for Hartley Coleridge, the saving grace of the conceits. Quoting stanza
XL of 'Appleton House' Gosse wrote:

> This is pretty and harmless, but perhaps just because it errs so gently against
> the canons of style, we ask ourselves how so seriously-minded a man as
> Marvell could run on in such a childish way. There is a good deal in Marvell
> that is of this species of wit, graceful and coloured, but almost infantile . . .
> His style, when he can put his conceits behind him, is extremely sharp and
> delicate, with a distinction of phrase that is quite unknown to most of his
> contemporaries . . . He is the last of the English romantic poets for several
> generations, and no one of them all, early or late, has regarded nature with
> a quicker or more loving attention than he.

Marvell was at least read, however. Edward Fitzgerald, translator of
The Rubaiyat of Omar Khayyam, called him 'an old favourite of mine',
and remembered how Tennyson found the couplet 'But at my back
I alwaies hear / Times winged Charriot hurrying near' 'sublime'.[1]
Palgrave recalled how Tennyson had 'special praise' for 'Bermudas'
and liked to read aloud 'To his Coy Mistress', and Hallam Tennyson
recorded how the poet liked to read aloud 'The Character of Holland'
and recall how he had made Carlyle helpless with laughter at it.[2] As
early as 1831 Leigh Hunt had compared Tennyson's poetry with
Marvell's,[3] and 'The Nymph' is echoed in 'Maud' and 'The Princess.'[4]
Hopkins found Marvell a 'most rich and nervous poet'.[5] Ruskin[6] and
R. L. Stevenson[7] had some familiarity with Marvell, and both Francis

---

[1] *Letters and Literary Remains of Edward Fitzgerald*, ed. W. A. Wright (1889) I 337, II 133.

[2] *Life and Works of Tennyson* (1889) IV 99–100, 308–9.

[3] *Tatler*, II (26 Feb 1831) 593.

[4] *Notes and Queries*, x (July 1963) 264–5, (Oct) 385.

[5] *Correspondence of Gerard Manley Hopkins and Richard Watson Dixon*, ed. C. C. Abbott (1935) p. 23.

[6] Oswald Doughty, *A Victorian Romantic* (1949) p. 324.

[7] Stevenson, *Letters*, ed. Sidney Colvin (1899) II 214.

Thompson[1] and Alice Meynell,[2] influenced in their own verse by the metaphysicals, wrote on Marvell briefly in reviews.

With the last decade of the nineteenth century Marvell became established, though he was not feted for another twenty years. A. C. Benson devoted an article to him in *Macmillan's Magazine* for January 1892. He objected to the conceits, the 'monotony' of subjects, and 'an uncertainty, an incompleteness' and lack of proportion, 'An Horatian Ode' being 'the one instance where Marvell's undoubted genius burned steadily through a whole poem'. But he also commented enthusiastically:

> The strength of Marvell's style lies in its unexpectedness. You are arrested by what has been well called a 'pre-destined' epithet, not a mere otiose addition, but a word which turns a noun into a picture; the 'hook-shouldered' hill 'to abrupter greatness thrust', 'the sugar's uncorrupting oil', 'the vigilant patrol of stars', 'the squatted thorns', 'the oranges like golden lamps in a green night', 'the garden's fragrant innocence', – these are but a few random instances of a tendency that meets you in every poem. Marvell had in fact the qualities of a consummate artist, and only needs to repress his luxuriance and to confine his expansiveness.

With the inclusion of G. A. Aitken's edition of Marvell in the Muses Library in 1892, the poet was at last conveniently accessible in a newly edited text. The reviewer in the *Athenaeum* (3 Sept 1892) thought Marvell 'monstrously overrated' and declared 'the *Golden Treasury* contains all of his work that is worth more than a single reading'. But with E. K. Chambers's review in the *Academy* (17 Sept 1892) acceptance was almost complete. He heard in Marvell 'the music of Puritanism – the Puritanism of Spenser and Sidney, not uncultivated, not ungracious, not unsensuous even, but always with the same dominant note in it, of moral strength and moral purity'. Natural sweetness had now been replaced by moral strength and purity, setting the tone for much of the twentieth-century criticism of Marvell. Chambers also marks an important stage in the acceptance of the conceit. 'Appleton House', he wrote,

[1] Thompson reviewed Birrell's *Andrew Marvell* in *Academy*, LXIX (23 Sept 1905) 976–7; on Marvell's influence on Thompson see J. C. Reid, *Francis Thompson Man and Poet* (1959) pp. 67, 99, and Everard Meynell, *Life of Francis Thompson* (1926) p. 123.

[2] Alice Meynell represented Marvell in her anthology *The Flower of the Mind* (1897) and wrote on him in the *Pall Mall Gazette* (14 July 1897) 3.

shows him at his best – and at his worst, in the protracted conceit, whereby a garden, its flowers and its bees, are likened to a fort with a garrison. And here I am minded to enter a plea against the indiscriminate condemnation of conceits in poetry. After all, a conceit is only an analogy, a comparison, a revealing of likeness in things dissimilar, and therefore of the very essence of poetic imagination. Often it illumines, and where it fails, it is not because it is a conceit, but because it is a bad conceit; because the thing compared is not beautiful in itself, or because the comparison is not flashed upon you, but worked out with such tedious elaboration as to be 'merely fantastical'. Many of Marvell's conceits are, in effect, bad; the well-known poem 'On a Drop of Dew', redeemed though it is by the last line and a half, affords a terrible example. But others are shining successes.

In 1900 Marvell was included in *The Oxford Book of English Verse* by Quiller-Couch, who also edited a brief volume of his lyrics in the Oxford 'Select English Classics'. H. C. Beeching's article on 'The Lyrical Poems of Andrew Marvell' in the *National Review* for July 1901 is a useful study, but its significance lies not so much in the sound observations it makes, but in the workmanlike, almost routine manner of proceeding. The discoveries have been made; analysis and classification now follow. Augustine Birrell's volume *Andrew Marvell* in the 'English Men of Letters' series (1905), though containing practically no critical observations, nonetheless marks the final admission of Marvell to the body of standard authors.

VII

Marvell's reputation, along with that of the other metaphysical poets, had importantly developed in America during the nineteenth century. J. E. Duncan notes that the American interest in the metaphysicals 'was relatively free from English influence. American critics generally appreciated the metaphysicals' transcendental qualities, their hard core of thought, and the union of body, mind and soul reflected in their poetry.'[1]

Marvell's early reputation as a defender of liberty persisted in America also. In 1773 his name was taken as a pseudonym in two pamphlets in a controversy over the site of a market in Philadelphia.[2] But his

---

[1] J. E. Duncan, *The Revival of Metaphysical Poetry* (Minneapolis, 1959) p. 69.
[2] Caroline Robbins in a letter to the *Times Literary Supplement*, 19 Dec 1958, p. 737.

poetry was well known early in the nineteenth century. Emerson was
reading Marvell in the 1820s. And he wrote in his journal for 1828:

> Is not the age gone by of the great splendour of English poetry, and will it
> not be impossible for any age soon to vie with the pervading etherial poesy
> of Herbert, Shakespeare, Marvell, Herrick, Milton, Ben Jonson; at least to
> represent anything like their peculiar form of ravishing verse? It is the head
> of human poetry . . . I have for them an affectionate admiration I have for
> nothing else. They set me on speculations. They move my wonder at myself.
> They suggest the great endowment of the spiritual man. They open glimpses
> of the heaven that is in the intellect.

Marvell figures in Emerson's reading lists for 1838 and 1842, and
Emerson's library includes an annotated copy of the 1857 Boston
edition of the poems. He represented Marvell in his anthology *Parnassus*
(Boston, 1877), and, as O. W. Holmes noted in 1885, was influenced by
Marvell in his own verse.[1]

In the *Southern Literary Messenger* for August 1836 Edgar Allan Poe,
reviewing Hall's *Book of Gems*, wrote a fine account of the 'Nymph
complaining', 'a beautiful poem, abounding in sweet pathos, in soft
and gentle images, in the most exquisitely delicate imagination':

> How truthful an air of deep lamentation hangs here upon every gentle
> syllable! It pervades all. It comes over the sweet melody of the words, over
> the gentleness and grace which we fancy in the little maiden herself, – even
> over the half-playful, half petulant air with which she lingers on the beauties
> and good qualities of her favorite, like the cool shadow of a summer cloud
> over a bed of lilies and violets, and 'all sweet flowers'. The whole thing is
> redolent with poetry of the very loftiest order. It is positively crowded with
> nature and with pathos. Every line is an idea, conveying either the beauty
> and playfulness of the faun, or the artlessness of the maiden, or the love
> of the maiden, or her admiration, or her grief, or the fragrance, and sweet
> warmth, and perfect appropriateness of the little nest-like bed of lilies and
> roses, which the faun devoured as it lay upon them, and could scarcely be
> distinguished from them by the once happy little damsel who went to seek
> her pet with an arch and rosy smile upon her face. Consider the great variety
> of *truth* and delicate thought in the few lines we have quoted – [lines 63–92]

[1] R. W. Emerson, *Journals* (Boston, 1914) II 253–4; O. W. Holmes, *Ralph Waldo
Emerson* (1885) p. 21; Walter Harding, *Emerson's Library* (1967) p. 185; Legouis, *André
Marvell* (1928) p. 236; Norman A. Brittin, 'Emerson and the Metaphysical Poets', in
American Literature, VIII (March 1936) 1–21.

the *wonder* of the maiden at the fleetness of her favourite – the 'little silver feet' – the faun challenging his mistress to the race, 'with a pretty skipping grace', running on before, and then, with head turned back, awaiting her approach only to fly from it again – can we not distinctively perceive all these things? The exceeding vigor, too, and beauty of the line, '*And trod as if on the four winds*', which are vividly apparent when we regard the artless nature of the speaker and the *four feet* of the favorite – *one for each wind*. Then the garden of 'my own', so overgrown – entangled – with lilies and roses as to be 'a little wilderness' – the faun loving to be there and there '*only*' – the maiden seeking it 'where it *should* lie', and not being able to distinguish it from the flowers until 'itself would rise' – the lying among the lilies 'like a bank of lilies' – the loving to 'fill' itself with roses, 'And its pure virgin limbs to fold/In whitest sheets of lilies cold' and these things being its 'chief' delights – and then the pre-eminent beauty and naturalness of the concluding lines – whose very outrageous hyperbole and absurdity only renders them the more true to nature and to propriety, when we consider the innocence, the artlessness, the enthusiasm, the passionate grief, and more passionate admiration of the bereaved child – '*Had it lived long it would have been/Lilies without – roses within.*'

It is a distinguished piece of criticism in its elucidatory sympathy and in its enthusiasm. Poe shows a far greater feeling for Marvell than any of the earlier, or the contemporary, critics of Marvell in Britain.

In the late 1840s Whittier wrote an essay on Marvell in the *National Era*, which was reprinted in *Old Portraits and Modern Sketches* (Boston, 1850). The image of Marvell as 'one of the inflexible defenders of English liberty, sowers of the seed, the fruits of which we are now reaping' naturally made an appeal to this great opponent of slavery. But Whittier also responded to 'his merits as a poet, by no means inconsiderable'.

His poems, written in the 'snatched leisure' of an active political life, bear marks of haste, and are very unequal. In the midst of passages of pastoral description worthy of Milton himself, feeble lines and hackneyed phases occur. His 'Nymph lamenting the Death of her Faun' is a finished and elaborate piece, full of grace and tenderness. 'Thoughts in a Garden' will be remembered by the quotations of that exquisite critic, Charles Lamb. . . . One of his longer poems, 'Appleton House,' contains passages of admirable description, and many not unpleasing conceits. . . . There is a splendid Ode to Cromwell – a worthy companion of Milton's glorious sonnet – which is not generally known, and which we transfer entire to our pages. Its simple dignity, and the melodious flow of its versification, commend themselves more to our feelings than its eulogy of war. It is energetic and impassioned, and probably affords a better idea of the author, as an actor in the stirring drama of his time, than the 'soft Lydian airs' of the poems that we have quoted.

'The Garden', 'Appleton House', 'Bermudas', 'Eyes and Tears' and 'Climb at Court' were the poems quoted, importantly making Marvell accessible as a poet – though it is on the defender of liberty theme that Whittier concludes: 'His memory is the inheritance of Americans as well as Englishmen. His example commends itself in an especial manner to the legislators of our Republic.'

Marvell became available in America not only in English anthologies, but in an increasing number of volumes published within the United States. As early as 1857 an edition of Marvell's poems was published in Boston – fifteen years before any English nineteenth-century edition. It contained an abridgement of Henry Rogers's essay, and some original editorial comment:

> Marvell possessed wit so sportful and airy, yet at the same time so recondite, that it is hard to find anywhere an instance in which the Court, the Tavern and the scholar's study are blended with such Corinthian justness of measure ... His mind presents the rare combination of wit with moral sense, by which the one is rescued from scepticism and the other from prosing. His poems form the synthesis of Donne and Butler.

The same year he was represented in R. W. Griswold's *Sacred Poets of England and America*, and he continued to be printed throughout the century – in *Favorite Odes and Poems by Collins, Dryden and Marvell* (Boston, 1875), *The Poetical Works of Milton and Marvell* (Boston, 1878), and later collections.

That Marvell's were among the 'favorite' poems suggests his popularity. Certainly he was known to Hawthorne, who took the last line of *The Scarlet Letter* (1850) from 'The Unfortunate Lover',[1] and to Melville, who alluded to 'Appleton House' in the first chapter of *Billy Budd* (1891);[2] Emily Dickinson shows some similarities of image and tone to Marvell, though the influence was probably indirect. While among the academic establishment Marvell's reputation was also high. James Russell Lowell wrote in an essay on Dryden in 1870:

[1] R. L. Brant, 'Hawthorne and Marvell', in *American Literature*, xxx (Nov 1958) 366.
[2] Mrs Duncan-Jones in Legouis, *Andrew Marvell* (1965) p. 236n; and see Michael Milgate, in *English Studies*, xlix (Feb 1968) 47–50.

Marvell's 'Horatian Ode', the most truly classic in our language, is worthy of its theme. The same poet's *Elegy* on Cromwell, in parts noble, and everywhere humanly tender, is worth more than all Carlyle's biography as a witness to the gentler qualities of the hero, and of the deep affection that stalwart nature could inspire in hearts of truly masculine temper. As it is little known, a few verses of it may be quoted to show the difference between grief that thinks of its object and grief that thinks of its rhymes.

VIII

The view that the metaphysicals were 'rediscovered' by T. S. Eliot – and by Grierson's anthology, which Eliot reviewed in the *Times Literary Supplement* (20 October 1921) – has now been convincingly qualified. We can see a gradual acceptance of the metaphysicals throughout the nineteenth century, accelerating with Grosart's editions of Cowley, Crashaw, Donne, Herbert and Marvell in the 1870s and culminating with Grierson's edition of Donne in 1912. With Marvell, Eliot was making no 'discovery', but dealing with a figure already established in the literary cultures of America, where he had been educated, and England, where he had settled. Yet Eliot's importance must not, in reaction, be underrated. Marvell's acceptance had not become total; objecting to his inclusion in the English Men of Letters series, the *Times Literary Supplement* commented on 22 September 1905 that 'Marvell was only in a limited sense an English Man of Letters'; 'amongst the poets Marvell is the thinnest end of the wedge yet admitted'.

Details of Eliot's essay on Marvell can be seen to have been prefigured. Leigh Hunt's observation that 'Marvell unites wit with earnestness', the 'combination of wit with moral sense' remarked in the Boston edition and in Chambers's review, led to Eliot. The gradual acceptance of the conceit – in Coleridge, Grosart, and Chambers – the realisation that it 'sprung out of a vital thought or emotion or fancy' and in 'revealing of likeness in things dissimilar' was 'of the very essence of poetic imagination' again point to Eliot's acceptance and understanding of conceits. And his acceptance of the colloquial rhythms, the deliberate metrical 'irregularities' of the metaphysicals had also been prefigured; indeed Isaac Rosenberg, in a letter written in 1917, just before his death in the trenches, wished Marvell's lines had been stronger:

Regular rhythms I do not like much, but of course it depends on where the stress and accent are laid. I think there is nothing finer than the vigorous opening of Lycidas for music; yet it is regular. Now I think if Andrew Marvell had broken up his rhythms more he would have been considered a terrific poet. As it is I like his poem urging his mistress to love because they have not a thousand years to love in and he can't afford to wait. (I forget the name of the poem) well I like it more than Lycidas.

But although elements of Eliot's criticism can be found in earlier writers (and J. E. Duncan usefully demonstrates forerunners to Eliot on the metaphysicals), they are elements less emphasised in their original contexts. It is in the selection and emphasis of particular characteristics as the salient characteristics of metaphysical poetry that Eliot's essays are distinctive. Their influence was immense and, as Frank Kermode has remarked, they introduced a fresh critical terminology whose use is not yet exhausted.[1]

The modern period of Marvell criticism is represented in the articles selected in this volume, and the curious reader can find supplementary references in the bibliography. But a sketch, necessarily brief, of some of the more influential trends, in so far as distinct trends can be discerned, may help place the articles in context. Herbert Grierson had represented Marvell in his immensely influential anthology *Metaphysical Lyrics and Poems of the Seventeenth Century* (Oxford, 1921) and commented, 'apart from Milton he is the most interesting personality between Donne and Dryden, and at his best a finer poet than either'. Eliot's 1921 valuation was similarly high, and though he qualified it in his 1923 *Nation* review of Marvell's poems, it has been this high valuation that has persisted, and persists, until the present day. J. B. Broadbent in *Poetic Love* (1964) has been one of the very few critics to question it.

From Eliot's emphasis on the metaphysicals as major figures in English poetry, other critics soon developed a system. George Williamson in *The Donne Tradition* (Cambridge, Mass., 1930) developed from Eliot's observations a 'tradition', in which Marvell is placed in the line of Donne; in England F. R. Leavis's 'Line of Wit' similarly developed from Eliot: 'The line, then, runs from Ben Jonson (and Donne) through Carew and Marvell to Pope.' Geoffrey Walton's *From Metaphysical to*

[1] *The Collected Works of Isaac Rosenberg*, ed. G. Bottomley and D. Harding (1937) p. 317 (noted in G. Walton, *From Metaphysical to Augustan* (1955)); *Andrew Marvell, Selected Poetry*, ed. F. Kermode (1967) p. viii; see also Frank Kermode, 'Dissociation of Sensibility', in *Kenyon Review*, XIX (Spring 1957) 169–94.

Augustan (1955) in its turn developed Leavis's line.[1] Marvell also attracted the attention of William Empson in *Seven Types of Ambiguity* (1930), possibly the most significant and fruitful English critical work of the first half of this century. In America, Cleanth Brooks followed a similar approach, seeing the comprehension within a poem of conflicting attitudes as a characteristic feature of the metaphysicals. The brief observations of these two critics (both later wrote sustained essays on Marvell) provided a valuable stimulation in Marvell criticism. More traditional, more conservative in critical method was Pierre Legouis's *André Marvell* (Paris, 1928: revised, abridged and translated, Oxford, 1965; 2nd ed. 1968). The first, and still the only, thorough and comprehensive survey of Marvell's life, writings and reputation, it established a basis and context from which later criticism could begin. To this, and to H. M. Margoliouth's two-volume edition of Marvell's poems and letters (Oxford, 1927; revised 1952) modern scholars are heavily indebted.

For a long time Eliot, Empson, Brooks and Leavis provided the main impetus in critical discussions of Marvell. The *explication de texte*, the practical criticism, the close reading favoured by the New Critics and their British counterparts, was a method particularly suitable for lyric poetry. Cleanth Brooks and R. P. Warren on 'Definition of Love' in *Understanding Poetry* (New York, 1938), Laurence Lerner on 'An Horatian Ode' in John Wain's *Interpretations* (1955) and Empson, Brooks and Hardy in their pieces in this volume, show the approach at its most rewarding. But it is not an exercise that can be indefinitely repeated.

Moreover, judgements of the uniqueness, the original vividness, the distinctiveness of the metaphysicals were soon countered by an array of qualifying scholarly studies. The 'modernity' of the metaphysicals, much emphasised in the 1920s and 1930s, was especially challenged. Rosemond Tuve in *Elizabethan and Metaphysical Imagery* (1947) was at pains to demonstrate that the metaphysicals were less innovators than heirs to tradition; and Louis Martz's *The Poetry of Meditation* (1954) examined a particular tradition – the Catholic meditation – which he demonstrated to be a significant structuring force on much of what had been thought distinctively 'metaphysical'. Both these studies make important reference to Marvell. At the same time, a number of shorter

---

[1] F. R. Leavis in *Scrutiny*, IV (Dec 1935) 249, reprinted in *Revaluation* (1936). A shorter version of Geoffrey Walton's discussion of Marvell appeared in *Politics and Letters*, I (Summer 1948) 22–35.

studies attempted to establish the genres to which Marvell's poems can be attached. M. C. Bradbrook's 'Marvell and the Poetry of Rural Solitude'[1] was one of the earliest of such studies, and a later example, Frank Kermode's reading of 'The Garden' is included here. Slowly an awareness of the literary contexts of Marvell's poetry has developed, and there has been a parallel concern to interpret the poetry in the light of the political context of Marvell's personality and milieu. Christopher Hill's Marxist approach included here is one of the first attempts to read the lyrics in political and social terms, and recently John M. Wallace in *Destiny His Choice* (1968) has attempted to redefine the political position of Marvell, and to relate it to the poetry.

The development of these approaches has led, of course, to some striking clashes of interpretation. The confrontation of the critic and scholar (historical, iconographical, rhetorical) has been a recurrent feature of the last two decades of Marvell studies. It can be seen in the debate between Cleanth Brooks and Douglas Bush over 'An Horatian Ode', and between F. W. Bateson and F. R. Leavis over 'A Dialogue between the Soul and Body', and in the perpetual discussion of 'vegetable love' in 'To his Coy Mistress'.

The volume of criticism on Marvell has developed considerably in the last ten years. Both Pierre Legouis and Frank Kermode have valuably pricked some of the absurdities of over-ingenious and unhelpful 'interpretation'.[1] But new absurdities continually appear, and much of the published work has nothing to offer of either criticism or scholarship. The 'simplicity' once remarked upon is a quality rarely noted or looked for by modern critics, and though they note his qualities of lightness, grace and wit, few have achieved these themselves. Fortunately Marvell seems as well able to survive the weight of commentary as his earlier neglect. His elusiveness, his obliqueness, his ironic, wry detachment save him from any firm critical categorisation. After the most formidable of critical accounts, we can turn again to his poetry and find it as untouched, as evasive, as enigmatic as ever.

[1] *Review of English Studies*, xvii (Jan 1941) 37–46.

[2] Pierre Legouis, 'Marvell and the New Critics', in *Review of English Studies*, viii (Nov 1957) 382–9; Frank Kermode, 'Marvell Transprosed', in *Encounter*, xxvii (Nov 1966) 77–84. There is another survey by Bruce King, 'In Search of Marvell', in *Review of English Literature*, viii (Oct 1967) 31–41.

EDITOR'S NOTE

The selection of essays for this volume has been restricted in two ways. Firstly, the Marvell represented is the Marvell of *Miscellaneous Poems* (1681). I have not attempted to represent discussions of either his prose or his satires, since these have provoked very few modern judgements. Secondly, I have not abstracted material from books or monographs devoted to Marvell. I have assumed that the serious reader would be likely to consult these anyway, and would not welcome the duplication of material. Books devoted to Marvell are listed separately in the Bibliography.

The major source for any study of the reputation of and development of critical interest in Marvell is the final chapter and the bibliography of Pierre Legouis, *André Marvell: poète, puritain, patriote, 1621–1678* (Paris, 1928), and the additional information in the abridgement and translation of this study, *Andrew Marvell: poet, puritan, patriot* (Oxford, 1965; rev. 2nd ed. 1968). In preparing the Introduction to this volume, my debt to Professor Legouis's exhaustive researches has been immense. I am indebted, also, for references to additional material to Joseph E. Duncan's valuable study, *The Revival of Metaphysical Poetry* (Minneapolis, 1959), and to additional notes by John Butt to J. B. Leishman, *The Art of Marvell's Poetry* (1966). I am very grateful indeed to Mrs E. E. Duncan-Jones, and to Mr H. Neville Davies, Mr R. M. Cummings, and Mr J. D. Peacock, for unpublished information they have allowed me to incorporate into the Introduction, and for helpful discussion of the selection of essays.

Unless otherwise stated, all quotations from Marvell are from the *Poems and Letters of Andrew Marvell*, ed. H. M. Margoliouth (Oxford, 1927; revised 1952).

MICHAEL WILDING

Chronology

1621 31 March, Andrew Marvell born, fourth child and first son of the 'facetious and yet Calvinistic' Rev. Andrew Marvell, and his wife, Anne Pease, at Winstead-in-Holderness, Yorkshire.

1624 October, Rev. Marvell chosen by burgesses of Hull to be lecturer in Holy Trinity Church and master of the Charterhouse.

1633 Andrew Marvell left Hull Grammar School, and 14 December matriculated as sizar of Trinity College, Cambridge. The poet Cowley was at Trinity with Marvell, 1637–41.

1637 Marvell contributed two poems (in Latin and Greek) to *Musa Cantabrigiensis*; contributors included Joseph Beaumont, Richard Crashaw, Cowley, Edward King.

1638 April, Marvell made a scholar of Trinity. 28 April his mother died. 27 November his father married Lucy Alured, a widow.

1639 Graduated B.A. Converted by 'Jesuits' and fled from Cambridge. His father discovered him 'in a *Bookseller's* Shop in *London*, and prevailed with him to return to the College'.

1641 23 January Rev. Marvell drowned crossing River Humber by boat. Marvell excluded from Trinity.

1642 About this time Marvell began, according to Milton, his 'four years abroad in Holland, France, Italy, and Spain' and acquired the four languages. At some stage he was in Rome, where he met Flecknoe, who was there 1645–7.

1645 'Thyrsis and Dorinda' set to music by William Lawes about this time, and presumably written somewhat earlier.

1648 Marvell wrote commendatory poem on the royalist Lovelace's *Lucasta*, and was perhaps author of elegy on Francis Villiers, killed taking part in a royalist uprising in July.

1649 Contributed an elegy to *Lachrymae Musarum* on death of Henry, Lord Hastings. Denham, Dryden and Herrick also contributed.

1650 'Tom May's Death' and 'An Horatian Ode'. Thomas, Lord
      Fairfax, former commander-in-chief of Parliamentary army,
      resigned from Parliament, disapproving of execution of king and
      proposed campaign against Scots; retired to his estates at Nun
      Appleton and Bilborough in Yorkshire. Marvell employed as
      tutor in languages to his daughter Mary, until end of 1652. 'Upon
      the Hill and Grove at Bill-borow' and 'Upon Appleton House'
      both dedicated to Fairfax.

1651 Latin and English commendatory verses to Doctor Witty, in his
      translation of Dr James Primrose's *Popular Errors*; both were
      doctors at Hull.

1653 February, Latin poem to Oliver St John. Wrote 'Character of
      Holland'. Milton, blind now for a year, unsuccessfully recom-
      mended Marvell to be assistant to him as Latin Secretary. By
      July, Marvell had been appointed tutor to William Dutton, son
      of a cavalier (d. 1646), protégé and from 1657 ward of Cromwell,
      who planned to marry his youngest daughter, Frances, to him.
      Marvell lived at Eton with Dutton in house of Oxenbridge,
      who had twice visited Bermudas, and perhaps inspired Marvell's
      poem.

1654 'The First Anniversary' written, published anonymously 1655.
      Marvell still at Eton, where he witnessed leases of two college
      houses in August.

1656 January, Marvell with Dutton at Saumur in France, and still
      there in August when royalist James Scudamore referred in a
      letter to them, 'Mr Dutton, called by the French Le Genre du
      Protecteur whose Governour is one Mervill, a notable English
      Italo-Machiavellian.'

1657 Fairfax's daughter Mary married Duke of Buckingham. Marvell
      wrote 'On the Victory obtained by Blake over the Spaniards'
      (June–July) and 'Two Songs at the Marriage of the Lord Faucon-
      berg and the Lady Mary Cromwell' (November). September,
      became Latin Secretary to the Commonwealth, assistant to
      Thurloe, the Secretary of State.

1658 Latin epitaph on Oxenbridge's wife, Jane. 'A Poem upon the
      Death of O.C.' written.

1659 Elected Member of Parliament for Hull, a seat he held for rest of
      his life. Still Latin Secretary. Granted lodgings in Whitehall, 14
      July. Member of Harrington's Rota Club 1659–60.

1660 Marvell returned as the junior member for Hull, April. 17
December, Marvell asked in Commons for release of Milton
from prison without payment of extortionate fees demanded.

1662 Exchanged blows in House of Commons with Thomas Clifford.
May, in Holland with Sir George Downing, the British Minister,
at the Hague.

1663 April, back in Westminster. July, left with Earl of Carlisle,
Ambassador Extraordinary to Russia, Sweden and Denmark, as
his secretary in a party of nearly eighty. Arrived Archangel, 19
August.

1664 24 June left Moscow for Stockholm; 13 October left for Copen-
hagen; 15 December returned overland via Hamburg to Calais.
John, son of Marvell's friend Sir John Trott, died; Latin epitaph
by Marvell.

1665 30 January, reached London. 'Became a sojourner in Oxford for
the sake of the public library, and continued there, I presume,
some months' (Wood). Parliament held in Oxford in October
because of plague in London. 100 lines of 'Character of Holland',
without his name and with a contemporary ending not by him,
published.

1667 'Last Instructions to a Painter', 'Clarindon's House-Warming',
'Letter to Sir John Trott'.

1670 Latin verses 'Inscribenda Luparæ' written in competition for
verses for Louvre. Perhaps author of 'The Kings Vows'.

1671 'Further Advice to a Painter', 'The Loyall Scot', Latin and English
verses on Blood's stealing the crown. Fairfax died.

1672 Charles II's Declaration of Indulgence. Marvell defends this
policy of religious toleration in *The Rehearsal Transpros'd*,
attacking Samuel Parker, archdeacon of Canterbury.

1673 Parliament forced Charles to accept Test Act against Roman
Catholics. *Rehearsal Transpros'd part II.*

1674 January–February, in Holland. Associated with Dutch fifth
column in England seeking to end Anglo-Dutch War. 'On Mr
Milton's Paradise lost' prefixed to 2nd edition of Milton's poem.

1675 'The Statue in Stocks-Market', 'The Statue at Charing Cross',
'A Dialogue between the two Horses', and parody of Charles's
speech opening Parliament.

1676 *Mr Smirke; Or, The Divine in Mode.*

1677 Marvell harboured from the law two bankrupt businessmen,

Edward Nelthorpe and Richard Thompson, lodging them in a house in Great Russell Street in London, leased by Mary Palmer. Marvell had to apologise for 'insolence' to Speaker in Commons. *An Account of the Growth of Popery, and Abritrary Government in England.* Marvell's 'intimate friend', James Harrington, died.

1678 March, *London Gazette* announced offer of reward for information of author or printer of *Growth of Popery*. *Remarks Upon a Late Disingenuous Discourse.* August 16, died in his house in Great Russell Street of an ague; some contemporary suspicions of poisoning. Buried at St Giles in the Fields.

1681 *Miscellaneous Poems* published, certified 15 October 1680 by Mary Marvell to be 'Printed according to the exact Copies of my late dear Husband'. No record of this marriage has been found, though Mary Marvell claimed it took place in May 1677. F. S. Tupper in 'Mary Palmer, alias Mrs Andrew Marvell', in *PMLA* LIII (June 1938) 367–82, argues the marriage was a fabrication.

T. S. ELIOT

Andrew Marvell — I (1921)

THE tercentenary of the former member for Hull deserves not only the celebration proposed by that favoured borough, but a little serious reflection upon his writing. That is an act of piety, which is very different from the resurrection of a deceased reputation. Marvell has stood high for some years; his best poems are not very many, and not only must be well known, from the *Golden Treasury* and the *Oxford Book of English Verse*, but must also have been enjoyed by numerous readers. His grave needs neither rose nor rue nor laurel; there is no imaginary justice to be done; we may think about him, if there be need for thinking, for our own benefit, not his. To bring the poet back to life – the great, the perennial, task of criticism – is in this case to squeeze the drops of the essence of two or three poems; even confining ourselves to these, we may find some precious liquor unknown to the present age. Not to determine rank, but to isolate this quality, is the critical labour. The fact that of all Marvell's verse, which is itself not a great quantity, the really valuable part consists of a very few poems indicates that the unknown quality of which we speak is probably a literary rather than a personal quality; or, more truly, that it is a quality of a civilization, of a traditional habit of life. A poet like Donne, or like Baudelaire or Laforgue, may almost be considered the inventor of an attitude, a system of feeling or of morals. Donne is difficult to analyse: what appears at one time a curious personal point of view may at another time appear rather the precise concentration of a kind of feeling diffused in the air about him. Donne and his shroud, the shroud and his motive for wearing it, are inseparable, but they are not the same thing. The seventeenth century sometimes seems for more than a moment to gather up and to digest into its art all the experience of the human mind which (from the same point of view) the later centuries seem to have been partly engaged in repudiating. But Donne would have been an individual at any time and place; Marvell's best verse is the product of European, that is to say Latin, culture.

Out of that high style developed from Marlowe through Jonson (for Shakespeare does not lend himself to these genealogies) the seventeenth century separated two qualities: wit and magniloquence. Neither is as simple or as apprehensible as its name seems to imply, and the two are not in practice antithetical; both are conscious and cultivated, and the mind which cultivates one may cultivate the other. The actual poetry, of Marvell, of Cowley, of Milton, and of others, is a blend in varying proportions. And we must be on guard not to employ the terms with too wide a comprehension; for like the other fluid terms with which literary criticism deals, the meaning alters with the age, and for precision we must rely to some degree upon the literacy and good taste of the reader. The wit of the Caroline poets is not the wit of Shakespeare, and it is not the wit of Dryden, the great master of contempt, or of Pope, the great master of hatred, or of Swift, the great master of disgust. What is meant is some quality which is common to the songs in *Comus* and Cowley's Anacreontics and Marvell's 'Horatian Ode'. It is more than a technical accomplishment, or the vocabulary and syntax of an epoch; it is, what we have designated tentatively as wit, a tough reasonableness beneath the slight lyric grace. You cannot find it in Shelley or Keats or Wordsworth; you cannot find more than an echo of it in Landor; still less in Tennyson or Browning; and among contemporaries Mr Yeats is an Irishman and Mr Hardy is a modern Englishman – that is to say, Mr Hardy is without it and Mr Yeats is outside of the tradition altogether. On the other hand, as it certainly exists in Lafontaine, there is a large part of it in Gautier. And of the magniloquence, the deliberate exploitation of the possibilities of magnificence in language which Milton used and abused, there is also use and even abuse in the poetry of Baudelaire.

Wit is not a quality that we are accustomed to associate with 'Puritan' literature, with Milton or with Marvell. But if so, we are at fault partly in our conception of wit and partly in our generalizations about the Puritans. And if the wit of Dryden or of Pope is not the only kind of wit in the language, the rest is not merely a little merriment or a little levity or a little impropriety or a little epigram. And, on the other hand, the sense in which a man like Marvell is a 'Puritan' is restricted. The persons who opposed Charles I and the persons who supported the Commonwealth were not all of the flock of Zeal-of-the-land Busy or the United Grand Junction Ebenezer Temperance Association. Many of them were gentlemen of the time who merely believed, with con-

siderable show of reason, that government by a Parliament of gentlemen was better than government by a Stuart; though they were, to
that extent, Liberal Practitioners, they could hardly foresee the tea-
meeting and the Dissidence of Dissent. Being men of education and
culture, even of travel, some of them were exposed to that spirit of the
age which was coming to be the French spirit of the age. This spirit,
curiously enough, was quite opposed to the tendencies latent or the
forces active in Puritanism; the contest does great damage to the poetry
of Milton; Marvell, an active servant of the public, but a lukewarm
partisan, and a poet on a smaller scale, is far less injured by it. His line
on the statue of Charles II, 'It is such a King as no chisel can mend', may
be set off against his criticism of the Great Rebellion: 'Men . . . ought
and might have trusted the King'. Marvell, therefore, more a man of
the century than a Puritan, speaks more clearly and unequivocally
with the voice of his literary age than does Milton.

This voice speaks out uncommonly strong in the 'Coy Mistress'.
The theme is one of the great traditional commonplaces of European
literature. It is the theme of 'O mistress mine', of 'Gather ye rosebuds',
of 'Go, lovely rose'; it is in the savage austerity of Lucretius and the
intense levity of Catullus. Where the wit of Marvell renews the theme
is in the variety and order of the images. In the first of the three para-
graphs Marvell plays with a fancy which begins by pleasing and leads
to astonishment.

> Had we but World enough, and Time,
> This coyness Lady were no crime.
> . . . I would
> Love you ten years before the Flood:
> And you should if you please refuse
> Till the Conversion of the *Jews*.
> My vegetable Love should grow
> Vaster than Empires, and more slow. . . .

We notice the high speed, the succession of concentrated images, each
magnifying the original fancy. When this process has been carried to
the end and summed up, the poem turns suddenly with that surprise
which has been one of the most important means of poetic effect since
Homer:

> But at my back I alwaies hear
> Times winged Charriot hurrying near:

> And yonder all before us lye
> Desarts of vast Eternity.

A whole civilization resides in these lines:

> Pallida Mors æquo pulsat pede pauperum tabernas,
> Regumque turris. . . .

And not only Horace but Catullus himself:

> Nobis, cum semel occidit brevis lux,
> Nox est perpetua una dormienda.

The verse of Marvell has not the grand reverberation of Catullus's Latin; but the image of Marvell is certainly more comprehensive and penetrates greater depths than Horace's.

A modern poet, had he reached the height, would very likely have closed on this moral reflection. But the three strophes of Marvell's poem have something like a syllogistic relation to each other. After a close approach to the mood of Donne,

> then Worms shall try
> That long preserv'd Virginity . . .
> The Grave's a fine and private place,
> But none I think do there embrace,

the conclusion,

> Let us roll all our Strength, and all
> Our sweetness, up into one Ball,
> And tear our Pleasures with rough strife,
> Thorough the Iron gates of Life.

It will hardly be denied that this poem contains wit; but it may not be evident that this wit forms the crescendo and diminuendo of a scale of great imaginative power. The wit is not only combined with, but fused into, the imagination. We can easily recognize a witty fancy in the successive images ('my *vegetable* love', 'till the conversion of the Jews'), but this fancy is not indulged, as it sometimes is by Cowley or Cleveland, for its own sake. It is structural decoration of a serious idea.

In this it is superior to the fancy of 'L'Allegro', 'Il Penseroso', or the lighter and less successful poems of Keats. In fact, this alliance of levity and seriousness (by which the seriousness is intensified) is a characteristic of the sort of wit we are trying to identify. It is found in

> Le squelette était invisible
> Au temps heureux de l'art païen!

of Gautier, and in the *dandysme* of Baudelaire and Laforgue. It is in the poem of Catullus which has been quoted, and in the variation by Ben Jonson:

> Cannot we deceive the eyes
> Of a few poor household spies?

> 'Tis no sin love's fruits to steal,
> But that sweet sin to reveal,
> To be taken, to be seen,
> These have sins accounted been.

It is in Propertius and Ovid. It is a quality of a sophisticated literature; a quality which expands in English literature just at the moment before the English mind altered; it is not a quality which we should expect Puritanism to encourage. When we come to Gray and Collins, the sophistication remains only in the language, and has disappeared from the feeling. Gray and Collins were masters, but they had lost that hold on human values, that firm grasp of human experience, which is a formidable achievement of the Elizabethan and Jacobean poets. This wisdom, cynical perhaps but untired (in Shakespeare, a terrifying clairvoyance), leads toward, and is only completed by, the religious comprehension; it leads to the point of the 'Ainsi tout leur a craqué dans la main' of Bouvard and Pécuchet.

The difference between imagination and fancy, in view of this poetry of wit, is a very narrow one. Obviously, an image which is immediately and unintentionally ridiculous is merely a fancy. In the poem 'Upon Appleton House', Marvell falls in with one of these undesirable images, describing the attitude of the house toward its master:

> Yet thus the laden House does sweat,
> And scarce indures the *Master* great:
> But where he comes the swelling Hall
> Stirs, and the *Square* grows *Spherical*;

which, whatever its intention, is more absurd than it was intended to be.
Marvell also falls into the even commoner error of images which are
over-developed or distracting; which support nothing but their own
misshapen bodies:

> But now the *Salmon-Fishers* moist
> Their *Leathern Boats* begin to hoist;
> And, like *Antipodes* in Shoes,
> Have shod their *Heads* in their *Canoes*.

Of this sort of image a choice collection may be found in Johnson's
Life of Cowley. But the images in the 'Coy Mistress' are not only witty,
but satisfy the elucidation of Imagination given by Coleridge:

> This power . . . reveals itself in the balance or reconcilement of opposite
> or discordant qualities: of sameness, with difference; of the general, with the
> concrete; the idea with the image; the individual with the representative;
> the sense of novelty and freshness with old and familiar objects; a more than
> usual state of emotion with more than usual order; judgement ever awake and
> steady self-possession with enthusiasm and feeling profound or vehement. . . .

Coleridge's statement applies also to the following verses, which are
selected because of their similarity, and because they illustrate the
marked caesura which Marvell often introduces in a short line:

> The tawny Mowers enter next;
> Who seem like *Israelites* to be,
> Walking on foot through a green Sea. . . .

> And now the Meadows fresher dy'd;
> Whose grass, with moister colour dasht,
> Seems as green Silks but newly washt. . . .

> He hangs in shades the Orange bright,
> Like golden Lamps in a green Night. . . .

> Annihilating all that's made
> To a green Thought in a green Shade. . . .

> Had it liv'd long, it would have been
> Lilies without, Roses within.

The whole poem, from which the last of these quotations is drawn ('The Nymph and the Faun'), is built upon a very slight foundation, and we can imagine what some of our modern practitioners of slight themes would have made of it. But we need not descend to an invidious contemporaneity to point the difference. Here are six lines from 'The Nymph and the Faun':

> I have a Garden of my own,
> But so with Roses over grown,
> And Lillies, that you would it guess
> To be a little Wilderness;
> And all the Spring-time of the year
> It onely loved to be there.

And here are five lines from 'The Nymph's Song to Hylas' in the 'Life and Death of Jason', by William Morris:

> I know a little garden close
> Set thick with lily and red rose.
> Where I would wander if I might
> From dewy dawn to dewy night,
> And have one with me wandering.

So far the resemblance is more striking than the difference, although we might just notice the vagueness of allusion in the last line to some indefinite person, form, or phantom, compared with the more explicit reference of emotion to object which we should expect from Marvell. But in the latter part of the poem Morris divaricates widely:

> Yet tottering as I am, and weak,
> Still have I left a little breath
> To seek within the jaws of death
> An entrance to that happy place;
> To seek the unforgotten face
> Once seen, once kissed, once reft from me
> Anigh the murmuring of the sea.

Here the resemblance, if there is any, is to the latter part of the 'Coy Mistress'. As for the difference, it could not be more pronounced. The effect of Morris's charming poem depends upon the mistiness of the feeling and the vagueness of its object; the effect of Marvell's upon its bright, hard precision. And this precision is not due to the fact that Marvell is concerned with cruder or simpler or more carnal emotions. The emotion of Morris is not more refined or more spiritual; it is merely more vague: if anyone doubts whether the more refined or spiritual emotion can be precise, he should study the treatment of the varieties of discarnate emotion in the *Paradiso*. A curious result of the comparison of Morris's poem with Marvell's is that the former, though it appears to be more serious, is found to be the slighter; and Marvell's 'Nymph and the Faun', appearing more slight, is the more serious.

> So weeps the wounded Balsome: so
> The holy Frankincense doth flow;
> The brotherless *Heliades*
> Melt in such Amber Tears as these.

These verses have the suggestiveness of true poetry; and the verses of Morris, which are nothing if not an attempt to suggest, really suggest nothing; and we are inclined to infer that the suggestiveness is the aura around a bright clear centre, that you cannot have the aura alone. The day-dreamy feeling of Morris is essentially a slight thing; Marvell takes a slight affair, the feeling of a girl for her pet, and gives it a connexion with that inexhaustible and terrible nebula of emotion which surrounds all our exact and practical passions and mingles with them. Again, Marvell does this in a poem which, because of its formal pastoral machinery, may appear a trifling object:

> *Clorinda.* Near this, a Fountaines liquid Bell
> Tinkles within the concave Shell.
>
> *Damon.* Might a Soul bath there and be clean,
> Or slake its Drought?

where we find that a metaphor has suddenly rapt us to the image of spiritual purgation. There is here the element of *surprise*, as when Villon says:

> Necessité faict gens mesprendre
> Et faim saillir le loup des boys,

the surprise which Poe considered of the highest importance, and also
the restraint and quietness of tone which make the surprise possible.
And in the verses of Marvell which have been quoted there is the
making the familiar strange, and the strange familiar, which Coleridge
attributed to good poetry.

The effort to construct a dream world, which alters English poetry
so greatly in the nineteenth century, a dream world utterly different
from the visionary realities of the *Vita Nuova* or of the poetry of Dante's
contemporaries, is a problem of which various explanations may no
doubt be found; in any case, the result makes a poet of the nineteenth
century, of the same size as Marvell, a more trivial and less serious
figure. Marvell is no greater personality than William Morris, but he
had something much more solid behind him: he had the vast and penetrating influence of Ben Jonson. Jonson never wrote anything purer
than Marvell's 'Horatian Ode'; this ode has that same quality of wit
which was diffused over the whole Elizabethan product and concentrated in the work of Jonson. And, as was said before, this wit which
pervades the poetry of Marvell is more Latin, more refined, than anything that succeeded it. The great danger, as well as the great interest
and excitement, of English prose and verse, compared with French, is
that it permits and justifies an exaggeration of particular qualities to the
exclusion of others. Dryden was great in wit, as Milton in magniloquence; but the former, by isolating this quality and making it by
itself into great poetry, and the latter, by coming to dispense with it
altogether, may perhaps have injured the language. In Dryden wit
becomes almost fun, and thereby loses some contact with reality;
becomes pure fun, which French wit almost never is.

> The midwife placed her hand on his thick skull,
> With this prophetic blessing: *Be thou dull.* . . .
> A numerous host of dreaming saints succeed,
> Of the true old enthusiastic breed.

This is audacious and splendid; it belongs to satire beside which Marvell's Satires are random babbling, but it is perhaps as exaggerated as:

> Oft he seems to hide his face,
> But unexpectedly returns,
> And to his faithful champion hath in place
> Bore witness gloriously; whence Gaza mourns,

And all that band them to resist
His uncontrollable intent.

How oddly the sharp Dantesque phrase 'whence Gaza mourns' springs
out from the brilliant contortions of Milton's sentence!

Who, from his private Gardens, where
He liv'd reserved and austere,
    As if his highest plot
    To plant the Bergamot
Could by industrious Valour climbe
To ruine the great Work of Time,
    And cast the Kingdome old
    Into another Mold.

.   .   .

The *Pict* no shelter now shall find
Within his party-colour'd Mind,
    But from this Valour sad
    Shrink underneath the Plad:

There is here an equipoise, a balance and proportion of tones, which,
while it cannot raise Marvell to the level of Dryden or Milton, extorts
an approval which these poets do not receive from us, and bestows a
pleasure at least different in kind from any they can often give. It is
what makes Marvell a classic; or classic in a sense in which Gray and
Collins are not; for the latter, with all their accredited purity, are
comparatively poor in shades of feeling to contrast and unite.

We are baffled in the attempt to translate the quality indicated by
the dim and antiquated term wit into the equally unsatisfactory
nomenclature of our own time. Even Cowley is only able to define
it by negatives:

Comely in thousand shapes appears;
    Yonder we saw it plain; and here 'tis now,
    Like spirits in a place, we know not how.

It has passed out of our critical coinage altogether, and no new term
has been struck to replace it; the quality seldom exists, and is never
recognized.

> In a true piece of Wit all things must be
>   Yet all things there agree;
> As in the Ark, join'd without force or strife,
> All creatures dwelt, all creatures that had life.
>   Or as the primitive forms of all
>   (If we compare great things with small)
> Which, without discord or confusion, lie
> In that strange mirror of the Deity.

So far Cowley has spoken well. But if we are to attempt even no more than Cowley, we, placed in a retrospective attitude, must risk much more than anxious generalizations. With our eye still on Marvell, we can say that wit is not erudition; it is sometimes stifled by erudition, as in much of Milton. It is not cynicism, though it has a kind of toughness which may be confused with cynicism by the tender-minded. It is confused with erudition because it belongs to an educated mind, rich in generations of experience; and it is confused with cynicism because it implies a constant inspection and criticism of experience. It involves, probably, a recognition, implicit in the expression of every experience, of other kinds of experience which are possible, which we find as clearly in the greatest as in poets like Marvell. Such a general statement may seem to take us a long way from 'The Nymph and the Faun', or even from the 'Horatian Ode'; but it is perhaps justified by the desire to account for that precise taste of Marvell's which finds for him the proper degree of seriousness for every subject which he treats. His errors of taste, when he trespasses, are not sins against this virtue; they are conceits, distended metaphors and similes, but they never consist in taking a subject too seriously or too lightly. This virtue of wit is not a peculiar quality of minor poets, or of the minor poets of one age or of one school; it is an intellectual quality which perhaps only becomes noticeable by itself, in the work of lesser poets. Furthermore, it is absent from the work of Wordsworth, Shelley, and Keats, on whose poetry nineteenth-century criticism has unconsciously been based. To the best of their poetry wit is irrelevant:

> Art thou pale for weariness
> Of climbing heaven and gazing on the earth,
> Wandering companionless
> Among the stars that have a different birth,
> And ever changing, like a joyless eye,
> That finds no object worth its constancy?

We should find it difficult to draw any useful comparison between these lines of Shelley and anything by Marvell. But later poets, who would have been the better for Marvell's quality, were without it; even Browning seems oddly immature, in some way, beside Marvell. And nowadays we find occasionally good irony, or satire, which lack wit's internal equilibrium, because their voices are essentially protests against some outside sentimentality or stupidity; or we find serious poets who seem afraid of acquiring wit, lest they lose intensity. The quality which Marvell had, this modest and certainly impersonal virtue – whether we call it wit or reason, or even urbanity – we have patently failed to define. By whatever name we call it, and however we define that name, it is something precious and needed and apparently extinct; it is what should preserve the reputation of Marvell. 'C'était une belle âme, comme on ne fait plus à Londres.'

SOURCE: *Times Literary Supplement*; reprinted in T. S. Eliot, *Selected Essays* (1932).

T. S. ELIOT

Andrew Marvell—II (1923)

THE Nonesuch Press, having produced an admirable edition of poems by John Donne, has now brought out a still more beautiful and wholly satisfactory edition of Marvell [*Miscellaneous Poems*, edition limited to 850 copies]. It is to be hoped that these will be followed by similar editions of other poets of the same epoch; for if seventeenth-century poetry is to be in fashion – and we suspect that the Nonesuch Press is a barometer of the tastes of at least 850 people – let it be a thoroughgoing fashion. Fashions can be turned to account, and in this fashion there is a great deal that is wholly commendable; but if it is to be fruitful, and not merely an expression of petulance against the nineteenth century, it must establish itself by a discriminating study of a considerable number of poets, an appreciation of what they have in common, and of what each has that he shares with none other.

A year or two ago, after the City of Hull, with more gratitude than most cities, had commemorated the tercentenary of a Parliamentarian who had served his constituency well, there appeared a memorial volume which did more credit to the City which subventioned it than to the writers whose critical essays on Andrew Marvell were there assembled. From such a collection some genuine agreement, or definite difference, concerning the place and significance in English literature of the author celebrated, ought to transpire: but it never does. Critics almost invariably treat a writer, on such solemn occasions, as if it were impiety to recognize that any other authors have existed, or have had any relation to the subject of the eulogy. Exactly the points which it is their business to ponder, and on which their consensus or discord would have some interest and value, are avoided; the critics neither agree nor disagree: they expatiate upon their own whimsies and fancies. Now, a poet must be very great, very individual indeed, for us to be more or less safe in isolating him in this way; and even then we have only the part of a true appreciation. And Marvell and his contemporaries

are not in this class. There is not one of them who is a safe model
for study, in the sense that Chaucer, that Pope, is a safe model. For they
are all more or less fantastical. This is no censure; there is no reason why
a poet should not be as fantastical as possible, if that is the only way for
him. But fantasticality must be that proper to its age, and the fantastic
which may be a proper expression for our own will not be the fantastic
of any other. Our conceits cannot be those of Marvell; they will spring,
equally genuine, from a different impulse, from a different level of
feeling.

Marvell is, without doubt, a very conceited poet. In a conceit two
things very different are brought together, and the spark of ecstasy
generated in us is a perception of power in bringing them together.
It is, in my opinion, a conceit of the very finest order when Marvell
says, of a spring of clear water:

> Might a Soul bath there and be clean,
> Or slake its Drought?

Our pleasure is in the suddenness of the transference from material to
spiritual water. But when Shakespeare says –

> She looks like sleep
> As she would catch another Antony
> In her strong toil of grace,

it is not a conceit. For instead of contrast we have fusion: a restoration
of language to contact with things. Such words have the inevitability
which make them appropriate to be spoken by any character. And
when a greater than Marvell – Bishop King – says –

> But hark! my pulse, like a soft drum,
> Beats my approach, tells thee I come,

that also is a conceit. If the drum were left out it would cease to be a
conceit – but it would lose the valuable associations which the drum
gives it. But when Dante says –

> Qual si fe Glauco, al gustar della erba,

or –

> l'impresa
> Che fe Nettuno ammirar l'ombra d'Argo,

or the best known –

> si ver noi aguzzevan le ciglia,
> come vecchio sartor fa nella cruna,

these are not conceits. They have a rational necessity as well as suggestiveness; they are, like the words of Shakespeare above, an *explication* of the meaning.

A conceit is not to be something practised by the poet and despised by the critic; it has its place; for a purpose, for a poet, for a whole age, it may be the proper thing. And we must understand that the conceits which seem to us to fail are formed by exactly the same method as the conceits which seem to us to succeed. For that understanding we must read the whole of Marvell. But we must not only read the whole of Marvell; we must read Cleveland as well. And for this reason, and for others, and for the simple pleasure in a well-made book, we hope that the Nonesuch Press will continue their editions of seventeenth-century poets.

SOURCE: *Nation and Athenaeum*, (29 September 1923).

WILLAM EMPSON

Marvell's 'Garden' (1932)

THE chief point of the poem is to contrast and reconcile conscious and unconscious states, intuitive and intellectual modes of apprehension; and yet that distinction is never made, perhaps could not have been made; his thought is implied by his metaphors. There is something very Far Eastern about this; I was reminded of it by Mr Richard's discussion, in a recent *Psyche*, of a philosophical argument out of Mencius. The Oxford edition notes bring out a crucial double meaning (so this at least is not my own fancy) in the most analytical statement of the poem, about the Mind:

> Annihilating all that's made
> To a green Thought in a green Shade.

'Either "reducing the whole material world to nothing material, i.e. to a green thought", or "considering the material world as of no value compared to a green thought" '; either contemplating everything or shutting everything out. This combines the idea of the conscious mind, including everything because understanding it, and that of the unconscious animal nature, including everything because in harmony with it. Evidently the object of such a fundamental contradiction (seen in the etymology: turning all *ad nihil*, to nothing, and *to* a thought) is to deny its reality; the point is not that these two are essentially different but that they must cease to be different so far as either is to be known. So far as he has achieved his state of ecstasy he combines them, he is 'neither conscious nor not conscious', like the seventh Buddhist stage of enlightenment. (It is by implying something like this, I think, that the puns in Donne's 'Extasie' too become more than a simple Freudian give-away.) But once you accept this note you may as well apply it to the whole verse.

> Mean while the Mind, from pleasure less,
> Withdraws into its happiness:

> The Mind, that Ocean where each kind
> Does streight its own resemblance find;
> Yet it creates, transcending these,
> Far other Worlds, and other Seas;
> Annihilating . . .

From pleasure less. Either 'from the lessening of pleasure' – 'we are quiet in the country, but our dullness gives a sober and self-knowing happiness, more intellectual than that of the overstimulated pleasures of the town' or 'made less by this pleasure' – 'The pleasures of the country give a repose and emotional release which make me feel less intellectual, make my mind less worrying and introspective.' This is the same opposition; the ambiguity gives two meanings to pleasure, corresponding to his Puritan ambivalence about it, and to the opposition between pleasure and happiness. *Happiness*, again, names a conscious state, and yet involves the idea of things falling right, happening so, not being ordered by an anxiety of the conscious reason. (So that as a rule it is a weak word; it is by seeming to look at it hard and bring out its implications that the verse here makes it act as a strong one.)

This same doubt gives all their grandeur to the next lines. The sea if calm reflects everything near it; the mind as knower is a conscious mirror. Somewhere in the sea are sea-lions and sea-horses and everything else, though they are different from land ones; the unconsciousness is unplumbed and pathless, and there is no instinct so strange among the beasts that it lacks its fantastic echo in the mind. In the first version thoughts are shadows, in the second (like the *green thought*) they are as solid as what they image; and yet they still correspond to something in the outer world, so that the poet's intuition is comparable to pure knowledge. (Keats may have been quoting the sixth verse, by the way, when he said that if he saw a sparrow on the path he pecked about on the gravel.) This metaphor may reflect back so that *withdraws* means the tide going down; the *mind* is less now, but will return and it is now that one can see the rock-pools. On the Freudian view of an Ocean, *withdraws* would make this repose in nature a return to the womb; anyway it may mean either 'withdraws into self-contemplation' or 'withdraws altogether, into its mysterious processes of digestion'. *Streight* may mean 'packed together', in the microcosm, or 'at once'; the beasts see their reflection (perhaps the root word of the metaphor) as soon as they look for it; the calm of nature gives the poet an immediate self-knowledge. But we have already had two entrancingly witty verses about the sublimation of sexual desire into a taste for Nature, and the *kinds* look for their *resemblance*, in practice, out of a desire for *creation*; in the mind, at this fertile time for the poet, they can do so 'at once', being 'packed together'. This profound transition, from the correspondences of thought with fact to those of thought with thought, to *find* which is to be *creative*, leads on to the next couplet, in which not only does the *mind transcend* the world it mirrors, but a sea, by a similar transition, transcends both land and sea too, which implies self-consciousness and all the antinomies of philosophy. And it is true that the sea reflects the *other worlds* of the stars. Yet even here the double meaning is not lost; all land-beasts have their sea-beasts, but the sea also has the kraken; in the depths as well as the transcendence of the mind are things stranger than all the kinds of the world.

Green takes on great weight here, as Miss Sackville-West pointed out, because it has been a pet word of Marvell's before; to list the uses before the satires may seem a trivial affectation of scholarship, but at least shows how often he used the word. In the Oxford text; pages 12, line 23: 17, line 18: 25, line 11: 27, line 4: 31, line 27: 38, line 3: 45, line 3: 70, line 376: 71, line 390: 74, line 510: 122, line 2. Less important, 15, line 18: 30, line 55: 42, line 14: 69, line 386: 74, line 484: 85, line 82: 89, line 94. It is connected here with grass, buds, children, and an as yet virginal prospect of sexuality,[2] a power of thought as yet only latent in sensibility, and the peasant stock from which the great families emerge. The 'unfathomable' grass both shows and makes a soil fertile; it is the humble, permanent, undeveloped nature which sustains everything, and to which everything must return; children are connected with this both as buds, because of their contact with Nature (as in Wordsworth), and unique fitness for Heaven (as in the Gospels).

> The tawny Mowers enter next,
> Who seem like Israelites to be,
> Walking on foot through a green Sea

connects greenness with oceans and gives it a magical security; though one must drown in it.

> And in the greenness of the Grass
> Did see its Hopes as in a Glass

connects greenness with mirrors and the partial knowledge of the mind. The complex of ideas he concentrates into this passage, in fact, had been worked out separately already.

To nineteenth-century taste the only really poetical verse of the poem is the central fifth of the nine; I have been discussing the sixth, whose dramatic position is an illustration of its very penetrating theory. The first four are a crescendo of wit, on the themes 'success or failure is not important, only the repose that follows the exercise of one's powers' and 'women, I am pleased to say, are no longer interesting to me, because nature is more beautiful'. One effect of the wit is to admit, and so make charming, the impertinence of the second of these, which indeed the first puts in its place; it is only for a time, and after effort among human beings, that he can enjoy solitude. The value of these moments made it fitting to pretend they were eternal; and yet the lightness of his expression of their sense of power is more intelligent, and so more convincing, than Wordsworth's solemnity on the same theme, because it does not forget the opposing forces.

> When we have run our Passions heat,
> Love hither makes his best retreat.
> The *Gods*, that mortal beauty chase,
> Still in a Tree did end their race.
> *Apollo* hunted *Daphne* so,
> Only that She might Laurel grow.
> And *Pan* did after *Syrinx* speed.
> Not as a Nymph, but for a Reed.

The energy and delight of the conceit has been sharpened or keyed up here till it seems to burst and transform itself; it dissolves in the next verse into the style of Keats. So his observation of the garden might mount to an ecstasy which disregarded it; he seems in this next verse to imitate the process he has described, to enjoy in a receptive state the exhilaration which an exercise of wit has achieved. But striking as the change of style is, it is unfair to empty the verse of thought and treat it as random description; what happens is that he steps back from overt classical conceits to a rich and intuitive use of Christian imagery. When people treat it as the one good 'bit' of the poem one does not know whether they have recognised that the Alpha and Omega of the verse are the Apple and the Fall.

> What wond'rous Life is this I lead!
> Ripe Apples drop about my head;
> The Luscious Clusters of the Vine
> Upon my Mouth do crush their Wine;
> The Nectaren, and curious Peach,
> Into my hands themselves do reach;
> Stumbling on Melons, as I pass,
> Insnar'd with Flow'rs, I fall on Grass.

Melon, again, is the Greek for apple; 'all flesh is *grass*', and its own *flowers* here are the snakes in it that stopped Eurydice. Mere grapes are at once the primitive and the innocent wine; the *nectar* of Eden, and yet the blood of sacrifice. *Curious* could mean 'rich and strange' (nature), 'improved by care' (art) or 'inquisitive' (feeling towards me, since nature is a mirror, as I do towards her). All these eatable beauties give themselves so as to lose themselves, like a lover, with a forceful generosity; like a lover they *ensnare* him. It is the triumph of his attempt to impose a sexual interest upon nature; there need be no more Puritanism in this use of sacrificial ideas than is already inherent in the praise of solitude; and it is because his repose in the orchard hints at such a variety of emotions that he is contemplating *all that's made*. Sensibility here repeats what wit said in the verse before; he tosses into the fantastic treasure-chest of the poem's thought all the pathos and dignity that Milton was to feel in his more celebrated Garden; and it is while this is going on, we are told in the next verse, that the mind performs its ambiguous and memorable *withdrawal*. For each of the three central verses he gives a twist to the screw of the microscope and is living in another world.

SOURCE: *Scrutiny, I* (1932), reprinted *Determinations*, ed. F. R. Leavis (1934).

NOTE

1. Cf 'giving a green gown' sixteenth century; 'having a bit of green' twentieth century'

CHRISTOPHER HILL

Society and Andrew Marvell[1] (1946)

A gentleman whose name is Mr Marvile; a man whom, both by report and the converse I have had with him, of singular desert for the State to make use of; who alsoe offers himselfe if there be any imployment for him.

(JOHN MILTON TO PRESIDENT BRADSHAW,
21 February 1653)

Amongst these lewd revilers the lewdest was one whose name was Marvell. . . . He . . . daily spewed infamous libels out of his filthy mouth against the King himself. If at any times the Fanatics had occasion for this libeller's help, he presently issued out of his cave like a gladiator or wild beast.

(SAMUEL PARKER, Bishop of Oxford, *History of his own Time*, quoted in Masson's *Life of Milton*,
VI 708).

I

AT first sight the poetry of Andrew Marvell seems to bear little relation to the age in which he lived. Marvell wrote a good deal of political satire, which is of considerable interest to the historian, but of less poetic value; his greatest poems (except the 'Horatian Ode upon Cromwel's return from Ireland') have no direct reference to the political and social revolution of the seventeenth century. Yet this revolution transformed the lives of Englishmen; it faced them with intellectual and moral decisions which it was difficult to evade. I believe that if we study Marvell with a knowledge of the political background of his life we can discover in the great lyrics new complexities which will increase our appreciation of those very sensitive and civilized poems.

Marvell was born near Hull in 1621, his father being a clergyman whom Andrew described as 'a conformist to the established rites of the Church of England, though none of the most over-running or eager in them'.[2] Marvell went to Cambridge, then much the more Puritan of the two universities, and remained there until 1640. He then travelled on the Continent for four or five years, during which period the Civil War between Charles I and his Parliament broke out. Most of Marvell's friends at this time seem to have been aristocratic young cavaliers of the type he was likely to meet in continental salons; and when he returned to England his own sympathies were apparently Royalist. But we have no real evidence for his activities, and little for his views, until 1650, the year after the execution of Charles I. Then he wrote the 'Horatian Ode upon Cromwel's return from Ireland', from which it is clear that he was prepared to accept the triumphant revolution. In the following year he became tutor to Mary Fairfax, daughter of the famous general who had led the Parliamentary armies to victory.[3] This suggests that he was already accepted as a sound Parliamentarian. The period in Yorkshire with the Fairfaxes and the years immediately following seem to have been those in which his greatest poetry was written.

In his early thirties Marvell emerged as a more active supporter of the new government. In 1653 he was personally recommended by no less a person than Milton as his assistant in the secretaryship for foreign tongues (see epigraph). Marvell failed to get this post then, becoming tutor to a ward of Oliver Cromwell instead. But in 1657 Marvell became Milton's colleague in the Foreign or Latin secretaryship. Like Pepys, he was one of the new type of civilian middle-class official who came into their own after the Civil War, during the soberer years of the Protectorate. In 1658 Marvell was elected M.P. for Hull, for which he continued to serve in successive parliaments until his death in 1678. His correspondence shows him to have been an indefatigable defender of the interests of his constituency. But his main activity was as a pamphleteer for the Parliamentary opposition to Charles II's governments and as a defender of religious liberty and freedom of thought, the struggle for which had originally attracted Milton and no doubt Marvell to the Parliamentary side.

Despite his early Royalist phase, then, Marvell became decidedly a partisan of the cause of Parliament: he was intimate with its noblest figures. He was not only the protégé of Milton, but also the friend of Harrington, shrewdest of the Parliamentarian political thinkers, and of Baxter, most resolute of Nonconformist divines. Marvell accepted the

Revolution only in his late twenties; he was no juvenile or light-hearted enthusiast. But unlike Dryden, who took service under the Protectorate at the same time as Marvell, and who wrote eulogies of Oliver Cromwell which afterwards proved embarrassing, Marvell did not leave the ship when it began to sink. In the dark days after 1660 he retained his dangerous friendship with Milton, and his partisanship became increasingly open. He invented the nickname Cabal, which has stuck to the government of Clifford, Arlington, Buckingham, Ashley, and Lauderdale. Marvell dealt roughly with the sycophantic Samuel Parker, whose brief character sketch is quoted above; and he ran great risks by the outspokenness of his attacks on the cynical extravagance of the Court, the brutalities of the advocates of religious persecution and the treacherous activities of the pro-French party at Court.

Marvell's oft-quoted remark about the Civil War, 'The Cause was too good to have been fought for', does not mean what those who cite it out of its context appear to think – that Marvell was disavowing 'the Good Old Cause'. He meant, on the contrary, that the war *should* not have been fought because it *need* not have been fought, because the victory of Parliament was inevitable, war or no war. Here Marvell was following the historical and political theory of his friend James Harrington,[4] in just the same way as Halifax did later in his *Letter to a Dissenter*: 'You Act very unskilfully against your visible Interest, if you throw away the Advantages, of which you can hardly fail in the next probable Revolution. Things tend naturally to what you would have, if you would let them alone, and not by an unseasonable Activity lose the Influences of your good star, which promiseth you every thing that is prosperous.'[5] For Marvell, after saying the cause was too good to have been fought for, continued – with an exaggeration pardonable if we recollect that he was writing under Charles II's censorship – 'The King himself, being of so accurate and piercing a judgement, would soon have felt where it stuck. For men may spare their pains when Nature is at work, and the world will not go the faster for our driving. Even as our present Majesty's happy restoration did itself come, all things else happen in their best and proper time, without any need of officiousness.'[6]

II

'The Warre was begun in our streets before the King or Parliament had any armies', wrote Baxter,[7] another of Marvell's friends, in whose defence some of his greatest pamphlets were later to be written. As the tension within society became more acute, so a new type of lyric arose, charged with the most intense feeling of the age. These lyrics, unlike the Elizabethan, were no longer intended to be sung: they had lost their social function, and existed only to resolve the conflict within the poet's mind. The poet has become an isolated individual in a divided society, and his own mind is divided too: we find this internal conflict in poets so dissimilar as Marvell's early friend Lovelace, Crashaw, and Vaughan.

A characteristic of the conceit, indeed, from Donne to Traherne (precisely the revolutionary period) is that it lays incompatibles side by side, that it unites the apparently unrelated and indeed the logically contradictory, that it obtains its effects by forcing things different in kind onto the same plane of reference. In this broad sense we may speak of the lyric of conflict, whose characteristics are an awareness in the poet's mind of the new and troubling (especially the new scientific discoveries) as well as the old and familiar, and an effort to fit them into a common scheme – first by the violent and forced juxtaposition of Donne, then by the unresolved conflict of the later metaphysicals; until finally, after the victory of the new political and intellectual forces, we get a new type of poetry drawing on new philosophical assumptions, and disturbed by none of the doubts which have tormented the sensitive since the days of Shakespeare.[8] The tortured conceit gives way to the neatly balanced rhymed couplet. This new equilibrium satisfied poets less and less in the second half of the eighteenth century, but was not finally upset until the fresh social and political crisis of the French Revolution – and Wordsworth.

The existence of a conflict of some sort in Marvell is apparent from the most careless reading of his poems. At the risk of alienating readers by an excessively crude and oversimplified statement, I wish to say briefly and dogmatically what I think may have underlain this conflict, and then to try to prove and illustrate this thesis. The suggestion is that Marvell's poetry is shot through with consciousness of a conflict between subjective and objective, between the idea and the reality, which it is perhaps not too far-fetched to link up (very indirectly, of course) with the social and political problems of his time. This conflict takes many forms, but we can trace a repeated pattern, a related series of symbols, which suggests that fundamentally all the conflicts are interrelated, and that this 'double heart' (Marvell's phrase) is as much the product of a sensitive mind in a divided society as is Day Lewis's 'divided heart'.[9] That of course is one reason why Marvell and the other 'metaphysical' poets have so attracted our generation.

One of Marvell's qualities which is most sympathetic to us is his humour, his refusal to take his agonies too seriously. This is in itself one of the aspects of the 'double heart', Marvell's ability to see both sides; but it also shows his attempt to come to terms with and to control the contradictions between his desires and the world he has to live in, his ideals and the brutal realities of the Civil War. Humour is for Marvell one way of bearing the unbearable: it is a sign of his enviable maturity, besides which Waller, Cowley, Dryden, and the other ex-Royalist and future Royalist panegyrists of Cromwell look so shabby. The opening lines of the 'Horatian Ode' perfectly illustrate this aspect of Marvell's manner:

> The forward Youth that would appear
> Must now forsake his *Muses* dear,
> Nor in the Shadows sing
> His Numbers languishing.

Less than three years after writing these lines Marvell offered his services to the Parliamentary cause, which he was never to desert in the remaining twenty-five years of his life. The light touch, the self-mockery, the hatred of the portentous which are obvious in these lines should not obscure for us the genuine doubts and struggles, conflicts and despairs, which had preceded Marvell's acceptance of the position which he here states with an irony made possible only by deep conviction. Marvell has come through when he has gained this tone.

III

But I propose to defer consideration of the 'Horatian Ode' until after we have looked at some of the lyrics, in which the political approach is less obvious. Let us begin with 'The Definition of Love', for here the points can be made merely by quotation:

> My Love is of a birth as rare
> As 'tis for object strange and high:
> It was begotten by despair
> Upon Impossibility.

Magnanimous Despair alone
Could show me so divine a thing,
Where feeble Hope could ne'r have flown
But vainly flapt its Tinsel Wing.

And yet I quickly might arrive
Where my extended Soul is fixt,
But Fate does Iron wedges drive,
And alwaies crouds it self betwixt. . . .

And therefore her Decrees of Steel
Us as the distant Poles have plac'd,
(Though Loves whole World on us doth wheel)
Not by themselves to be embrac'd. . . .

As Lines so Loves *oblique* may well
Themselves in every Angle greet:
But ours so truly *Paralel*,
Though infinite can never meet.

Therefore the Love which us doth bind,
But Fate so enviously debarrs,
Is the Conjunction of the Mind,
And Opposition of the Stars.

This is a very sophisticated poem, playing about with newly fashionable geometrical theories. The main point, obviously, is the one that I have already suggested as typical of Marvell – the conflict between Love and Fate, desire and possibility. Fate 'defines' Love in both senses of the word – it both limits it and expresses its full significance. But the poem is far more than a clever conceit. The image in lines 11 and 12 is perfect for the age of Civil War. Fate is symbolized by the products of one of the industries which were transforming rural Britain, by the conventional symbol for warlike arms; and it 'crowds itself betwixt' with irresistible force: here Fate is thought of as a tumultuous multitude of human individuals, as well as abstract military and industrial processes. Nor is Fate merely an external force. As Miss Bradbrook and Miss Lloyd Thomas said, 'Material Fate and spiritual Love, though apparently in complete opposition, are in reality two aspects of the same situation:

> Magnanimous Despair alone
> Could show me so divine a thing.

If "the Stars" were not so completely opposed, the love could not reach such heroic stature.'[10]

The individual exposed to and triumphing over and through the buffetings of Fate is the theme of the bombastic rhodomontade of 'The Unfortunate Lover':

> See how he nak'd and fierce does stand,
> Cuffing the Thunder with one hand;
> While with the other he does lock,
> And grapple, with the stubborn Rock: ...
>
> This is the only *Banneret*
> That ever Love created yet:
> Who though, by the Malignant Starrs,
> Forced to live in Storms and Warrs:
> Yet dying leaves a Perfume here,
> And Musick within every Ear:
> And he in Story only rules,
> In a Field *Sable* a Lover *Gules*.

Marvell too had been forced 'by the Malignant Starrs' 'to live in Storms and Warrs'; his finest music was wrung out of him in the grapple with a stubborn world.

Let us examine some of the other poems with these symbols and our main thesis in mind.

The titles of many speak for themselves: 'A Dialogue Between the Resolved Soul, and Created Pleasure', 'A Dialogue between the Soul and Body'. In the first of these the conflict is between a militantly Puritan soul, conscious of its mission, its calling, its arduous pilgrimage to heaven, on the one hand, and the distracting and illusory pleasures of the senses and of idleness on the other. In the second poem the conflict is more subtle:

> *Soul.* O who shall, from this Dungeon, raise
> A Soul inslav'd so many wayes?
> With bolts of Bones, that fetter'd stands
> In Feet; and manacled in Hands.

> Here blinded with an Eye; and there
> Deaf with the drumming of an Ear.
> A Soul hung up, as t'were, in Chains
> Of Nerves, and Arteries, and Veins.[11]
> Tortur'd, besides each other part,
> In a vain Head, and double Heart. . . .
>
> *Body.* But Physick yet could never reach
> The Maladies Thou me dost teach;
> Whom first the Cramp of Hope does Tear:
> And then the Palsie Shakes of Fear.
> The Pestilence of Love does heat:
> Or Hatred's hidden Ulcer eat.
> Joy's chearful Madness does perplex:
> Or Sorrow's other Madness vex.
> Which Knowledge forces me to know;
> And Memory will not foregoe.
> What but a Soul could have the wit
> To build me up for Sin so fit?
> So Architects do square and hew,
> Green Trees that in the Forest grew.

Here the antithesis is not just between soul and body, for the soul may betray the body as well as the body the soul; it is a complex, four-handed conflict, which blends the familiar themes of puritan asceticism against sensual pleasure with action against rest. (The symbolism of the last two lines is a favourite of Marvell's: the loss of certain natural qualities that the civilizing process makes inevitable. There seems, as will be shown later, to be a direct connection between this symbolism and the more obvious conflict of the Civil War.) Marvell's sympathies are here less decisively on one side than they were in the 'Dialogue Between the Resolved Soul, and Created Pleasure', where the moral issue was clear: here opposite concepts are jostling in Marvell's mind. (He is indeed one of the few Parliamentarian writers – if we except Winstanley on the extreme left – who frankly enjoys and praises the pleasures of the body.)[12]

The same complexity occurs in 'Upon Appleton House':

> As first our *Flesh* corrupt within
> Tempts impotent and bashful *Sin.*

This is not just good against evil, but evil that is also good against good that is also evil. In these complicated problems and relationships there are no easy solutions or evasions:

> To what cool Cave shall I descend,
> Or to what gelid Fountain bend?
> Alas! I look for Ease in vain,
> When Remedies themselves complain,

cried Damon the Mower. The Soul lamented to the Body that it was

> Constrain'd not only to indure
> Diseases, but, whats worse, the Cure.

Again, in complex form, though with a different solution, conflict pervades 'To his Coy Mistress'. It is no longer soul against body, but the sensual pleasures up against the hard facts of an uncongenial world in which effort is demanded. The moral is not 'Gather ye rosebuds while ye may'. It is –

> Let us roll all our Strength, and all
> Our sweetness, up into one Ball:
> And tear our Pleasures with rough strife,
> Thorough the Iron gates of Life.
> Thus, though we cannot make our Sun
> Stand still, yet we will make him run.

That, as has been well said, is a Puritan rather than a libertine conclusion:[13] the sensual pleasures are put into a subordinate place:

> Had we but World enough, and Time,
> This coyness Lady were no crime.

But as we have neither world nor time enough, coyness *is* a crime. The gates of life are iron, time's winged chariot is hurrying near:

> And yonder all before us lye
> Desarts of vast Eternity.

We may compare Marvell's own lines on 'The First Anniversary of the Government under O. C.':

> 'Tis he the force of scattered Time contracts,
> And in one Year the work of Ages acts:
> While heavy Monarchs make a wide Return,
> Longer, and more Malignant then *Saturn*:
> And though they all *Platonique* years should raign,
> In the same Posture would be found again.

It should not surprise us by now to find Marvell censuring 'heavy Monarchs' in the same vein as a coy mistress, or praising Cromwell's political activity in the same terms as those in which he had invited the lady to 'sport us while we may'.

'To his Coy Mistress' strikes a note we shall find repeated. The individual and his desires come up against the outer world, life and time. The mock-serious moral of that flippant and very un-Puritan poem 'Daphnis and Chloe' is the obverse of that of 'To his Coy Mistress'; it is better to forgo a pleasure than to be casual or half-hearted about it.

> Gentler times for Love are ment
> Who for parting pleasure strain
> Gather Roses in the rain,
> Wet themselves and spoil their Sent.

In the 'Coy Mistress' the mere epicureanism of the Court poets is *rejected*. The poem's moral, paradoxically, has more in common with the rigorous concentration and effort typical of Puritanism and commercialism. And again iron symbolizes the harsh impersonality of this world which we *must* accept.[14]

IV

The Mower, whose iron scythe cuts down himself as well as the grass, the innocent as well as the guilty, is a favourite symbol with Marvell. He appears in 'The Mower against Gardens', 'Damon the Mower', 'The Mower to the Glo-Worms', 'The Mower's Song', and 'Upon Appleton House'. The theme of 'The Mower against Gardens' is one which frequently recurs: it contrasts natural and artificial cultivation; the coarse toil and sweat of the mowers is set against the leisured sophistication, the luxury products of the garden. 'Luxurious Man', the Mower says

—first enclos'd within the Gardens square
   A dead and standing pool of Air:
And a more luscious Earth for them did knead,
   Which stupifi'd them while it fed.
The Pink grew then as double as his Mind. . . .
'Tis all enforc'd; the Fountain and the Grot;
   While the sweet Fields do lye forgot.

And over all this ostentatious opulence the Mower stands brooding like Fate, confident in his power:

   The *Gods* themselves with us do dwell.

But the nostalgia for a simpler pre-commercial age is qualified by an irony of humorous over-statement which shows that Marvell was arguing a case in which he did not wholly believe:

   And *Fauns* and *Faryes* do the Meadows till,
   More by their presence then their skill.

There is the same semi-serious regret in 'The Nymph complaining for the death of her Faun'.

The formal garden, as something essential to any gentleman's mansion, was relatively new in seventeenth-century England. There was still something exotically luxurious about it. 'God Almighty first planted a garden', but they began to become common in England as a result of the Tudor peace, of the internal order and security which allowed manor houses to replace baronial castles and created the conditions in which lesser gentry, yeomen, and merchants were able to prosper. In *The Faerie Queene* the garden is a symbol of the sheltered and opulent life of courtly society: Spenser follows in this the tradition of the mediaeval allegory of love.[15] Bacon wrote his essay to tell the very wealthy how a garden should be laid out. Stuart gardens, as the Mower has already told us, were still very formal: they were 'the greatest refreshment to the spirit of man', as Bacon put it, *because* of their contrast with rude Nature in the unenclosed waste outside. It is thus easy to see how the garden became a symbol of security, property, ease, repose, and escape:[16] it was shut off from the commons, the open fields, the sweaty vulgar outside, from the Mower. For other seventeenth-century poets as well as Marvell and Milton the garden is normally Eden rather than Gethsemane.[17]

If we take the garden as Marvell's equivalent of the ivory tower, the mere title of 'The Mower against Gardens' is a political tract in itself. The Mower symbolizes Fate, the historic process which lowers over these artificial and walled-off paradises, as Milton's Satan broods over the Garden of Eden.

The Mower is always a portentous figure:

> Sharp like his Sythe his Sorrow was,
> And wither'd like his Hopes the Grass.
>   ('Damon The Mower')

When he is lost he is guided by glow-worms:

> —Country Comets, that portend
> No War, nor Princes funeral,
> Shining unto no higher end
> Then to presage the Grasses fall.
>   ('The Mower to the Glo-Worms')

War and the death of kings are never very far away, even if they only point a contrast. In this poem and in 'The Mower's Song' the Mower is overcome by the power of love: Juliana –

> What I do to the Grass, does to my Thoughts and Me.

(cf the Fate and Love motive in 'The Definition of Love' and 'The Unfortunate Lover'). But in 'Upon Appleton House', as we shall shortly see, the Mower is directly related to the blind forces of the Civil War.[18]

The garden had its deep attractions for Marvell in the years before he plunged into public life. For he had his escapism, of which the opening of 'The Garden' is typical:

> How vainly men themselves amaze
> To win the Palm, the Oke, or Bayes;
> And their uncessant Labours see
> Crown'd from some single Herb or Tree.
> Whose short and narrow verged Shade
> Does prudently their Toyles upbraid;
> While all Flow'rs and all Trees do close
> To weave the Garlands of repose.

But even here the poet is tripped up: 'Insnar'd with flow'rs, I fall on Grass.' The calm and peace are transient, an interlude: 'Temporis O suaves lapsus!' says the Latin version. The garden is a place of temporary repose and refreshment, not a permanent haven. The mind seeks an intenser satisfaction than the merely physical pleasures of the garden: it

> creates, transcending these,
> Far other Worlds, and other Seas.

The soul looks forward to further activity even while the body is at rest:

> Casting the Bodies Vest aside,
> My Soul into the boughs does glide:
> There like a Bird it sits, and sings,
> Then whets, and combs its silver Wings;
> And, till prepar'd for longer flight,
> Waves in its Plumes the various Light.

Whilst the soul thus anticipates eternity, the garden itself recalls Paradise before the Fall. But the ambiguous phrase 'Garden-state' hints at England, and the terms of the comparison remind us that Marvell's garden is in and of this world:

> 'twas beyond a Mortal's share
> To wander solitary there.

'Society is all but rude'; yet its needs impinge remorselessly upon the ideal world of escape, prevent it being final. Already in the second verse Marvell had doubted whether quiet and innocence were to be found at all on earth. The poem began by mocking at the vanity of human effort; in the last verse 'th' industrious Bee' is introduced, who – lest we should have missed the significance of the adjective – 'computes its time as well as we'. The garden clock, for all its fragrance, reminds us of 'Times winged Chariot'. We cannot think ourselves out of time any more than we can escape from fallen humanity.

'The Nymph complaining for the death of her Faun' pictures a garden-Eden shattered by violence from without: the violence of soldiers:

> The wanton Troopers riding by
> Have shot my Faun and it will dye.

Marvell plays with the idea later to be elaborated in the 'Horatian Ode', of the innocent victim sacrificially redeeming the users of violence, but here rejects it:

> Though they should wash their guilty hands
> In this warm life-blood, which doth part
> From thine, and wound me to the Heart,
> Yet could they not be clean: their Stain
> Is dy'd in such a Purple Grain.
> There is not such another in
> The World, to offer for their Sin.

There is no easy redemption. But the tone of the complaint is curious: 'Ev'n Beasts must be with justice slain.' The Faun symbolizes an escape, and is not uncritically regarded:

> Thenceforth I set my self to play
> My solitary time away,
> With this: and very well content,
> Could so mine idle Life have spent. . . .
>   Had it liv'd long, I do not know
> Whether it too might have done so
> As *Sylvio* did: his Gifts might be
> Perhaps as false or more than he.

As always in Marvell, the conflict is far from simple: he cannot wholly praise 'a fugitive and cloistered virtue'.

In 'The Coronet', the poet seeks 'through every Garden, every Mead' for flowers to crown his Saviour (flowers 'that once adorn'd my Shepherdesses head'). But –

> Alas I find the Serpent old
> That, twining in his speckled breast,
> About the flow'rs disguis'd does fold,
> With wreaths of Fame and Interest.

And the conclusion is

> let these wither, so that he may die,
> Though set with Skill and chosen out with Care.

The garden is not enough.

V

In 'Upon Appleton House', Marvell's longest poem, all this symbolism becomes specific. The house had been a nunnery, which had come to the Fairfax family at the Reformation. In the poem the retirement, the cultured and indeed opulent ease of the nunnery is frankly opposed to the claims of a Protestant and commercial civilization. The words which Marvell writes of the earlier Fairfax who acquired the Church lands clearly presage the dilemma of the Fairfaxes, father and son, when they had to take sides in the Civil War:

> What should he do? He would respect
> Religion, but not Right neglect.

The elder Fairfax built his family mansion and his fortune on the site of the nunnery; the younger Fairfaxes took up arms in the name of liberty against the Lord's Anointed.

In the poem England before the Civil War is depicted as a garden, in which Fairfax

> did with his utmost Skill,
> *Ambition* weed, but *Conscience* till.

(That other great Parliamentary general, Oliver Cromwell left 'his private Gardens, where He liv'd reserved and austere', at the call of duty in the Civil War.)

Fairfax's garden (or England) is clearly linked up with the Garden of Eden (stanzas XLI–XLIII), concluding:

> What luckless Apple did we tast,
> To make us Mortal, and The Wast?

The symbolism of the Mower, who blindly massacres all that he meets in 'the Abbyss . . . of that unfathomable Grass', is repeated in stanzas XLVI–LIII, and the reference to the Civil War is again explicit:

> The Mower now commands the Field; . . .
> A Camp of Battail newly fought:
> Where, as the Meads with Hay, the Plain
> Lyes quilted ore with Bodies slain:

> The Women that with forks it fling,
> Do represent the Pillaging.[19]

War is no respecter of persons, cuts down the innocent and uncon-
cerned together with the guilty:

> Unhappy Birds! what does it boot
> To build below the Grasses Root;
> Where Lowness is unsafe as Hight,
> And Chance o'retakes what scapeth spight? . . .
>
> Or sooner hatch or higher build. . . .

The Levellers 'take Pattern at' 'this naked equal Flat', – 'A new and
empty Face of things'.

> The Villagers in common chase
> Their Cattle, which it closer rase;
> And what below the Sith increast
> Is pincht yet nearer by the Beast.

This direct reference to the Levellers, and hint at the destructive com-
munism of 'the many-headed monster', is symbolically followed by a
sudden inundation. Marvell 'takes Sanctuary in the Wood'. But
escapism brings no neutrality: the forces shaping our lives can neither
be controlled nor evaded. This reintroduces Marvell's other theme of
the need for equalizing desire and opportunity, the conflict brought
to a crisis by the brutal external force of the Mower. Thus Marvell's
key ideas are linked in one symbol, suggesting the possibility that all
his poems really deal with a single complex of problems.

In 'Upon Appleton House' there is humorously ironical escapism
again (stanzas LXXI–LXXXI). The whole passage is of the greatest interest as evidence of Marvell's 'double heart'. On a careless reading the
picture is one of ideal happiness, a Garden-of-Eden life, an escape,
particularly, from war:

> How safe, methinks, and strong, behind
> These Trees have I incamp'd my Mind;
> Where Beauty, aiming at the Heart,
> Bends in some Tree its useless Dart;

> And where the World no certain Shot
> Can make, or me it toucheth not.
> But I on it securely play,
> And gaul its Horsemen all the Day.

But again Marvell makes continual digs at his own dream-world:

> Strange *Prophecies* my Phancy weaves. ....

> I in this light *Mosaick* read.
> Thrice happy he who, not mistook,
> Hath read in *Natures mystick Book*.

(The heavy emphasis their position gives to 'methinks' and 'not mistook' can hardly be entirely without significance.)

> Thus I, *easie Philosopher*,
> Among the *Birds* and *Trees* confer. ....

> The Oak-Leaves me embroyder all,
> Between which Caterpillars crawl:
> And Ivy, with familiar trails,
> Me licks, and clasps, and curles, and hales.
> Under this *antick Cope* I move
> Like some great *Prelate of the Grove*.

'Easie' prepares us for incomplete acceptance, and the political note would strike for contemporaries the requisite undertone of disapproval in the last lines quoted, even without the hint of 'Caterpillars'. A bishop and his vestments could not but call up reactions of hostility in a good Parliamentarian (cf 'Safe from the Storms, and Prelat's rage' in 'Bermudas').

There is a snare hinted in the very placidity of this garden-world, in the attractions of its philosophy:

> And where I Language want, my Signs
> The Bird upon the Bough divines;
> And more attentive there doth sit
> Than if She were with Lime-twigs knit.

(Cf 'The Garden' and the passage about the falconer in the 'Horatian Ode'.) For all its fair seeming, this Eden does not really satisfy the poet:

> languishing with ease, I toss
> On Pallets swoln of Velvet Moss;
> While the Wind, cooling through the Boughs,
> Flatters with Air my panting Brows.

('In this time', Hobbes wrote in *Leviathan* in 1651, 'that men call not onely for Peace, but also for Truth', flattery was not enough.) Chains are not less chains because men cling to them, nor are half-truths truths because sincerely held:

> Bind me ye *Woodbines* in your 'twines,
> Curle me about ye gadding *Vines*,
> And Oh so close your Circles lace,
> That I may never leave this Place:
> But, lest your Fetters prove too weak,
> Ere I your Silken Bondage break,
> Do you, *O Brambles*, chain me too,
> And courteous *Briars* nail me through.

The idyllic scene suddenly suggests the Crucifixion.[20] And the succeeding stanzas show that escapism is not in fact Marvell's ultimate ideal. It is not the highest wisdom to discover 'I was but an inverted Tree'. For now Mary Fairfax enters. Whatever she symbolizes (and it is clear from stanza LXXXXI that she is associated with Puritan 'Goodness' as well as Fairfaxian 'Discipline'), there can be no doubt of the condemnation of 'loose Nature' (cf 'easie Philosopher') in the lines describing her advent:

> See how loose Nature, in respect
> To her, it self doth recollect;
> And every thing so whisht and fine,
> Starts forth with to its *Bonne Mine*. . . .

> But by her *Flames*, in Heaven try'd,
> *Nature* is wholly *vitrifi'd*.

> 'Tis *She* that to these Gardens gave
> That wondrous Beauty which they have;
> *She* streightness on the Woods bestows; . . .
> *She* yet more Pure, Sweet, Streight, and Fair,
> Then Gardens, Woods, Meads, Rivers are. . . .

> For *She*, to higher Beauties rais'd,
> Disdains to be for lesser prais'd.
> *She* counts her Beauty to converse
> In all the Languages as *hers*.

Her wisdom subsumes and includes the wisdom of the garden, just as her discipline and morals reduce its luxuriance to order.[21]

> Go now fond Sex that on your Face
> Do all your useless Study place,
> Nor once at Vice your Brows dare knit
> Lest the smooth Forehead wrinkled sit:
> Yet your own Face shall at you grin,
> Thorough the Black-bag of your Skin;
> When *knowledge* only could have fill'd
> And *Virtue* all those *Furrows* till'd.[22]

The new standards and discipline transmute the old cosmos by putting it into its place, and a new reality emerges, so different that we might be at the Antipodes:

> 'Tis not, what once it was, the *World*;
> But a rude heap together hurl'd;
> All negligently overthrown,
> Gulfes, Deserts, Precipices, Stone.
> Your lesser *World* contains the same,
> But in more decent Order tame;
> *Your Heaven's Center, Nature's Lap,*
> *And Paradice's only Map.*

(cf 'Clorinda and Damon' –

> *Damon.*   These once had been enticing things,
>   *Clorinda*, Pastures, Caves, and Springs.
> *Clorinda.* And what late change?
> *Damon.*   The other day
>   *Pan* met me. . . .)

In many of the poems Marvell is concerned to show the mutual indispensability of apparent opposites. He says of Fairfax in 'The Hill and Grove at Bill-borow' –

> Therefore to your obscurer Seats
> From his own Brightness he retreats:
> Nor he the Hills without the Groves,
> Nor Height but with Retirement loves.

In 'Bermudas' the garden-island (which is also an idealized England) is not an escape from struggle, but its reward. It is 'far kinder' than the prelates' England, but the emigrants have had to pass through storms to reach it, and the song is sung by men at work. The picture of the perfect haven is set between two quatrains which remind us unobtrusively of the difficulty of getting there.[23]

VI

The conflict in the poet's own mind between the attractions of evading reality in communion with Nature, and the necessity of coming to terms with the world, is shown in its most interesting form in the 'Horatian Ode upon Cromwel's Return from Ireland'. This poem was probably written before the great lyrics, before Marvell entered the Fairfax household, but it is convenient to consider it here since to some extent it sums up the argument by its direct political reference.

> The forward Youth that would appear
> Must now forsake his *Muses* dear,
>   Nor in the Shadows sing
>   His Numbers languishing . . .
> 'Tis Madness to resist or blame
> The force of angry Heavens flame:
>   And, if we would speak true,
>   Much to the Man is due,
> Who, from his private Gardens, where
> He liv'd reserved and austere,
>   As if his highest plot
>   To plant the Bergamot,
> Could by industrious Valour climbe
> To ruine the great Work of Time,
>   And cast the Kingdome old
>   Into another Mold.
> Though Justice against Fate complain,
> And plead the ancient Rights in vain:
>   But those do hold or break
>   As Men are strong or weak.

The poet is clearly arguing with himself rather than with Cromwell; note the garden symbol again. Then there comes the famous passage in which the Parliamentarian Marvell shows his sympathy for the old-world virtues of the executed Charles I,[24] consoling himself with the vision of new life through sacrificial death:

> A bleeding Head where they begun,
> Did fright the Architects to run;
> And yet in that the *State*
> Foresaw it's happy Fate.

Again Marvell takes up the struggle with himself, and hints back at the lost ideals of the Garden in a passage where the needs of the state are again shown as triumphing over the private interests of the individual:

> So when the Falcon high
> Falls heavy from the Sky,
> She, having kill'd, no more does search,
> But on the next green Bow to pearch;
> Where, when he first does lure,
> The Falckner has her sure.

(The falconer is England, the state; but he is also Fate, the reality which has to be accepted, the historical process: he recalls the Mower.) Marvell concludes reasonably on the side of action, the impossibility of neutrality:

> But thou the Wars and Fortunes Son
> March indefatigably on;
> And for the last effect
> Still keep thy Sword erect:
> Besides the force it has to fright
> The Spirits of the shady Night,
> The same *Arts* that did *gain*
> A *Pow'r* must it *maintain*.

('Shady', it will be observed, continues the symbolism; cf 'Shadows' in line 3.)

Critics have frequently commented on the rather left-handed compliment to Cromwell in this poem: his use of force and fraud is indeed a little openly praised. I suggest that this is part of Marvell's own internal struggle, and is evidence of his desire to be honest with himself. The artist in him dislikes the unpleasant actions which alone can 'cast the Kingdome old into another Mold'; but like his master, Milton, Marvell has come to realize that the immortal garland is to be run for not without dust and heat. He has come down from the ivory tower into the arena.

In so far as Marvell is thinking of Cromwell at all, he is not treating him as an individual: the general is for the poet the personification of the Revolution, of victory over the King.

> Nature that hateth emptiness,
> Allows of penetration less:
>   And therefore must make room
>   Where greater Spirits come.

Cromwell draws his greatness from the events of which he has been the instrument – a view of history with which the Protector would have agreed and which Milton assumes in *Samson Agonistes*. For Marvell the Revolution is 'the force of angry Heavens flame', ruining 'the great Work of Time', something real which must inevitably be accepted, which cannot be wished away nor even excluded from the garden. ' 'Tis Madness to resist or blame' an elemental power of this kind. 'The world will not go the faster for our driving', but it will also not go the slower for our regrets. Wisdom is 'To make their Destiny their *Choice*' ('Appleton House', 744). In the 'Horatian Ode' Marvell is clearly aware of a fusion of opposites: the life of the community demands the death of the individual, rest is obtainable only through and by means of effort, eternal vigilance is the price of liberty, freedom is the knowledge of necessity.[25]

But this paradox, this dialectical thought, recurs throughout Marvell's poems. The soul, in 'On a Drop of Dew',

> Does, in its pure and circling thoughts, express
> The greater Heaven in an Heaven less. . . .
>   Moving but on a point below,
>   It all about does upwards bend. . . .
> Congeal'd on Earth: but does, dissolving run,
> Into the Glories of th'Almighty Sun.

We find it in 'Ametas and Thestylis making Hay-Ropes', ironically,

as in the 'Coy Mistress' seriously. The solution of the conflict may not
be the victory of either side, but a fusion of aspects of both from which
something new emerges. We find the synthesis again in 'Eyes and
Tears':

> How wisely Nature did decree,
> With the same Eyes to weep and see!
> That, having view'd the object vain,
> They might be ready to complain. . . .
>
> I have through every Garden been,
> Amongst the Red, the White, the Green;
> And yet, from all the flow'rs I saw,
> No Hony, but these tears could draw. . . .[26]
>
> Thus let your Streams o'reflow your Springs,
> Till Eyes and Tears be the same things:
> And each the other's difference bears;
> These weeping Eyes, those seeing Tears.

VII

The suggestion then is that all Marvell's problems are interconnected.
They are the problems of an individual in an age of revolutionary
change. I do not think the following lines from 'The Fair Singer' were
intended to be taken at more than their surface value (though one never
knows with Marvell); but they could be interpreted as a perfect
allegory of the influence of society on the individual:

> I could have fled from One but singly fair:
> My dis-intangled Soul it self might save,
> Breaking the curled trammels of her hair.
> But how should I avoid to be her Slave,
> Whose subtile Art invisibly can wreath
> My Fetters of the very Air I breath?[27]

Soul and body, Love and Fate, illusion and reality, escape or action –
all the poems in the last analysis deal with the adjustment of individual
conduct to external conditions and forces. Marvell's life and his poetry
form a single whole. I would also suggest that the resolution of the
personal conflict revealed in the lyrics is almost exactly parallel to the

resolution of the political conflict revealed in the political poems: the individual soul never can disentangle itself from society, never can save itself in isolation; 'the very Air I breath' even in the remotest garden comes from outside. Since we cannot escape we must submit.

The significance of this solution of his own crisis for Marvell is shown by the number of times he recurs to it. The moral of 'The First Anniversary of the Government under O. C.' is exactly the same as that of the 'Horatian Ode':

> For all delight of Life thou then didst lose,
> When to Command, thou didst thyself Depose;
> Resigning up thy Privacy so dear,
> To turn the headstrong Peoples Charioteer;
> For to be *Cromwell* was a greater thing,
> Then ought below, or yet above a King:
> Therefore thou rather didst thy Self depress,
> Yielding to Rule, because it made thee Less.[28]

The subordination of self to political purposes which he believed to be right: that is the lesson Marvell had taught himself once he found that he could not escape from the disagreeable realities of the world. It was not only Cromwell

> whom Nature all for Peace had made,
> But angry Heaven unto War had sway'd.
>   ('Death of O. C.' 15–16)

Like so many other Parliamentarians, Marvell had been pushed reluctantly to approve of revolution and regicide since otherwise 'religion and liberty' could not be secured. Here again the wise and virtuous man 'makes his destiny his choice'.

> Far different Motives yet, engag'd them thus,
> Necessity did them, but Choice did us.
>   ('On Blake's Victory, 141–2)

Marvell was a true Cromwellian, truer perhaps than Milton, who could not accept the new tactics of the Restoration. For Marvell, as we have seen, the Restoration illustrated the point that 'things happen . . . without any need of officiousness'. He had Cromwell's carelessness of

forms of government, provided the root of the matter were secure. Yet
Marvell had Milton's sense – a conception surely born of the agonies
and triumphs and sufferings of the Revolution? – of good through evil,
of the impossibility of good without evil, of the meaninglessness of
rejecting good because of concomitant evil. It was from the rind of one
apple tasted in a garden that the knowledge of good and evil came into
the world. Tearing our pleasures 'with rough strife Thorough the Iron
gates of Life' makes them greater, not less.

> Thus, though we cannot make our Sun
> Stand still, yet we will make him run.

That is the final triumph over circumstance. The highest praise of
Cromwell was that he

> as the *Angel* of our Commonweal,
> Troubling the Waters, yearly mak'st them Heal.
>   ('First Anniversary' 401–2)

Or as Endymion, who wanted the moon, said to Cynthia:

> Though I so high may not pretend,
> It is the same so you descend.
> ('Marriage of Lord Fauconberg and Lady Mary Cromwell')

By the time of 'The First Anniversary' and 'On Blake's Victory over
the Spaniards', all Marvell's problems are solved: and the great poetry
ceases.[29] Marvell became a public servant, and his experience in writing
compact business prose helped him, with Pepys and Dryden, to contribute a fresh element of conciseness and clarity to English prose style.
Though the Restoration was to bring new complications, the inward
assurance Marvell had so hardly won in the fifties was never lost. The
poet became a pamphleteer as soon as he saw some of the returned
Cavaliers trying to set the clock back to before 1640, trying to interfere
with liberty of thought. With a purity of style reminiscent of Pascal,
Marvell laughed down the enemies of religious toleration. The irre-
ligious fashionable world enjoyed his polished and sophisticated wit
no less than Paris had enjoyed the *Lettres provinciales* in which Pascal
had exposed the Jesuits. It is no part of my purpose to discuss Marvell's
admirable prose, but it is perhaps worth recording the judgement of

Miss Bradbrook and Miss Lloyd Thomas that its wit and ridicule are based on 'a security of unquestioned and untroubled belief which gives him a standard by which he can relate the different levels of feeling, with their intensity'.[30] That is what we should have expected from our study of the poems.

This security, this stability in his political principles, this poised maturity and urbanity, are Marvell's peculiar strength: and they were won in the conflicts of the early fifties to which the great lyrics testify. In a lengthy simile in 'The First Anniversary', primitive man, terrified by the setting of the sun and the shadows, continues to look for light in the west, and is beginning to despair—

> When streight the Sun behind him he descry'd,
> Smiling serenely from the further side.

That is the dialectic of life and change as Marvell came to know it.

SOURCE: *Modern Quarterly*, no. 4 (1946), reprinted in *Puritanism and Revolution* (1958).

NOTES

1. See F. W. Bateson, *English Poetry* (1950) pp. 96–101, for criticisms of this essay.
2. *The Works of Andrew Marvell*, ed. A. B. Grosart, III (1873) p. 322.
3. Alas! the girl whom Marvell used as a symbol of ideal virtue in 'Upon Appleton House' (see p. 82) came to no good end. She was married to the second Duke of Buckingham (Dryden's Zimri) in 1657. The marriage caused something of a sensation at the time. For Buckingham, son of Charles I's hated minister and himself a notorious Cavalier, used the Fairfax marriage as a means for recovering his confiscated estates, the General giving Parliament his personal security for his son-in-law's good behaviour. It was hoped that other Royalists would follow Buckingham's example in thus making terms with the Protectorate. But Oliver Cromwell died in 1658, and after the Restoration Buckingham in his turn was able to protect Fairfax.
4. Marvell was a member of Harrington's Rota Club in 1659–60.
5. The Marquess of Halifax, *Complete Works* (1912) III pp. 139–40.
6. *Works*, III 212. Marvell's view of history is further analysed in sections VI and VII.
7. *A Holy Commonwealth* (written by Richard Baxter at the invitation of James Harrington, Esq., 1659) p. 457.
8. Swift, of course, is an exception to this general acceptance of the new synthesis; but I think his personal and political abnormalities could be explained in terms which would confirm rather than weaken the generalization.
9. Cf Richard Sibbes: 'A kind of doublenesse of heart, whereby wee would bring two things together that cannot suit' *The Soules Conflict* (1635) p. 469. The phrase no doubt derives from James 1:8.
10. M. C. Bradbrook and M. G. Lloyd Thomas, *Andrew Marvell* (1940) p. 45. Their whole analysis of the dialectics of this intricate poem is most interesting.

11. In one of Quarles's *Emblemes* (Book v, no. 7) the soul is shown literally imprisoned within a skeleton, crying out 'who shall deliver me from the body of this death?' Cf Rosemary Freeman, *English Emblem Books* (1948) p. 119.

12. Aubrey tells us of Marvell that 'he kept bottles of wine at his lodging, and many times he would drink liberally by himself to refresh his spirits and exalt his muse' (*Aubrey's Brief Lives* (1898) II 53).

13. Cf Bishop Joseph Hall: 'A good man must not be like Ezechias Sunne, that went backward, nor like Joshuahs Sunne, that stood still, but Davids Sunne, that (like a Bridegroome) comes out of his Chamber, and as a Champion rejoyceth to runne his Race' – *Meditations and Vows* (1901) p. 7. Cf also the *Enchiridion* of Francis Quarles, first published in 1641: 'He only (if any) hath the art to lengthen out his taper, that puts it to the best advantage' (fourth century, no. LV).

14. Cf Bradbrook and Lloyd Thomas, op. cit., pp. 43–4, 73, on the structure of 'To his Coy Mistress' and of the 'Horatian Ode': the authors find in each 'a triple movement, the Hegelian thesis, antithesis, and synthesis'. See also T. S. Eliot's 1921 essay, reprinted in this volume, especially p. 48.

15. C. S. Lewis, *The Allegory of Love* (1936) p. 119.

16. 'I . . . write . . . to those only, that are weather-beaten in the sea of this world, such as having lost the sight of their gardens and groves study to sail on a right course among rocks and quicksands' – Sir Fulke Greville, *Life of Sir Philip Sidney* (1907) p. 224. Cf also Shakespeare's *Richard II*, III iv. George Puttenham, *The Art of English Poesie* (1589) compared the poet to a gardener who improved on nature. The garden as an image of order and harmony was a favourite of Bunyan's – J. Brown, *John Bunyan*, (1885) pp. 50–1; H. Talon, *John Bunyan* (1951) pp. 302–3. Cf also Gerrard Winstanley, *Fire in the Bush* (1650), passim. John Evelyn's *Elysium Britannicum*, begun about 1653, compared England to the Garden of Eden.

17. Maren-Sofie Røstvig, in *The Happy Man* (Oslo, 1954), studies the evolution of the cult of rural retirement in seventeenth-century England. She dates its beginning from the political crisis of the late 1620s and 1630s, rising to its peak in the forties and fifties with Mildmay Fane, Edward Benlowes and Henry Vaughan. She quotes a wide range of poets who deal with garden themes in the second quarter of the century. I would add to her list only Nathaniel Whiting, 'Upon Bellama's Walking in the Garden' (*Albino and Bellama*, 1638), George Wither, Hymn 30 (*Hallelujah*, 1641), Shirley 'The Garden' (*Poems*, 1646), Nicholas Hookes, 'To Amanda walking in the garden' (*Amanda*, 1653). I should not myself altogether agree with Miss Røstvig's absolute opposition of the Royalist 'Hortulan Saint' to 'the grim figure of the Puritan pilgrim' (*The Happy Man*, p. 441). The case of Marvell suggests that it was more complicated than that.

18. All Marvell's symbols, of course, are used partly unconsciously, and so their significance varies: the Mower is now the power of Love, now the scythe of Death or Fate; now the armies of the Civil War; at other times he stands for a pre-commercial simplicity which acquires an elemental force in contrast to the sophistication of the garden. So too the garden itself stands for different things in different poems: but I do not think this makes analysis impossible, provided we are careful to apply no rule-of-thumb symbol-equivalents. All Marvell's writing is packed with alternative meanings.

19. At Edgehill, Royalist Welsh infantry, very badly equipped 'with scythes, pitchforks and even sickles . . . cheerfully took the field, and literally like reapers descend[ed] to that harvest of death' – quoted in J. R. Phillips, *Memoirs of the Civil War in Wales and the Marches* (1874) I 128. In 1649 scythes were a part of the equipment sent over to the English army in Ireland, for the rather different purpose of cutting down corn in order to starve the Irish into submission – J. P. Prendergast, *The Cromwellian Settlement of Ireland* (1865) p. 14.

20. Cf Lewis Bayley, 'A Divine Colloquy between the Soul and her Saviour': 'Soul –

Lord, wherefore wouldest thou begin thy Passion in a Garden? Christ – Because that in a Garden thy Sin took first Beginning' – *The Practice of Piety*, 55th ed. (1723) p. 451.

21. Similarly, 'little T. C.' had been adjured to 'reform the errours of the Spring'; and the mind in 'The Garden' created worlds and seas which transcended reality. Cf Lancelot Andrewes: 'Christ rising was indeed a Gardiner.... He it is that . . . shal turne all our grass into garden-plots' – *XCVI Sermons*, 2nd ed. (1631) p. 538.

22. Black-bag = mask. Death, the final eternal reality, equally reinforces the moral whether the invitation – as here – is to virtue, or – as in the 'Coy Mistress' – to pleasure.

23. I owe some of these points to Mr C. H. Hobday.

24. Did Marvell see the execution? The lines—

> Nor call'd the *Gods* with vulgar spight
> To vindicate his helpless Right,
> But bow'd his comely Head,
> Down as upon a Bed

read like an eyewitness's recollection of a fact recorded by the Venetian Ambassador which Marvell's editors seem to have missed: 'As they doubted that His Majesty might resist the execution of the sentence, refusing to lay his neck upon the block, they fixed into the block at his feet two iron rings through which they passed a cord which, placed on His Majesty's neck, would necessarily make him bend by force, and offer his head to the axe, if he did not voluntarily resign himself to the humiliation of the fatal blow. But the King, warned of this, without coming to such extremes, said that they should use no violence; he would readily submit to the laws of necessity and the rigours of force' – E. Momigliano, *Cromwell*, English translation (1930) p. 282; cf also Sir P. Warwick, *Memoirs of the Reign of Charles I* (1701) p. 385, and E. Warburton, *Memoirs of Prince Rupert and the Cavaliers*, III (1849) p. 400.

25. 'The thesis is the impersonal power of Cromwell . . . The antithesis is the personal dignity and comeliness of Charles, which may offset Cromwell's achievement: and the synthesis is the acceptance of Cromwell, both his "forc'd Pow'r" and his personal unattractiveness. . . . The poem may well represent the steps of reasoning by which the friend of Lovelace threw in his lot with the Roundheads' (Bradbrook and Lloyd Thomas, *Andrew Marvell*, p. 73).

26. Here again the garden fails to meet the poet's needs.

27. Marvell may have noticed 'curld Trammels of thy hayre' in Drayton's *Second Nimphall*.

28. Lines 221–8. Cf 'A letter to Doctor Ingelo', where Cromwell is described as 'Ducere sive sequi nobile laetus iter': on a noble course his joy was equal whether leading or following.

29. We do not *know* this. Miss Bradbrook and Miss Lloyd Thomas point out that some of the religious and philosophical poems might be dated after Marvell's state service began (op. cit., p. 9). But I think the indirect internal evidence is strong enough to justify allotting all the great poems to the same period, roughly 1650–5. I should like to think that the order of the lyrical poems in the 1681 edition (which Margoliouth uses) is chronological. Then we could trace the chronological as well as the logical sequence of Marvell's inner struggles. But the point is not material.

30. Op. cit., p. 116. They contrast Swift – but that is another story. Swift, incidentally, was a great admirer of Marvell's prose.

[Editor's note.] Fuller notes appear in the original publication of this essay.

CLEANTH BROOKS

Marvell's 'Horatian Ode' (1946)

THE easiest error into which we may fall in defining the relationship between historical and critical studies is illustrated by the preface of Maurice Kelley's interesting book on Milton, *This Great Argument*. For Kelly, the problem of exegesis is almost amusingly simple: we will read Milton's *Christian Doctrine* to find out what Milton's ideas are, and then we shall be able to understand his *Paradise Lost*, explaining the tangled and difficult poetic document by means of the explicit prose statement. But Kelley's argument rests not only upon the assumption that the Milton who wrote the *Christian Doctrine* was precisely and at all points the same man who composed *Paradise Lost* – a matter which, for all practical purposes, may well be true; it rests upon the further and much more dangerous assumption that Milton was able to *say* in *Paradise Lost* exactly what he intended to say: and that what he supposed he had put into that poem is actually to be found there. In short, Mr Kelley tends to make the assumption about poetry which most of us constantly make; namely, that a poem is essentially a decorated and beautified piece of prose.

But I propose to deal here with a more modest example than Milton's epic. I propose to illustrate from Marvell's 'Horatian Ode'. If we follow the orthodox procedure, the obvious way to understand the 'Ode' is to ascertain by historical evidence – by letters and documents of all kinds – what Marvell really thought of Comwell, or, since Marvell apparently thought different things of Cromwell at different times, to ascertain the date of the 'Ode', and then neatly fit it into the particular stage of Marvell's developing opinion of Cromwell. But this is at best a relatively coarse method which can hope to give no more than a rough approximation of the poem; and there lurk in it some positive perils. For to ascertain what Marvell the man thought of Cromwell, and even to ascertain what Marvell as poet consciously intended to say in his poem, will not prove that the poem actually says this, or all this, or merely this. This last remark, in my opinion, does not imply too metaphysical a notion of the structure of a poem. There is surely a sense in which any one must agree that a poem has a life of its own, and a sense in which it provides in itself the only criterion by which what it says can be judged. It is a commonplace that the poet sometimes writes better than he knows, and, alas, on occasion, writes worse than he knows. The history of English literature will furnish plenty of examples of both cases.

As a matter of fact, Marvell's 'Ode' is not a shockingly special case. Indeed, I have chosen it for my example, not because it is special – not because I hope to reveal triumphantly that what it really says is something quite opposed to what we have supposed it to be saying – but because it seems to me a good instance of the normal state of affairs. Yet, even so, the 'Ode' will provide us with problems enough. To the scholar who relies upon the conventional approach, the problems become rather distressingly complicated.

Let us review the situation briefly. Hard upon his composition of the 'Ode' in 1650, Marvell had published in 1649 a poem 'To his Noble Friend Mr Richard Lovelace', and a poem 'Upon the Death of the Lord Hastings'. Both Margoliouth and Legouis find these poems rather pro-Royalist in sentiment and certainly it is difficult to read them otherwise. If we add to these poems the 'Elegy upon the Death of My Lord Francis Villiers', a Cavalier who was killed fighting for the King in 1649, the Royalist bias becomes perfectly explicit. As Margoliouth puts it: 'If [the elegy on Villiers] is Marvell's, it is his one unequivocal royalist utterance; it throws into strong relief the transitional character of "An Horatian Ode" where royalist principles and admiration for Cromwell the Great Man exist side by side.'

A transition in views there must have been, but the transition certainly cannot be graphed as a steadily rising curve when we take into account Marvell's next poem, 'Tom May's Death'. May died in November 1650. Thus we have the 'Horatian Ode', which was almost certainly written in the summer of 1650, preceding by only a few months a poem in which Marvell seems to slur at the Commander of the Parliamentary armies – either Essex or Fairfax – as 'Spartacus', and to reprehend May himself as a renegade poet who has prostituted the mystery of the true poets. The curve of Marvell's political development shows still another surprising quirk when we recall that only a few months after his attack on May, Marvell was to be living under Spartacus Fairfax's roof, acting as tutor to his little daughter Mary.

Let me interrupt this summary to say that I am not forcing the evidence so as to crowd the historian into the narrowest and most uncomfortable corner possible. On the contrary, whatever forcing of the evidence has been done has been done by the editors and the historians. If we limit ourselves to historical evidence, it is possible to suppose that 'Tom May's Death' was actually written on the Hill at Billborrow; and Margoliouth chooses early 1651 as the probable date for Marvell's arrival at Appleton House only because, as he says, ' "Tom May's Death" is not the sort of poem Marvell would have written under Fairfax's roof.'

There is no need, in view of our purposes, to extend the review of Marvell's political development through the late 1650s with their Cromwellian poems or through the Restoration period with its vexed problems concerning which of the anti-Court satires are truly, and which are falsely, ascribed to Marvell. The problem of Marvell's attitude through the years 1649–51 will provide sufficient scope for this examination of some of the relations and interrelations of the historical approach and the critical approach. For there is still another complication, which has received less attention than it deserves. It is the curious fact that the 'Horatian Ode' in which Marvell seems to affirm the ancient rights of the monarchy –

> Though Justice against Fate complain,
> And plead the antient Rights in vain . . .

is full of echoes of the poetry of Tom May, the poet whom Marvell was, a few months later, to denounce for having failed poetry in the hour of crisis:

> When the Sword glitters ore the Judges head,
> And fear the Coward Churchmen silenced,
> Then is the Poets time, 'tis then he drawes,
> And single fights forsaken Vertues cause.
> He, when the wheel of Empire whirleth back,
> And though the World's disjointed Axel crack,
> Sings still of *ancient Rights* and better Times,
> Seeks wretched good, arraigns successful Crimes.

The echoes of May's poetry, of course, may well have been unconscious: to me it is significant that they are from May's translation of
Lucan's poem on the Roman civil wars. (The relevant passage from
Margoliouth's notes will be found on pp. 112–13) I must say that I
find the parallels quite convincing and that I am a little surprised at
Margoliouth's restraint in not pushing his commentary further. For
one is tempted to suppose that in the year or so that followed the
execution of Charles, Marvell was obsessed with the problem of the
poet's function in such a crisis; that the poet May was frequently in his
mind through a double connection – through the parallels between the
English and the Roman civil war, Lucan's poem on which May had
translated, and through May's conduct as a partisan of the Commonwealth; and that the 'Horatian Ode' and 'Tom May's Death', though
so different in tone, are closely related and come out of the same
general state of mind. But to hazard all this is to guess at the circumstances of Marvell's composition of these poems. It can be only a guess,
and, in any case, it takes us into a consideration of what must finally be
a distinct problem: how the poem came to be: whereas our elected
problem is rather: what the poem is. I am, by the way, in entire sympathy with the essay 'The Intentional Fallacy', by W. K. Wimsatt and
M. C. Beardsley, in the *Sewanee Review* [LIV (Summer 1946) 468–88].
We had best not try to telescope the separate problems of 'the psychology of composition' and that of 'objective evaluation'. I have no
intention of trying to collapse them here.

   Well, what is 'said' in the 'Horatian Ode'? What is the speaker's
attitude toward Cromwell and toward Charles? M. Legouis sees in the
'Ode' a complete impartiality, an impartiality which is the product of
Marvell's non-participation in the wars. Legouis can even speak of the
poem as 'ce monument d'indifférence en matière de régime politique'.
But the 'Ode', though it may be a monument of impartiality, is not a
monument of indifference. To read it in this fashion is to miss what
seems to me to be a passionate interest in the issues, an interest which is
manifested everywhere in the poem. It is true that we have no evidence
that Marvell ever served in the civil war, but we had better not leap to
conclusions of his indifference from that. My own guess is that some
young Cavaliers who shed their blood for the King thought and felt
less deeply about the issues than does the speaker of this poem. The
tone is not that of a 'plague o' both your houses' nor is it that of 'the
conflict provided glory enough to be shared by both sides.'

Mr Margoliouth comes much closer to the point. He sums up as follows: 'The ode is the utterance of a constitutional monarchist, whose sympathies have been with the King, but who yet believes more in men than in parties or principles, and whose hopes are fixed now on Cromwell, seeing in him both the civic ideal of a ruler without personal ambition, and the man of destiny moved by and yet himself driving a power which is above justice.' This statement is plausible and, for its purposes, perhaps just. But does it take us very far – even on the level of understanding Marvell the man? What sort of constitutional monarchist is it who 'believes more in men than in . . . principles'? Or who can accept a 'power which is above justice'? I do not say that such a monarchist cannot exist. My point is that Margoliouth's statement raises more problems than it solves. Furthermore, in what sense are the speaker's hopes 'fixed . . . on Cromwell'? And how confident is he that Cromwell is 'without personal ambition'? I have quoted earlier Margoliouth's characterization of the 'Ode' as a poem 'where royalist principles and admiration for Cromwell the Great Man exist side by side'. I think that they do exist side by side, but if so, how are they related? Do they exist in separate layers, or are they somehow unified? Unified, in some sense, they must be if the 'Ode' is a poem and not a heap of fragments.

I hope that my last statement indicates the kind of question which we finally have to face and answer. It is a problem of poetic organization. As such, it addresses itself properly to the critic. The historical scholars have not answered it, for it is a question which cannot be answered in terms of historical evidence. (This is not to say, of course, that the same man may not be both historical scholar and critic.) Moreover, I have already taken some pains to indicate how heavily the critic, on his part, may need to lean upon the historian. To put the matter into its simplest terms: the critic obviously must know what the words of the poem mean, something which immediately puts him in debt to the linguist; and since many of the words in this poem are proper nouns, in debt to the historian as well. I am not concerned to exalt the critic at the expense of specialists in other disciplines: on the contrary, I am only concerned to show that he has a significant function, and to indicate what the nature of the function is.

But I am not so presumptuous as to promise a solution to the problem. Instead, the reader will have to be content with suggestions – as to what the 'Ode' is not saying, as to what the 'Ode' may be saying – in short, with explorations of further problems. Many critical problems, of course, I shall have to pass over and some important ones I shall only touch upon. To illustrate: there is the general Roman cast given to the 'Ode'. Marvell has taken care to make no specifically Christian references in the poem. Charles is Caesar; Cromwell is a Hannibal; on the scaffold, Charles refuses to call with 'vulgar spight', not on God, but on 'the Gods', and so on. Or to point to another problem, metaphors drawn from hunting pervade the poem. Charles chases himself to Carisbrooke; Cromwell is like the falcon; Cromwell will soon put his dogs in 'near/The *Caledonian* Deer'. Or, to take up the general organization of the poem: Marvell seems to have used the celebrated stanzas on Charles's execution to divide the poem into two rather distinct parts: first, Cromwell's rise to power; and second, Cromwell's wielding of the supreme power. This scheme of division, by the way, I intend to make use of in the discussion that follows. But I shall try, in general, to limit it to the specific problem of the speaker's attitude towards Cromwell, subordinating other critical problems to this one, which is, I maintain, essentially a critical problem too.

From historical evidence alone we would suppose that the attitude towards Cromwell in this poem would have to be a complex one. And this complexity is reflected in the ambiguity of the compliments paid to him. The ambiguity reveals itself as early as the second word of the poem. It is the 'forward' youth whose attention the speaker directs to the example of Cromwell. 'Forward' may mean no more than 'high-spirited', 'ardent', 'properly ambitious'; but the *New English Dictionary* sanctions the possibility that there lurks in the word the sense of 'presumptuous', 'pushing'. The forward youth can no longer now

> in the Shadows sing
> His numbers languishing.

In the light of Cromwell's career, he must forsake the shadows and his 'Muses dear' and become the man of action.

The speaker, one observes, does not identify Cromwell himself as the 'forward youth', or say directly that Cromwell's career has been motivated by a striving for fame. But the implications of the first two stanzas do carry over to him. There is, for example, the important word 'so' to relate Cromwell to these stanzas:

> So restless *Cromwel* could not cease . . .

And 'restless' is as ambiguous in its meanings as 'forward', and in its darker connotations even more damning. For, though 'restless' can mean 'scorning indolence', 'willing to forgo ease', it can also suggest the man with a maggot in the brain. 'To cease', used intransitively, is 'to take rest, to be or remain at rest', and the *New English Dictionary* gives instances as late as 1701. Cromwell's 'courage high' will not allow him to rest 'in the inglorious Arts of Peace'. And this thirst for glory, merely hinted at here by negatives, is developed further in the ninth stanza:

> Could by industrious Valour climbe
> To ruine the great Work of Time . . .

'Climbe' certainly connotes a kind of aggressiveness. In saying this we need not be afraid that we are reading into the word some smack of such modern phrases as 'social climber'. Marvell's translation of the second chorus of Seneca's *Thyestes* sufficiently attests that the work could have such associations for him:

> Climb at *Court* for me that will
> Tottering favors Pinacle;
> All I seek is to lye still.

Cromwell, on the other hand, does not seek to lie still – has sought something quite other than this. His valor is called – strange collocation – an 'industrious valour', and his courage is too high to brook a rival:

> For 'tis all one to Courage high
> The Emulous or Enemy;
> And with such to inclose,
> Is more then to oppose.

The implied metaphor is that of some explosive which does more violence to that which encloses it, the powder to its magazine, for instance, than to some wall which merely opposes it – against which the charge is fired.

But the speaker has been careful to indicate that Cromwell's motivation has to be conceived of as more complex than any mere thirst for glory. He has even pointed this up. The forward youth is referred to as one who 'would appear' – that is, as one who wills to leave the shadows of obscurity. But restless Cromwell 'could not cease' – for Cromwell it is not a question of will at all, but of a deeper compulsion. Restless Cromwell could not cease, if he would.

Indeed, the lines that follow extend the suggestion that Cromwell is like an elemental force – with as little will as the lightning bolt, and with as little conscience:

> And, like the three-fork'd Lightning, first
> Breaking the Clouds where it was nurst,
>   Did thorough his own Side
>   His fiery way divide.

We are told that the last two lines refer to Cromwell's struggle after Marston Moor with the leaders of the Parliamentary party. Doubtless they do, and the point is important for our knowledge of the poem. But what is more important is that we be fully alive to the force of the metaphor. The clouds have bred the lightning bolt, but the bolt tears its way through the clouds, and goes on to blast the head of Caesar himself. As Margoliouth puts it: 'The lightning is conceived as tearing through the side of his own body the cloud.' In terms of the metaphor, then, Cromwell has not spared his own body: there is no reason therefore to be surprised that he has not spared the body of Charles.

I do not believe that I over-emphasized the speaker's implication that Cromwell is a natural force. A few lines later the point is reinforced with another naturalistic figure, an analogy taken from physics:

> Nature that hateth emptiness,
> Allows of penetration less:
>   And therefore must make room
>   Where greater Spirits come. . . .

The question of right, the imagery insists, is beside the point. If nature will not tolerate a power vacuum, no more will it allow two bodies to occupy the same space. (It is amusing, by the way, that Marvell has boldly introduced into his analogy borrowed from physics the nonphysical term 'Spirits'; yet I do not think that the clash destroys the figure. Since twenty thousand angels can dance on the point of a needle, two spirits, even though one of them is a greater spirit, ought to be able to occupy the same room. But two spirits, as Marvell conceives of spirits here, will jostle one another, and one must give way. True, the greater spirit is immaterial, but he is no pale abstraction – he is all

air and fire, the 'force of angry Heavens flame'. The metaphor ought
to give less trouble to the reader of our day than it conceivably gave
to readers bred up on Newtonian physics.)

What are the implications for Charles? Does the poet mean to imply
that Charles has angered heaven – that he has merited his destruction?
There is no suggestion that Cromwell is a thunderbolt hurled by an
angry Jehovah – or even by an angry Jove. The general emphasis on
Cromwell as an elemental force is thoroughly relevant here to counter
this possible misreading. Certainly, in the lines that follow there is
nothing to suggest that Charles has angered heaven, or that the Justice
which complains against his fate is anything less than justice.

I began this examination of the imagery with the question, 'What is
the speaker's attitude toward Cromwell?' We have seen that the speaker
more than once hints at his thirst for glory:

> So restless *Cromwel* could not cease . . .
> Could by industrious Valour climbe . . .

But we have also seen that the imagery tends to view Cromwell as a
natural phenomenon, the bolt bred in the cloud. Is there a contradiction? I think not. Cromwell's is no vulgar ambition, If his valor is an
'industrious Valour', it contains plain valor too of a kind perfectly
capable of being recognized by any Cavalier:

> What Field of all the Civil Wars,
> Where his were not the deepest Scars?

If the driving force has been a desire for glory, it is a glory of that kind
which allows a man to become dedicated and, in a sense, even selfless
in his pursuit of it. Moreover, the desire for such glory can become so
much a compulsive force that the man does not appear to act by an
exercise of his personal will but seems to become the very will of something else. There is in the poem, it seems to me, at least one specific
suggestion of this sort:

> But through adventrous War
> Urged his active Star. . . .

Cromwell is the marked man, the man of destiny, but he is not merely
the man governed by his star. Active though it be, he cannot remain

passive, even in relation to it: he is not merely urged by it, but himself urges it on.

Yet, if thus far Cromwell has been treated as naked force, something almost too awesome to be considered as a man, the poet does not forget that after all he is a man too – that 'the force of angry Heavens flame' is embodied in a human being:

> And, if we would speak true,
> Much to the Man is due.

The stanzas that follow proceed to define and praise that manliness – the strength, the industrious valor, the cunning. (You will notice that I reject the interpretation which would paraphrase 'Much to the Man is due' as 'After all, Cromwell has accomplished much that is good'. Such an interpretation could sort well enough with Legouis's picture of Marvell as the cold and detached honest broker between the factions: unfortunately it will not survive a close scrutiny of the grammar and the general context in which the passage is placed.) One notices that among the virtues comprising Cromwell's manliness, the speaker mentions his possession of the 'wiser art':

> Where, twining subtile fears with hope,
> He wove a Net of such a scope,
>   That *Charles* himself might chase
>   To *Caresbrooks* narrow case.

On this point Cromwell has been cleared by all the modern historians (except perhaps Mr Hilaire Belloc). Charles's flight to Carisbrooke Castle, as it turned out, aided Cromwell, but Cromwell could have hardly known that it would; and there is no evidence that he cunningly induced the King to flee to Carisbrooke. Royalist pamphleteers, of course, believed that Cromwell did, and used the item in their general bill of damnation against Cromwell. How does the speaker use it here – to damn or to praise? We tend to answer, 'To praise.' But then it behoves us to notice what is being praised. The things praised are Cromwell's talents as such – the tremendous disciplined powers which Cromwell brought to bear against the King.

For the end served by those powers, the speaker has no praise at all. Rather he has gone out of his way to insist that Cromwell was deaf to the complaint of Justice and its pleading of the 'antient Rights'. The power achieved by Cromwell is a 'forced Pow'r' – a usurped power. On this point the speaker is unequivocal. I must question therefore Margoliouth's statement that Marvell sees in Cromwell 'the man of destiny moved by . . . a power that is above justice'. Above justice, yes, in the sense that power is power and justice is not power. The one does not insure the presence of the other. Charles has no way to vindicate his 'helpless Right', but it is no less Right because it is helpless. But the speaker, though he is not a cynic, is a realist. A kingdom cannot be held by mere pleading of the 'antient Rights':

> But those do hold or break
> As Men are strong or weak.

In short, the more closely we look at the 'Ode', the more clearly apparent it becomes that the speaker has chosen to emphasize Cromwell's virtues as a man, and likewise, those of Charles as a man. The poem does not debate which of the two was right, for that issue is not even in question. In his treatment of Charles, then, the speaker no more than Charles himself attempts to vindicate his 'helpless Right'. Instead, he emphasizes his dignity, his fortitude, and what has finally to be called his consummate good taste. The portraits of the two men beautifully supplement each other. Cromwell is – to use Aristotle's distinction – the man of character, the man of action, who 'does both act and know'. Charles, on the other hand, is the man of passion, the man who is acted upon, the man who knows how to suffer. The contrast is pointed up in half a dozen different ways.

Cromwell, acted upon by his star, is not passive but actually urges his star. Charles in 'acting' – in chasing away to Carisbrooke – actually is passive – performs the part assigned to him by Cromwell. True, we can read 'chase' as an intransitive verb (the *New English Dictionary* sanctions this use for the period): 'that Charles himself might hurry to Carisbrooke'. But the primary meaning asserts itself in the context: 'that Charles might chase himself to Carisbrooke's narrow case'. For this hunter, now preparing to lay his dogs in 'near/The *Caledonian* Deer', the royal quarry has dutifully chased itself.

Even in the celebrated stanzas on the execution, there is ironic realism as well as admiration. In this fullest presentation of Charles as king, he is the player king, the king acting in a play. He is the 'Royal Actor' who knows his assigned part and performs it with dignity. He truly adorned the 'Tragick Scaffold'

> While round the armed Bands
> Did clap their bloody hands

The generally received account is that the soldiers clapped their hands so as to make it impossible for Charles's speech to be heard. But in the context this reference to hand-clapping supports the stage metaphor. What is being applauded? Cromwell's resolution in bringing the King to a deserved death? Or Charles's resolution on the scaffold as he suffered that death? Marvell was too good a poet to resolve the ambiguity. It is enough that he makes the armed bands applaud.

It has not been pointed out, I believe, that Robert Wild, in his poem on 'The Death of Mr Christopher Love', has echoed a pair of Marvell's finest lines. Love was beheaded by Cromwell on 22 August 1651. In Wild's poem, Marvell's lines

> But with his keener Eye
> The Axes edge did try

become: 'His keener words did their sharp Ax exceed.' The point is of no especial importance except that it indicates, since Wild's poem was evidently written shortly after Love's execution, that in 1651 the 'Horatian Ode' was being handed about among the Royalists. For Wild was that strange combination, an English Presbyterian Royalist.

I have pointed out earlier that the second half of the poem begins here with the reference to

> that memorable Hour
> Which first assur'd the forced Pow'r.

Cromwell is now the *de facto* head of the state, and the speaker, as a realist, recognizes that fact. Cromwell is seen henceforth, not primarily in his character as the destroyer of the monarchy, but as the agent of the new state that has been erected upon the dead body of the King. The thunderbolt simile, of the first part of the poem, gives way here to the falcon simile in this second part of the poem. The latter figure revises and qualifies the former: it repeats the suggestion of ruthless energy and power, but Cromwell falls from the sky now, not as the thunderbolt, but as the hunting hawk. The trained falcon is not a wanton destroyer, nor an irresponsible one. It knows its master: it is perfectly disciplined:

> She, having kill'd, no more does search,
> But on the next green Bow to pearch . . .

The speaker's admiration for Cromwell the man culminates, it seems to me, here. Cromwell might make the Fame his own; he *need* not present kingdoms to the state. He might assume the crown rather than crowning each year. Yet he forbears:

> Nor yet grown stiffer with Command,
> But still in the *Republick's* hand . . .

Does the emphasis on 'still' mean that the speaker is surprised that Cromwell has continued to pay homage to the republic? Does he imply that Cromwell may not always do so? Perhaps not: the emphasis is upon the fact that he need not obey and yet does. Yet the compliment derives its full force from the fact that the homage is not forced, but voluntary and even somewhat unexpected. And a recognition of this point implies the recognition of the possibility that Cromwell will not always so defer to the commonwealth.

And now what of the republic which Cromwell so ruthlessly and efficiently serves? What is the speaker's attitude toward it? To begin with, the speaker recognizes that its foundations rest upon the bleeding head of Charles. The speaker is aware, it is true, of the Roman analogy, and the English state is allowed the benefit of that analogy. But it is well to notice that the speaker does not commit himself to the opinion that the bleeding head is a happy augury:

> And yet in that the *State*
> Foresaw it's happy Fate.

The Roman state was able to take it as a favorable omen, and was justified by the event. With regard to the speaker himself, it seems to me more to the point to notice what prophecy he is willing to commit himself to. He does not prophesy peace. He is willing to predict that England, under Cromwell's leadership, will be powerful in war, and will strike fear into the surrounding states:

> What may not then our *Isle* presume
> While Victory his Crest does plume!
> What may not others fear
> If thus he crown each year!

Specifically, he predicts a smashing victory over the Scots.

But what of the compliments to Cromwell on his ruthlessly effective campaign against the Irish? Does not the speaker succumb, for once, to a bitter and biased patriotism, and does this not constitute a blemish upon the poem?

> And now the *Irish* are asham'd
> To see themselves in one Year tam'd:
>   So much one Man can do,
>   That does both act and know.
> They can affirm his Praises best,
> And have, though overcome, confest
>   How good he is, how just . . .

Margoliouth glosses the word 'confessed' as follows: 'Irish testimony in favor of Cromwell at this moment is highly improbable. Possibly there is a reference to the voluntary submission of part of Munster with its English colony.' But surely Margoliouth indulges in understatement. The most intense partisan of Cromwell would have had some difficulty in taking the lines without some inflection of grim irony. The final appeal in this matter, however, is not to what Marvell the Englishman must have thought, or even to what Marvell the author must have intended, but rather to the full context of the poem itself. In that context, the lines in question can be read ironically, and the earlier stanzas sanction that reading. Cromwell's energy, activity, bravery, resolution – even what may be called his efficiency – are the qualities that have come in for praise, not his gentleness or his mercy. The Irish, indeed, are best able to affirm such praise as has been accorded to Cromwell; and they know from experience 'how good he is, how just', for they have been blasted by the force of angry Heaven's flame, even as Charles has been. But I do not mean to turn the passage into sarcasm. The third quality which the speaker couples with goodness and justice is fitness 'for highest Trust', and the goodness and justice of Cromwell culminate in this fitness. But the recommendation to trust has reference not to the Irish, but to the English state. The Irish are quite proper authorities on Cromwell's trustworthiness in this regard, for they have come to know him as the completely dedicated instrument of that state whose devotion to the purpose in hand is unrelenting and unswerving.

To say all this is not to suggest that Marvell shed any unnecessary tears over the plight of the Irish, or even to imply that he was not happy, as one assumes most Englishmen were, to have the Irish rebellion crushed promptly and efficiently. It is to say that the passage fits into the poem – a poem which reveals itself to be no panegyric on Cromwell but an unflinching analysis of the Cromwellian character.

The wild Irish have been tamed, and now the Pict will no longer be able to shelter under his particolored mind. It is the hour of decision, and the particolored mind affords no protection against the man who 'does both act and know'. In Cromwell's mind there are no conflicts, no teasing mixture of judgements. Cromwell's is not only an 'industrious valour', but a 'sad valour'. Margoliouth glosses 'sad' as 'steadfast', and no doubt he is right. But sad can mean 'sober' also, and I suspect that in this context, with its implied references to Scottish plaids, it means also drab of hue. It is also possible that the poet here glances at one of Virgil's transferred epithets, *maestum timorem*, sad fear, the fear that made the Trojans sad. Cromwell's valor is *sad* in that the Scots will have occasion to rue it.

Thus far the speaker has been content to view Cromwell from a distance, as it were, against the background of recent history. He has referred to him consistently in the third person. But in the last two stanzas he addresses Cromwell directly. He salutes him as 'the Wars and Fortunes Son'. It is a great compliment: Cromwell is the son of the wars in that he is the master of battle, and he seems fortune's own son in the success that has constantly waited upon him. But we do not wrench the lines if we take them to say also that Cromwell is the creature of the wars and the product of fortune. The imagery of the early stanzas which treats Cromwell as a natural phenomenon certainly lends support to this reading. Cromwell can claim no sanction for his power in 'antient Rights'. His power has come out of the wars and the troubled times. I call attention to the fact that we do not have to choose between readings: the readings do not mutually exclude each other: they support each other, and this double interpretation has the whole poem behind it.

Cromwell is urged to march 'indefatigably on'. The advice is good advice; but it is good advice because any other course of action is positively unthinkable. Indeed, to call it advice at all is perhaps to distort it: though addressed to Cromwell, it partakes of quiet commentary as much as of exhortation. After all, it is restless Cromwell who is being addressed. If he could not cease 'in the inglorious Arts of Peace' when his 'highest plot' was 'to plant the Bergamot', one cannot conceive of his ceasing now in the hour of danger.

And for the last effect
Still keep thy Sword erect . . .

Once more the advice (or commentary) is seriously intended, but it carries with it as much of warning as it does of approval. Those who take up the sword shall perish by the sword: those who have achieved their power on contravention of ancient rights by the sword can only expect to maintain their power by the sword.

What kind of sword is it that is able to 'fright the spirits of the shady night'? Margoliouth writes: 'The cross hilt of the sword would avert the spirits. . . .' But the speaker makes it quite plain that it is not merely the spirits of the shady night that Cromwell will have to fight as he marches indefatigably on. It will not be enough to hold the sword aloft as a ritual sword, an emblematic sword. The naked steel will still have to be used against bodies less diaphanous than spirits. If there is any doubt as to this last point, Marvell's concluding lines put it as powerfully and explicitly as it can be put:

The same *Arts* that did *gain*
A *Pow'r* must it *maintain.*

But, I can imagine someone asking, What is the final attitude toward Cromwell? Is it ultimately one of approval or disapproval? Does admiration overbalance condemnation? Or, is the 'Ode', after all, merely a varied Scottish plaid, the reflection of Marvell's own particolored mind – a mind which had not been finally 'made up' with regard to Cromwell? I think that enough has been said to make it plain that there is no easy, pat answer to such questions. There is a unified total attitude, it seems to me; but it is so complex that we may oversimplify and distort its complexity by the way in which we put the question. The request for some kind of summing up is a natural one, and I have no wish to try to evade it. For a really full answer, of course, one must refer the questioner to the poem itself; but one can at least try to suggest some aspects of the total attitude.

I would begin by re-emphasizing the dramatic character of the poem. It is not a statement – an essay on 'Why I cannot support Cromwell' or on ' Why I am now ready to support Cromwell.' It is a poem essentially dramatic in its presentation, which means that it is diagnostic rather than remedial, and eventuates, not in a course of action, but in contemplation. Perhaps the best way therefore in which to approach it is to conceive of it as, say, one conceives of a Shakespearean tragedy. Cromwell is the usurper who demands and commands admiration. What, for example, is our attitude toward Macbeth? We assume his guilt, but there are qualities which emerge from his guilt which properly excite admiration. I do not mean that the qualities palliate his guilt or that they compensate for his guilt. They actually come into being through his guilt, but they force us to exalt him even as we condemn him. I have chosen an extreme example. I certainly do not mean to imply that in writing the 'Ode' Marvell had Shakespeare's tragedy in mind. What I am trying to point to is this: that the kind of honesty and insight and whole-mindedness which we associate with tragedy is to be found to some degree in all great poetry and is to be found in this poem.

R. P. Warren once remarked to me that Marvell has constantly behind him in his poetry the achievement of Elizabethan drama with its treatment of the human will as seen in the perspective of history. He had in mind some of the lyrics, but the remark certainly applies fully to the 'Ode'. The poet is thoroughly conscious of the drama, and consciously makes use of dramatic perspective. Charles, as we have seen, becomes the 'Royal Actor', playing his part on the 'Tragick Scaffold'. But the tragedy of Charles is merely glanced at. The poem is Cromwell's – Cromwell's tragedy, the first three acts of it, as it were, which is not a tragedy of failure but of success.

Cromwell is the truly kingly man who is *not* king – whose very virtues conduce to kingly power and almost force kingly power upon him. It is not any fumbling on the poet's part which causes him to call Cromwell 'a Caesar' before the poem ends, even though he has earlier appropriated that name to Charles. *Both* men are Caesar, Charles the wearer of the purple, and Cromwell, the invincible general, the inveterate campaigner, the man 'that does both act and know'. Cromwell is the Caesar who must refuse the crown – whose glory it is that he is willing to refuse the crown – but who cannot enjoy the reward and the security that a crown affords. The tension between the speaker's admiration for the kingliness which has won Cromwell the power and his awareness that the power can be maintained only by a continual exertion of these talents for kingship – this tension is never relaxed. Cromwell is not of royal blood – he boasts a higher and a baser pedigree: he is the 'Wars and Fortunes Son'. He cannot rest because he is restless Cromwell. He must march indefatigably on, for he cannot afford to become fatigued. These implications enrich and qualify an insight into Cromwell which is as heavily freighted with admiration as it is with a great condemnation. But the admiration and the condemnation do not cancel each other. They define each other; and because there is responsible definition, they reinforce each other.

Was this, then, the attitude of Andrew Marvell, born 1621, sometime student at Cambridge, returned traveller and prospective tutor, toward Oliver Cromwell in the summer of 1650? The honest answer must be: I do not know. I have tried to read the poem, the 'Horatian Ode', not Andrew Marvell's mind. That seems sensible to me in view of the fact that we have the poem, whereas the attitude held by Marvell at any particular time must be a matter of inference – even though I grant that the poem may be put in as part of the evidence from which we draw inferences. True, we do know that Marvell was capable of composing the 'Ode' and I must concede that that fact may tell us a great deal about Marvell's attitude toward Cromwell. I think it probably does. I am not sure, for reasons given earlier in this paper, that it tells us everything: there is the problem of the role of the unconscious in the process of composition, there is the possibility of the poet's having written better than he knew, there is even the matter of the happy accident. I do not mean to overemphasize these matters. I do think, however, that it is wise to maintain the distinction between what total attitude is manifested in the poem and the attitude of the author as citizen.

Yet, though I wish to maintain this distinction, I do not mean to hide behind it. The total attitude realized in the 'Ode' does not seem to me monstrously inhuman in its complexity. It could be held by human beings, in my opinion. Something very like it apparently was. Listen, for example, to the Earl of Clarendon's judgement on Cromwell:

> He was one of those men, quos vitupare ne inimici quidem possunt, nisi ut simul laudent [whom not even their enemies can inveigh against without at the same time praising them], for he could never have done halfe that mischieve, without great partes of courage and industry and judgement, and he must have had a wonderful understandinge in the nature and humours of men, and as greate a dexterity in the applyinge them, who from a private and obscure birth (though of a good family), without interest of estate, allyance or frenshippes, could rayse himselfe to such a height, and compounde and kneade such opposite and contradictory humours and interests, into a consistence, that contributed to his designes and to ther owne distruction,

whilst himselfe grew insensibly powerful enough to, cut off those by whom
he had climed, in the instant, that they projected to demolish ther owne
buildinge. . . .

He was not a man of bloode, and totally declined Machiavells methode
. . . it was more then once proposed, that ther might be a generall massacre
of all the royall party, as the only expedient to secure the government, but
Crumwell would never consent to it, it may be out of to much contempt of
his enimyes; In a worde, as he had all the wikednesses against which damnation is denounced and for which Hell fyre is praepared, so he had some virtues,
which have caused the memory of some men in all ages to be celebrated,
and he will be looked upon by posterity, as a brave, badd man.

The resemblance between Clarendon's judgement and that reflected
in the 'Ode' is at some points so remarkable that one wonders whether
Clarendon had not seen and been impressed by some now lost manuscript of the 'Ode': 'Who from a private and obscure birth' – 'Who,
from his private Gardens, where/He liv'd reserved and austere' – 'could
rayse himself to such a height . . . by whome he had climed' – 'Could
by industrious Valour climbe', and so on and so forth. But I do not
want to press the suggestion of influence of Marvell on Clarendon.
Indeed, it makes for my general point to discount the possibility. For
what I am anxious to emphasize is that the attitude of the 'Ode' is not
inhuman in its Olympian detachment, that something like it could be
held by a human being, and by a human being of pronounced Royalist
sympathies.

I have argued that the critic needs the help of the historian – all the
help that he can get – but I have insisted that the poem has to be read
as a poem – that what it 'says' is a question for the critic to answer, and
that no amount of historical evidence as such can finally determine
what the poem says. But if we do read the poem successfully, the critic
may on occasion be able to make a return on his debt to the historian.
If we have read the 'Ode' successfully – *if*, I say for I am far from confident – it may be easier for us to understand how the man capable of
writing the 'Ode' was also able to write 'Tom May's Death' and 'Upon
Appleton House' and indeed, years later, after the Restoration, the
statement: 'Men ought to have trusted God; they ought and might
have trusted the King.'

Since completing this essay, I have come upon a further (see p. 104)
item which would suggest that the 'Horatian Ode' was circulating

among Royalists – not Puritans – in the early 1650s. The stanza form of
the 'Horatian Ode' was used only once by Marvell (in this poem) and
does not seem to occur in English poetry prior to Marvell. Margoliouth
and Legouis think it probable that this stanza was Marvell's own invention. Perhaps it was. But in Sir Richard Fanshawe's translation of
Horace's Odes – *Selected Parts of Horace* . . . *Now newly put into English*
(1652) – the 'Horatian Ode' stanza is used several times. If Marvell
invented the stanza in the summer of 1650, he must have been in close
association with Fanshawe for Fanshawe to have borrowed and made
use of the stanza so frequently in poems which were to be in print two
years later. I suspect that Marvell borrowed the stanza from Fanshawe.
Fanshawe had begun to publish translations of Horace (though none in
this stanza pattern) as early as 1648 in the volume which contained his
translation of *Il Pastor Fido*.[1] But in either case a Royalist connection
for Marvell is implied, for Fanshawe (1608–66) was a fervent and active
Royalist throughout the war, and after the Restoration was a trusted
servant of Charles II.

The following notes appear in H. M. Margoliouth's edition of The
Poems and Letters of Andrew Marvell (Oxford: Clarendon Press, 1927) 1
237–8:

A correspondent in *The Times Literary Supplement* (29 January 1920)
compares with lines 9–16 of this Ode Lucan, *Pharsalia*, i 144 et seq. . . .
Marvell perhaps had in mind both the Latin (cf successus urgere suos and
'Urg'd his active Star') and Tom May's translation, which here reads as
follows (2nd edition, 1631):

> But restlesse valour, and in warre a shame
> Not to be Conquerour; fierce, not curb'd at all,
> Ready to fight, where hope, or anger call,
> His forward Sword; confident of successe,
> And bold the favour of the gods to presse:
> Orethrowing all that his ambition stay,
> And loves that ruine should enforce his way;
> As lightning by the wind forc'd from a cloude
> Breakes through the wounded aire with thunder loud,
> Disturbes the Day, the people terrifyes,
> And by a light oblique dazels our eyes,
> Not *Joves* owne Temple spares it; when no force,
> No barre can hinder his prevailing course,
> Great waste, as foorth it sallyes and retires,
> It makes and gathers his dispersed fires.

Note the verbal resemblances, 'restlesse valour' and 'industrious Valour', 'forward Sword' and 'The forward Youth', 'lightning . . . from a cloude Breakes' and 'Lightning . . . Breaking the Clouds'. Further I suggest with diffidence that the striking phrase 'active Star' owes something to the chance neighbourhood of the two words in another passage in the same book of May's translation (*Pharsalia*, i 229–32):

> . . . the active Generall
> Swifter than Parthian back-shot shaft, or stone
> From Balearick Slinger, marches on
> T' invade Ariminum; when every star
> Fled from th' approaching Sunne but Lucifer . . .

Caesar is up betimes, marching when only the morning star is in the sky: Cromwell urges *his* 'active star'.

Sir Edward Ridley, carrying on the correspondence in *The Times Literary Supplement* (5 February 1920), points out further a likeness between Marvell's account of the death of Charles I and *Pharsalia*, viii 613–17 (the death of Pompey):

> ut vidit comminus ensem
> involvit vultus atque indignatus apertum
> fortunae praestare caput, tunc lumina pressit
> continuitque animam, ne quas effundere voces
> posset et aeternam fletu corrumpere famam . . .

SOURCE: *English Institute Essays 1946* (1947).

NOTE

1. [Editor's note.] See William Simeone, 'A Probable Antecedent of Marvell's "Horatian Ode" ', in *Notes and Queries*, CXCVII (July 1952) 316–18.

DOUGLAS BUSH

Marvell's 'Horatian Ode' (1952)

THE 'Horatian Ode' is commonly regarded not only as one of Marvell's finest poems but as an embodiment of two usually distinct poetic modes, the classical and the 'metaphysical'. For all its metaphysical texture and originality, it is the nearest approach in English to the form and the *gravitas* of Horace's patriotic odes. There is the further fact that the poem is not a conventional eulogy but a subtle portrait of its subject, warts and all. At a time when Cromwell aroused violently conflicting passions among Englishmen (as indeed he has ever since), Marvell was able to contemplate both him and King Charles with a mixture of warm admiration and cool, analytical detachment. To read the poem as poetry is also to read it as an historical document, for we must ask what Marvell is saying, in and between the lines, about Cromwell.

In *English Institute Essays 1946*, Professor Cleanth Brooks, attacking 'the specific problem of the speaker's attitude toward Cromwell', gives an elaborate and acute analysis of the ode which is intended to illustrate, in contrast to the 'coarse' method of historical criticism, the critic's obligation to interpret the poem as it stands, to bring out all the conscious and unconscious hints and complexities that it contains, and thereby to define Marvell's view of Cromwell from the inside. One might stop to quarrel with such an arbitrary doctrine of criticism, since the critic's obligation is surely to use all helpful evidence of any kind (and Mr Brooks himself, when he wishes, goes outside the poem), but in this case one may be quite willing to suspend disbelief and consider the ode on Mr Brooks's terms. Accepting the judgement of Marvell's editor, Mr Margoliouth, that 'royalist principles and admiration for Cromwell the Great Man exist side by side', Mr Brooks holds that the problem is a subtle one of poetic organization and therefore addresses itself properly to the critic.

But the moment we enter upon Mr Brooks's exegesis we see that, far from making a disinterested inquiry into the evidence provided by the poem, he is forcing the evidence to fit an unspoken assumption – namely, that a sensitive, penetrating, and well-balanced mind like Marvell could not really have admired a crude, single-minded, and ruthless man of action like Cromwell. This is a prejudice natural enough in a good modern liberal, who is bound to see Cromwell, even the Cromwell of 1650, as a sort of Puritan Stalin, but it is a prejudice; and it leads, as I have said, to frequent straining or distortion of what Marvell says and to the supplying of things he does not say. Indeed, if people in 1681 would have read the poem with Mr Brooks's eyes, as in the main a condemnation of Cromwell, there would not have been much reason for the poem's being cut out of the first edition of Marvell, since such a view of Cromwell would have been welcome enough to the Restoration. But that is irrelevant historical speculation, and we must look at the poem.

Mr Brooks's special pleading begins with his gloss on the first lines:

> The forward Youth that would appear
> Must now forsake his *Muses* dear,
>   Nor in the Shadows sing
>   His Numbers languishing.
> 'Tis time to leave the Books in dust,
> And oyl th' unused Armours rust:
>   Removing from the Wall
>   The Corslet of the Hall.

To the unprejudiced reader, the lines say that, in these troubled times, the young man of spirit must leave bookish and poetical pursuits for military action. Says Mr Brooks (p. 98):* ' "Forward" may mean no more than "high-spirited", "ardent", "properly ambitious"; but the *New English Dictionary* sanctions the possibility that there lurks in the word the sense of "presumptuous", "pushing" ', and 'It is the "forward" youth whose attention the speaker directs to the example of Cromwell.' Thus the critic has already made up his mind about the poet's view of Cromwell, and, instead of taking 'forward' in its common and natural sense, must grasp at a pejorative possibility (the meaning 'presumptuous', to judge from the *New English Dictionary*, has been commoner in modern times than it was in Marvell's).

* Page references have been amended to those of this volume.

After the prelude, Marvell shifts to Cromwell, stressing his tremendous, superhuman energy, with the aid of a violent and elaborate simile:

> So restless *Cromwel* could not cease
> In the inglorious Arts of Peace,
>   But through adventrous War
>   Urged his active Star.
> And, like the three-fork'd Lightning, first
> Breaking the Clouds where it was nurst,
>   Did thorough his own Side
>   His fiery way divide.
> For 'tis all one to Courage high
> The Emulous or Enemy;
>   And with such to inclose
>   Is more then to oppose.
> Then burning through the Air he went,
> And Pallaces and Temples rent:
>   And *Caesars* head at last
>   Did through his Laurels blast.

Here, as before, Mr Brooks makes a pejorative choice among 'ambiguous' possibilities. ' "Restless" is as ambiguous in its meanings as "forward", and in its darker connotations even more damning' (p. 99). The critic finds Cromwell's thirst for glory hinted at in many phrases – '*could* not cease', 'the inglorious Arts of Peace', in the fact that, instead of being led by his star, Cromwell 'Urged' his (pp. 99, 102). Mr Brooks may, theoretically, or ultimately, be correct, but has Marvell, so far, given warrant for these 'darker connotations'? At any rate Mr Brooks is consistent in always loading the dice against Cromwell.

The simile, says Mr Brooks (p. 100), makes Cromwell 'like an elemental force – with as little will as the lightning bolt, and with as little conscience'. Cromwell manifestly is likened to an elemental force, but, again, has Marvell given any warrant for the interpretative phrases, or are they a prejudiced addition? Does a lightning bolt have 'Courage high' ? But comment on the full meaning of the simile must wait for a moment. The nature of Mr Brooks's special pleading becomes conspicuous in his treatment of the next two lines, which are, for his problem, perhaps the most significant lines in the whole poem:

> 'Tis Madness to resist or blame
> The force of angry Heavens flame.

Mr Brooks writes (p. 101):

> Does the poet mean to imply that Charles has angered heaven – that he has
> merited his destruction? There is no suggestion that Cromwell is a thunder-
> bolt hurled by an angry Jehovah – or even by an angry Jove. The general
> emphasis on Cromwell as an elemental force is thoroughly relevant here to
> counter this possible misreading. Certainly, in the lines that follow there is
> nothing to suggest that Charles has angered heaven, or that the Justice which
> complains against his fate is anything less than justice.

I do not know what to make of such a statement as 'There is no suggestion that Cromwell is a thunderbolt hurled by an angry Jehovah –
or even by an angry Jove', since that is what Marvell unmistakably says.
In keeping with the pagan tone of a Horatian ode, of course, he nowhere permits a Christian allusion, but the poem is not a period piece
of artificial classicism and the reader makes an obvious transfer from
pagan Rome to Christian England. Even if Cromwell be conceived
only as a traditional 'Scourge of God', he is the agent of the Providence
whose will, in the common view of history, has worked in human
affairs. Mr Brooks seems to be merely rejecting evidence that is signally
inconvenient for his reading of the poem.

Since, as we observed, Mr Brooks himself, in spite of his premise,
goes outside the poem for desired data, one may venture to do likewise – although the poem itself is sufficiently clear and emphatic
in presenting Cromwell as the agent of angry heaven. We need not
assume that Marvell's view of men and events remained quite unaltered
up to the time, between four and five years later, when he wrote so
wholly eulogistic a poem as 'The First Anniversary of the Government
under O. C.', but it is altogether unlikely either that he had made a
volte-face or that he had become a mere time-server. We might take
a few bits from the later poem as glosses on 'angry Heavens flame'
which – however inferior the poetry – are not less reliable than a modern
critic's inferences:

> While indefatigable *Cromwell* hyes,
> And cuts his way still nearer to the Skyes,
> Learning a Musique in the Region clear,
> To tune this lower to that higher Sphere. (45–8)

> Hence oft I think, if in some happy Hour
> High Grace should meet in one with highest Pow'r,
> And then a seasonable People still
> Should bend to his, as he to Heavens will,
> What we might hope, what wonderful Effect
> From such a wish'd Conjuncture might reflect. (131-6)

> What since he did, an higher Force him push'd
> Still from behind, and it before him rush'd,
> Though undiscern'd among the tumult blind,
> Who think those high Decrees by Man design'd.
> 'Twas Heav'n would not that his Pow'r should cease,
> But walk still middle betwixt War and Peace;
> Choosing each Stone, and poysing every weight,
> Trying the Measures of the Bredth and Height;
> Here pulling down, and there erecting New,
> Founding a firm State by Proportions true. (239-48)

And, especially for the sake of one phrase, we might add a couplet from the opening of Marvell's 'Poem upon the Death of O. C.':

> And he whom Nature all for Peace had made,
> But angry Heaven unto War had sway'd. . . .

In these later poems Cromwell is unquestionably the instrument of God, and if in the earlier one the lines about 'angry Heavens flame' do not say the same thing, one does not know what they do say. The modern liberal – who normally reacts against Toynbee and Butterfield – can seldom fully understand the providential conception of history which was traditional in Marvell's age (witness Ralegh's *History of the World*) and which was indeed a necessary part of Christian belief; and Marvell, however liberal and emancipated from common prejudices, was a Christian. All this is not to say that he takes, here or elsewhere, a simple, one-sided view of either Cromwell or Charles, but one must emphasize the central importance of Cromwell's being a divine agent and hence endowed with the power of a force of nature.

In the next few lines Cromwell is associated with peaceful rural nature:

> And, if we would speak true,
> Much to the Man is due.

> Who, from his private Gardens, where
> He liv'd reserved and austere,
>   As if his highest plot
>   To plant the Bergamot . . .

The first two lines are something more than a transition. 'Much to the Man is due', in focusing on the actual person in himself, helps to define the previous conception of the being who was an instrument of Providence. The next quatrain is clearly intended to link Cromwell the man with the simple, frugal heroes of Roman tradition, like Cincinnatus, called from the plough to rule the state. In what they say, and in the affinity they imply, the lines are a quiet refutation of some of Mr Brooks's darker inferences.

Then we come to a passage where the warts may seem to protrude. The man who lived as if only to plant the bergamot

> Could by industrious Valour climbe
> To ruine the great Work of Time,
>   And cast the Kingdome old
>   Into another Mold.
> Though Justice against Fate complain,
> And plead the antient Rights in vain:
>   But those do hold or break
>   As Men are strong or weak.
> Nature that hateth emptiness
> Allows of penetration less:
>   And therefore must make room
>   Where greater Spirits come.
> What Field of all the Civil Wars
> Where his were not the deepest Scars? . . .

Mr Brooks thinks that 'climbe' 'certainly connotes a kind of aggressiveness' and a thirst for glory, and that, in the lines on 'Nature', 'The question of right, the imagery insists, is beside the point', since the question of power alone is being weighed (pp. 99, 100). He admits that Marvell recognizes Cromwell's martial valor, even a dedicated rather than a merely selfish sense of glory, and the role of a man of destiny; and he points out, following Margoliouth and Firth, that there is no ground for the contemporary charge, which Marvell repeats, that Cromwell had engineered Charles's flight to Carisbrooke Castle. But the critic maintains nevertheless that Cromwell has 'thus far . . . been

treated as naked force' (p. 102); he has been praised for 'the tremendous
disciplined powers' he has brought to bear against the king. However,
Mr Brooks proceeds,

> For the end served by those powers, the speaker has no praise at all. Rather
> he has gone out of his way to insist that Cromwell was deaf to the complaint
> of Justice and its pleading of the 'antient Rights'. The power achieved by
> Cromwell is a 'forced Pow'r' – a usurped power. On this point the speaker is
> unequivocal. I must question therefore Margoliouth's statement that Marvell
> sees in Cromwell 'the man of destiny moved by . . . a power that is above
> justice'. Above justice, yes, in the sense that power is power and justice is not
> power. The one does not insure the presence of the other. Charles has no way
> to vindicate his 'helpless Right', but it is no less Right because it is helpless.
> But the speaker, though he is not a cynic, is a realist. A kingdom cannot be
> held by mere pleading of the 'antient Rights':

> > But those do hold or break
> > As Men are strong or weak.

> In short, the more closely we look at the 'Ode', the more clearly apparent
> it becomes that the speaker has chosen to emphasize Cromwell's virtues as a
> man, and likewise, those of Charles as a man. The poem does not debate
> which of the two was right, for that issue is not even in question. (pp. 102–3)

This may be the right, or a tenable, view of the central passage we
have arrived at, and of the whole poem, yet it seems open to query. In
the first place, if the issue of 'right' is not even in question, how can
anyone be concerned, as Mr Brooks is all along, with distinguishing
right from power, with sifting moral praise and blame, and, in short,
making the strongest possible case for the prosecution? In the second
place, although elsewhere he is on the watch for sinister ambiguities,
even in words that appear innocent, here words of at least equal
ambiguity have become moral absolutes that condemn Cromwell.
The word 'right' ('the antient Rights', 'his helpless Right') may mean
not only abstract rightness but traditional claims which may or may
not be wholly right. 'Justice' may be absolute justice, or it may be the
limited vision of human law that must give way before the divine will
('Fate', in Roman terms). The 'great Work of Time' that Cromwell
has ruined is not necessarily or wholly the good work of time; a great
nation may have nourished wrongs that must, at whatever cost, be
righted. Marvell was assuredly not of 'Machiavellian' outlook, but in
his view of Cromwell he may – with some important differences –

have somewhat resembled Machiavelli: while Machiavelli's ideal was the old Roman republic, a republic could not bring order out of chaos, and the strong man who could must be welcomed. Though Marvell does not go into the causes of the civil war but concentrates on Cromwell and his royal opponent, he indicates that he sees 'the Kingdome old' as undergoing the pangs of both death and rebirth, and, with all his admiration for the royal actor, he bows to the man of action who can, however violently, establish order. And, as we have seen, he bows not only to the heroic individual but to the Providence who has raised him up.

After the account of Charles's execution – which for too many readers disturbs the center of gravity of the poem – the poet turns, as Mr Brooks says, from Cromwell the destroyer of the monarchy to 'the agent of the new state that has been erected upon the dead body of the King' (p. 104). The execution was 'that memorable Hour Which first assur'd the forced Pow'r'. But while Cromwell has been an illegal regicide, the effect of 'forced Pow'r' is partly countered by what follows, the incident from Roman history in which 'the State Foresaw it's happy Fate'. If the execution was evil, it can bring forth good. As Mr Brooks sees it, Marvell 'does not commit himself to the opinion that the bleeding head is a happy augury', but makes this the popular opinion. I doubt if Marvell – whatever he privately felt – is here consciously disassociating himself from 'the State'. If he were, would he go so far elsewhere in the poem in celebrating Cromwell with his own voice?

There follows at once a passage that is probably more embarrassing than any other part of the ode to anyone intent upon proving that Marvell's main attitude toward Cromwell is hostility or at most unwilling respect for unscrupulous strength and courage:

> And now the *Irish* are asham'd
> To see themselves in one Year tam'd:
>   So much one Man can do,
>   That does both act and know.
> They can affirm his Praises best,
> And have, though overcome, confest
>   How good he is, how just,
>   And fit for highest Trust.

Mr Margoliouth remarks that 'Irish testimony in favour of Cromwell at this moment is highly improbable' (though he sees a possible reference to the voluntary submission of part of Munster), and we may, with Mr Brooks, take the remark as an understatement. For Mr Brooks the appeal 'is not to what Marvell the Englishman must have thought, or even to what Marvell the author must have intended, but rather to the full context of the poem itself' (p. 106). One may not quite understand these several possibilities, since the poem did not get itself written by some agency outside of Marvell. However, Mr Brooks is driven to what may be thought the desperate solution of finding the lines ironical, a view he thinks sanctioned by the earlier stanzas because the Irish have learned of the qualities in Cromwell that Marvell had praised, energy, activity, and the like. 'The Irish, indeed, are best able to affirm such praise as has been accorded to Cromwell; and they know from experience "how good he is, how just", for they have been blasted by the force of angry Heaven's flame, even as Charles has been' (p. 106).

Since I cannot follow much of Mr Brooks's reading of the earlier stanzas, I cannot follow such an explanation. Nothing in the wording seems to me to carry the faintest trace of irony; it is as straightforward a statement as we could have, however little we like it. Nor do I see how irony could pass at once into what Mr Brooks accepts as eulogy without the slightest hint of a change of tone. Although, as he says, the recommendation of trust has reference to the English state, it is the Irish who have 'confest' it, and I see nothing in the text to support Mr Brooks's oblique interpretation of Marvell's account of Irish feelings: 'The Irish are quite proper authorities on Cromwell's trustworthiness in this regard, for they have come to know him as the completely dedicated instrument of that state whose devotion to the purpose in hand is unrelenting and unswerving' (p. 106). But, instead of twisting Marvell's plain words into irony, and thereby molding him into the likeness of a modern liberal, we really must accept the unpalatable fact that he wrote as an Englishman of 1650; and, in regard to what seems to us a strange assertion, we must say that he is indulging in some wishful thinking – Cromwell is so great a conqueror that even the Irish must share English sentiment and accept the course of history. In the poem on Cromwell's death, it may be added, Marvell glanced at his Irish campaign with nothing but admiration for his religious zeal and martial prowess (lines 179 ff). It may be added further that Milton was far closer to Marvell than any modern reader can be (and Milton was bold enough, a few years later when Cromwell was at the height of his power, to rebuke him for turning a republic into a dictatorship), and we have only to look at Milton's *Observations on the Articles of Peace* (1649) to see what the English attitude was. That is not to say that Marvell thought just as Milton thought; it is to say that the text of Marvell's poem means what it says, and that the suggestion of irony raises a much more difficult problem, within the poem, than the one it seeks to explain.

Early in his essay Mr Brooks observed that 'the critic obviously must know what the words of the poem mean, something which immediately puts him in debt to the linguist' (p. 97), but he neglects this sound precept in his comment on the next lines:

> Nor yet grown stiffer with Command,
> But still in the *Republick's* hand.

Says Mr Brooks:

> Does the emphasis on 'still' mean that the speaker is surprised that Cromwell has continued to pay homage to the republic? Does he imply that Cromwell may not always do so? Perhaps not: the emphasis is upon the fact that he need not obey and yet does. Yet the compliment derives its full force from the fact that the homage is not forced but voluntary and even somewhat un-expected. And a recognition of this point implies the recognition of the possibility that Cromwell will not always so defer to the commonwealth. (p. 105)

But such 'darker connotations' are quite gratuitous. 'Still' here – as later in 'Still keep thy Sword erect' – has its normal seventeenth-century meaning, 'always', and Marvell's words afford no ground for an ominous hint of a possible change of heart in Cromwell.

We need not concern ourselves with the rest of the ode, in which Marvell sees Cromwell as the obedient servant of Parliament, the prospective conqueror of the Scots, and a leader to be feared by Europe. But we may notice the last lines, where Mr Brooks again finds sinister implications:

> But thou the Wars and Fortunes Son
> March indefatigably on;
> And for the last effect
> Still keep thy Sword erect:
> Besides the force it has to fright
> The Spirits of the shady Night,
> The same Arts that did *gain*
> A *Pow'r* must it *maintain*.

The salutation in the first line means, as Mr Brooks says (p. 107), that 'Cromwell is the son of the wars in that he is the master of battle, and he seems fortune's own son in the success that has constantly waited upon him'. But he goes on to say that 'we do not wrench the lines if we take them to say also that Cromwell is the creature of the wars and the product of fortune'. I think this is a very decided wrenching of the lines; we must remember that Marvell has seen Cromwell as the agent of heaven. And there is some further wrenching in Mr Brooks's comment on 'Still keep thy Sword erect': 'Those who take up the sword shall perish by the sword: those who have achieved their power on contravention of ancient rights by the sword can only expect to maintain their power by the sword' (p. 108). Does Marvell give any hint toward such an interpretation?

Mr Brooks always offers general and particular insights that sharpen our perceptions, and this essay, like his others, is precise and provocative. His readers, if they came to it with the notion that Marvell's ode is a simple poem, could never again be misled in that way. But they could be misled into finding a greater degree of complexity than the text warrants. There is surely a line between legitimate and illegitimate ambiguity, a line to be respected by both poet and critic, and Mr Brooks seems continually to overstep that line. He sees the poem as expressing a 'unified total attitude', though a very complex one, yet it would be hard to merge his findings into any total unity unless Marvell is more or less lifted out of his age into ours. As we have seen, the result, if not the aim, of Mr Brooks's inquiry is, in large measure, to turn a seventeenth-century liberal into a modern one. That is one reason why historical conditioning has a corrective as well as a positive value, although in this case we do not need to go outside the poem to recognize fallacies and distortions in what purports to be a purely critical and unprejudiced analysis.

SOURCE: *Sewanee Review*, LX (1952).

EDITOR'S NOTE

Cleanth Brooks replies to these comments in 'A Note on the Limits of "History" and the Limits of "Criticism"', in *Sewanee Review*, LXI (Winter 1953) 129–35, reprinted in *Seventeenth Century English Poetry*, ed. W. R. Keast (New York, 1962) pp. 352–8.

FRANK KERMODE

The Argument of Marvell's 'Garden' (1952)

I

'THE Garden' is an *étude d'exécution transcendante* which has been interpreted by so many virtuosi in the past few years that a stiff-fingered academic rendering is unlikely to be very entertaining. However, since it appears that the brilliant executants have been making rather too many mistakes, there may be some value in going slowly over the whole piece.

I may be useful to point out in advance that these mistakes are of three kinds. The first is historical, as when Mr Milton Klonsky, writing in the *Sewanee Review* – LVIII (Winter 1950), 16–35 – seizes on a passage in Plotinus as the sole key to the poem. He is wrong, not because there is no connection at all between Plotinus and Marvell's lyric, but because he has misunderstood the relationship and consequently exaggerated its importance. He fails to observe that Marvell, like other poets of the period, uses philosophical concepts, including those of Neoplatonism in a special way, with reference not to the body of formal doctrine in which those concepts are originally announced, but to genres of poetry which habitually and conventionally make use of them. The process is familiar enough; for example, the nature of the relationship between pastoral poetry and philosophic material such as the debates on Action and Contemplation, Art and Nature, is tolerably well understood. It is not customary to find the only key to the works of Guarini or Fletcher in some Greek philosopher; but these poets have not, like Donne and Marvell, been distorted by the solemn enthusiasm of modern exegetes. In a sense all philosophical propositions in Marvell are what Professor Richards used to call 'pseudo-statements', and his is a 'physical' rather than a 'platonic' poetry. However, rather than risk myself in these deep waters, I shall support myself on a raft of Mr Wellek's construction: 'The work of art . . . appears as an object *sui generis* . . .

a system of norms of ideal concepts which are intersubjective . . .'
Above all, it is possible 'to proceed to a classification of works of art
according to the norms they employ' and thus 'we may finally arrive at
theories of genre'.[1] The point is that we must not treat these 'norms'
as propositions, for if we do we shall fall into the toils of Mr Klonsky.
Miss Ruth Wallerstein, who has worked so hard and so sanely to
liberate seventeenth-century poetry from modern error, is none the
less guilty of Mr Klonsky's fault, in her *Studies in Seventeenth Century
Poetic* (Madison, 1950). Not only the indolent cry out against the
suggestion that 'The Garden' needs to be explicated in terms of Hugo of
St Victor and Bonaventura. Doubtless there is, for the historian of
ideas, a real connection between the poem and the Victorine and Neo-
Platonic systems of symbolic thought; for there is a connection between
Plato and 'Trees'. However interesting this may be, it has nothing to do
with what most of us call criticism. If we read 'The Garden' as historians of poetry, and not as historians of ideas, we shall resist all such
temptation to treat the 'norms' as ideas, even if it proceeds from Dio-
tima herself, to whom Professor Richards succumbed in a recent
lecture on the poem.

The second kind of mistake is one which, particularly when it
assumes its more subtle shape, we are all liable to yield to, though it
appears to be seductive even in its usual grossness. Sufficient, however,
to say that 'The Garden' must not be read as autobiography. 'What
was Marvell's state of mind as he wandered in Fairfax's Yorkshire
garden?' is a very bad question to ask, but it is obviously one which
comes readily to the minds of learned and subtle interpreters; both
Marvell and Donne have suffered greatly from this form of misapplied
scholarship, and it is comforting to reflect that the date of 'The Garden'
is quite unknown, so that it cannot be positively stated to be the direct
record of some personal experience at Nun Appleton. It could conceivably have been written much later. The pseudo-biographical critic
is wasteful and deceptive; he diverts attention from the genre just as
certainly as Mr Klonsky does when he presents a picture of the poet
torturing himself with Chinese boxes of Forms, or Mr Empson when
he invites us to reflect upon the Buddhist enlightenment (*Some Versions
of Pastoral*, pp. 119–20; in U.S.A., *English Pastoral Poetry*).

The third kind of critical failure is clearly, in this case, the most
important, for the others would not have occurred had there not been
this cardinal error. It is the failure to appreciate the genre (the system of

'norms' shared by other poems) to which 'The Garden' belongs.
Despite the labours of Miss Bradbrook, Miss Lloyd Thomas,[2] and Miss
Wallerstein, poets like Théophile, Saint-Amant, Randolph, Lovelace,
Fane and Stanley have simply not been put to proper use in the criticism of Marvell. This is the central difficulty, and the one which this
paper is intended to diminish. The first necessity is to distinguish
between the genre and the history of the ideas to which the genre is
related.

II

'We cannot erre in following Nature': thus Montaigne, 'very rawly
and simply', with this addition: 'I have not (as *Socrates*) by the power
and vertue of reason, corrected my natural complexions, nor by Art
hindered mine inclination.'[3] This is a useful guide to that aspect of
'naturalism' in the thought of the late Renaissance which here concerns
us. The like consideration governs all the speculations of the older
Montaigne; Nature is to be distinguished from Custom; the natural
inclinations are good, and sensual gratifications are not the dangerous
suggestions that other and more orthodox psychologies hold them to
be. Sense and instinct seek and find their own temperance without the
interference of reason. It is good to satisfy a natural appetite, and it is
also, of course, innocent. Thus men behaved, says Montaigne, in the
Golden World, and thus they still behave in the Indies.

The question how far Montaigne believed in his own 'primitivism'
seems to me a difficult one, but it scarcely concerns us at the moment.
It is legitimate to use him as spokesman for naturalism; and before we
leave him it will be prudent to glance at some of his references to Plato,
in order to have at hand some record of the naturalist reaction to the
Platonic theory of love. In short, as the foregoing quotation implies,
Platonic love is rejected. No longer 'an appetite of generation by the
mediation of beauty', love is in fact 'nothing else but an insatiate thirst
of enjoying a greedily desired subject' (III 105). 'My Page makes love,
and understands it feelingly; Read *Leon Hebraeus* or *Ficinus* unto him;
you speake of him, of his thoughts and of his actions, yet understands he
nothing what you meane . . .' (III 102). Much more sympathetic are
'the ample and lively descriptions in *Plato*, of the loves practised in his
dayes' (III 82). If one is not over-careful – if, for instance, one fails to
discriminate between the orations of Socrates and those who precede

him, one may without much difficulty extract from the *Symposium* itself very different theories of love from those developed by Ficino or Milton. In Marvell's own youth antithetical versions of Platonism flourished contemporaneously at Cambridge and at Whitehall.

So far we have concerned ourselves, very briefly, with the informal naturalism of Montaigne, and hinted at a naturalistic version of Plato. What of the poetry which concerns itself with similar issues? One thinks at once of Tasso, and specifically of that chorus in his *Aminta, O bella età de l'oro* which was so often imitated and debated in the poetry of the age. In the happy Golden Age lovers concerned themselves with their own love and innocence, and not with honour, that tyrant bred of custom and opinion, that enemy of nature. In the garden of the unfallen just, whatever pleases is lawful. The paradise of these fortunate innocents is abundant in its appeal to the senses; law and appetite are the same, and no resolved soul interferes with the banquet of sense offered by created pleasure. Thus an ancient pastoral tradition accommodates new poetic motives, and poetry, though affirming nothing, strengthens its association with the freer thought of its time. The formal opposition to Tasso's statement is properly made in poetry which belongs to the same genre; and it may be found in the chorus in Act IV of Guarini's *Il Pastor Fido*. Parallel debates could go on in the great world, and in the little world of poetry: the debate about naturalism was a serious one, since it involved theological censures. The poetical debate is of a different quality. The proper answer to Tasso is Guarini's. A genre of poetry developed which assumed the right to describe the sensuality of a natural Eden, and a specialized kind concentrated on sexual gratifications as innocent, and the subject of unreasonable interference from Honour. The proper reply is, again, in terms of the 'norms' of the genre, and there is evidence that the very poets who stated the extreme naturalist case were quite capable of refuting it. One might call the 'norms' of the refutation an anti-genre. 'The Garden' is a poem of the anti-genre of the naturalist paradise.

Marvell therefore rejects the naturalist account of love, and with it that Platonism which was associated with the delights of the senses. The poets of the Renaissance were profitably aware of the possible antitheses in Platonic theories of love, just as they were aware of Plato's argument against their status as vessels of the truth.[4] Spenser makes comfortable bedfellows of two Platonisms in his 'Hymns'; the two Aphrodites easily change into each other in poem and emblem. Nothing is more characteristic of Renaissance poetry than the synthesis of spiritual and erotic in poetic genre and image. It was encouraged by centuries of comment on the *Canticum Canticorum* and the eclecticism of mystics as well as by the doctrinaire efforts of Bruno to spiritualize the erotic Petrarcan conceits. Much more evidence could be brought, if it were necessary, to establish the existence of genre and anti-genre in Platonic love-poetry. They not only co-exist, but suggest each other. Marvell could pass with ease from the libertine garden to the garden of the Platonic *solitaire*, soliciting the primary *furor* of spiritual ascent. (The ease of such transitions was partly responsible for the development of another genre – that of the palinode.)

'The Garden' stands in relation to the poetry of the gardens of sense as the 'Hymn of Heavenly Beauty' stands in relation to the 'Hymn of Beauty'. It is poetry written in the language of, or using the 'norms' of, a genre in a formal refutation of the genre. In fact, this was a method Marvell habitually used, sometimes almost with an affectation of pedantry, as I have elsewhere shown of 'The Mower against Gardens'.[5]

III

The garden is a rich emblem, and this is not the place to explore it in any detail; indeed I shall say nothing of the symbolic gardens of the Middle Ages which were still alive in the consciousness of the seventeenth century. The gardens to which Marvell most directly alludes in his poem are the Garden of Eden, the Earthly Paradise, and that garden to which both Stoic and Epicurean, as well as Platonist, retire for solace or meditation. The first two are in many respects one and the same; the third is the garden of Montaigne, of Lipsius, and of Cowley. I shall not refer to the *hortus conclusus*, though at one point in my explication of Marvell's poem I allude to a Catholic emblem-writer. Doubtless the notion of Nature as God's book affects the poetic tradition; it certainly occurs in poems about solitude at this period. But I think it is misleading to dwell on the history of the idea.

Of the complexity of the Earthly Paradise, with all its associated images and ideas, it is not necessary to say much: it is of course a staple of pastoral poetry and drama, and the quality of Marvell's allusions to it will emerge in my explication. But a word is needed about the garden of the solitary thinker, which Marvell uses in his argument against the libertine garden of innocent sexuality.

It is to be remembered that we are not dealing with the innocence of Tasso's Golden Age, where there is a perfect concord between appetite and reason, or with the garden of innocent love that Spenser sketches in *Faerie Queene*, IV x, where 'thousand payres of louers walkt, Praysing their god and yeelding him great thankes', and, 'did sport Their spot-lesse pleasures, and sweet loues content'. The libertines use the argu-ment of the innocence of sense to exalt sensuality and to propose the abolition of the tyrant Honour, meaning merely female chastity. This is the situation of the *Jouissance* poetry which was fashionable in France, and of which Saint-Amant's well-known example, excellently trans-lated by Stanley, is typical. It is equally the situation of Randolph's 'Upon Love Fondly Refused' and his 'Pastoral Courtship', Carew's 'Rapture' and Lovelace's 'Love Made in the first Age'. In Randolph's Paradise there is no serpent – 'Nothing that wears a sting, but I'[6] – and in Lovelace's

> No Serpent kiss poyson'd the Tast
> Each touch was naturally Chast,
> And their mere Sense a Miracle.[7]

And so it is throughout the libertine versions of sensual innocence. The garden, the place of unfallen innocence, is identified with a natura-list glorification of sensuality. The garden which is formally opposed to this one by Marvell is the garden where sense is controlled by reason and the intellect can contemplate not beauty but heavenly beauty.

It was Montaigne, this time in his Stoic role, who gave wide cur-rency to the pleasures of *solitary* seclusion. The relevant ideas and attitudes were developed into a poetic genre. Many poets certainly known to Marvell practised this genre, among them Fane and Fairfax and the French poets, notably Saint-Amant, whose *Solitude* demon-strates how easily he moved in this, the antithesis of the *Jouissance* mode. This famous poem was translated by Fairfax and by Katharine Phillips. This is the poetry of the meditative garden, whether the meditation be pseudo-Dionysian, or Ciceronian, or merely pleasantly Epicurean, like Cowley's. There is, of course, a play of the senses in which woman has no necessary part, though the equation of all appetite with the sexual appetite in the libertines tends to ignore it; this unamorous sensuality is firmly castigated by Lipsius in his treatment of gardens. If the garden is treated merely as a resort of pleasure, for the 'inward tickling and delight of the senses' it becomes 'a verie sepulchre of slothfulnes'. The true end of the garden is 'quietnes, withdrawing from the world, meditation', the subjection of the distressed mind to right reason.[8] The true ecstasy is in being rapt by intellect, not by sex.

Retirement; the study of right reason; the denial of the sovereignty of sense; the proper use of created nature: these are the themes of Marvell's poem laboriously and misleadingly translated into prose. As poetry the work can only be studied in relation to its genre, though that genre may be related to ethical debates. To the naturalist *Jouissance* Marvell opposes the meditative *Solitude*. The fact that both these opposed conceptions are treated in the work of one poet, Saint-Amant, and a little less explicitly in Théophile and Randolph also, should warn against the mistaking of seriousness for directness of reference to ethical propositions. 'The Garden' uses and revalues the 'norms' of the genre: it is not a contribution to philosophy, and not the direct account of a contemplative act.

IV

Henry Hawkins, the author of the emblem-book *Partheneia Sacra*, adopts a plan which enables him, in treating the emblematic qualities of a garden, to direct the attention of the pious reader away from the delights of the sense offered by the plants to a consideration of their higher significance. As in Marvell, sensual pleasure has to give way to meditation.[9] We now proceed to the explication of Marvell's poem, with a glance at Hawkins's wise disclaimer: 'I will not take upon me to tel al; for so of a Garden of flowers, should I make a Labyrinth of discourse, and should never be able to get forth' (p. 8).

The poem begins by establishing that of all the possible gardens it is dealing with that of retirement, with the garden of the contemplative man who shuns action. The retired life is preferred to the active life in a witty simplification: if the two ways of life are appraised in terms of the vegetable solace they provide it will be seen that the retired life is quantitatively superior. The joke is in the substitution of the emblem of victory for its substance. If you then appraise action in terms of plants you get single plants, whereas retirement offers you the solace of not one but *all* plants. This is a typical 'metaphysical' use of the figure called by Puttenham the Disabler. The first stanza, then, is a witty dispraise of the active life, though it has nothing to distinguish it sharply from other kinds of garden-poetry such as libertine or

Epicurean – except possibly the hint of a secondary meaning 'celibate' in the word *single* and a parallel sexual pun on *close*,[10] which go very well with the leading idea that woman has no place in this garden.

The Innocence of the second stanza cannot itself divide the poem from other garden-poems; for Innocence of a sort is a feature of the libertine paradise, as well as of the Epicurean garden of Cowley and indeed most gardens.

> Your sacred Plants, if here below,
> Only among the Plants will grow –

lines which are certainly a much more complicated statement than that of *Hortus* – seem to have stimulated Mr Klonsky to astonishing feats. But the idea is not as difficult as all that. Compare 'Upon Appleton House' –

> For he did, with his utmost Skill,
> *Ambition* weed, but *Conscience* till.
> *Conscience*, that Heaven-nursed Plant,
> Which most our Earthly Gardens want. (XLV)

Your sacred plants, he says, addressing Quiet and Innocence, are unlike the palm, the oak and the bays in that if you find them anywhere on earth it will be among the plants of the garden. The others you can find 'in busie Companies'. The joke here is to give Quiet and her sister plant-emblems like those of the active life, and to clash the emblematic and the vegetable plants together. The inference is that Innocence may be found only in the green shade (*concolor Umbra* occurs at this point in the Latin version). Society (with its ordinary connotations by 'polish' and 'company') is in fact all but rude (unpolished) by comparison with Solitude, which at first appears to be lacking in the virtues Society possesses, but which possesses them, if the truth were known, in greater measure (the Ciceronian-Stoic 'never less alone than when alone' became so trite that Cowley, in his essay 'Of Solitude', apologized for referring to it).

We are now ready for a clearer rejection of libertine innocence. Female beauty is reduced to its emblematic colours, red and white (a commonplace, but incidentally one found in the libertine poets) and unfavourably compared with the green of the garden as a dispenser of sensual delight. This is to reject Saint-Amant's 'crime innocent, à quoi la Nature consent'.[11] A foolish failure to understand the superiority of green causes lovers to insult trees (themselves the worthier object of love) by carving on them the names of women. (This happens in Saint-Amant's *Jouissance*.) Since it is the green garden, and not women that the poet chooses to regard as amorous, it would be farcically logical for him to carve on the trees their own names. The garden is not to have women or their names or their love in it. It is natural (green) and amorous (green – a 'norm' of the poem) in quite a different way from the libertine garden.

Love enters this garden, but only when the pursuit of the white and red is done, and we are without appetite. (Love is here indiscriminately the pursued and the pursuer. Weary with the race and exertion (*heat*) it 'makes a retreat' in the garden; hard-pressed by pursuers it carries out a military retreat.) The place of retreat has therefore Love, but not women: they are metamorphosed into trees. The gods, who might be expected to know, have been misunderstood; they pursued women not as women but as potential trees, for the green and not for the red and white. Marvell, in this witty version of the metamorphoses, continues to 'disable' the idea of sexual love. Here one needs quite firmly to delimit the reference, because it is confusing to think of *laurel* and *reed* as having symbolic significations. It is interesting that this comic metamorphosis (which has affinities with the fashionable mock-heroic) was practised for their own ends by the libertine poets; for example, in Saint-Amant's 'La Metamorphose de Lyrian et de Sylvie', in Stanley's Marinesque 'Apollo and Daphne', in Carew's 'Rapture', where Lucrece and other types of chastity become sensualists in the libertine paradise, and very notably in Lovelace. Thus, in 'Against the Love of Great Ones':

> *Ixion* willingly doth feele
> The Gyre of his eternal wheele,
> Nor would he now exchange his paine
> For Cloudes and Goddesses againe. (*Poems*, p. 75)

The sensuous appeal of this garden is, then, not sexual, as it is in the libertines. It has, nonetheless, all the enchantment of the Earthly Paradise, and all its innocence: this is the topic of the fifth stanza. The trees and plants press their fruit upon him, and their gifts are in strong contrast to those of the libertine garden,

> Love then unstinted, Love did sip,
> And Cherries pluck'd fresh from the Lip,
> On Cheeks and Roses free he fed;

> Lasses like *Autumne* Plums did drop,
> And Lads, indifferently did crop
>   A Flower, and a Maiden-head. (*Poems*, p. 146)

The fruits of green, not of red and white, are offered in primeval abundance, as they are in the Fortunate Islands or in any paradise. Everything is by nature lush and fertile; the difference between this and a paradise containing a woman is that here a Fall is of light consequence, and without tragic significance. ('Insnar'd with *flowers*, I fall on grass.') In the same way, Marvell had in 'Upon Appleton House' (LXXVII) bound himself with the entanglements not of wanton limbs, in the libertine manner of Carew, Randolph and Stanley, but of woodbine, briar and bramble. The same imagery is still in use for amorous purposes in the poetry of Leigh.

In this garden both man and nature are unfallen; it is therefore, for all its richness, not a trap for virtue but a paradise of perfect innocence. Even the fall is innocent; the sensuous allurements of the trees are harmless, and there is no need to 'fence The Batteries of alluring Sense'. It is evident that Empson and King were quite right to find here a direct allusion to the Fall.

Modern commentators all agree that the sixth stanza, central to the poem, is a witty Platonism, and of course this is so. The danger is that the Platonism can be made to appear doctrinal and even recherché, when in fact it is reasonably modest, and directly related to genre treatments of love in gardens. There is, however, a famous ambiguity in the first two lines: how are we to take 'from pleasure less'? It can mean simply (1) reduced by pleasure, or (2) that the mind retires because it experiences less pleasure than the senses, or (3) that it retires from the lesser pleasure to the greater. The first of these might be related to the doctrine of the creation in *Paradise Lost*, VII 168 ff – 'I am who fill Infinitude, nor vacuous the space. Though I uncircumscrib'd myself retire, And put not forth my goodness . . .' This would be consistent with the analogy later drawn between the human and the divine minds. But the second is more likely to be the dominant meaning, with a proper distinction between mind and sense which is obviously relevant to the theme ('None can chain a mind Whom this sweet Chordage cannot bind'). The third meaning is easily associated with this interpretation. The mind withdraws from the sensual gratification offered in order to enjoy a happiness of the imagination. In terms of the

genre, it rejects the *Jouissance* for the *Solitude* – indeed, Saint-Amant, in
a poem which prefers the contemplative garden, writes of it thus:

> Tantost, faisant agir mes sens
> Sur des sujets *de moindre estofe,*
> De marche en autre je descens
> Dans les termes du philosophe;
> Nature n'a point de secret
> Que d'un soin libre, mais discret,
> Ma curiosité ne sonde;
> Et, dans ma recherche profonde,
> Je loge en moy tout l'univers.
> Là, songeant au flus et reflus,
> *Je m'abisme dans cette idée;*
> Son mouvement me rend perclus,
> Et mon âme en est obsedée. (1 32; my italics)

To put it another way, one prefers a different kind of ecstasy from that
of the libertine, described by the same poet in his *Jouissance,* which
Stanley translated. Saint-Amant represents his solitary as acquiring
from nature knowledge of the forms, and the next two lines of Marvell's stanza seem to do likewise. The metaphor is not unfamiliar –
'Some have affirm'd that what on earth we find The sea can parallel for
shape and kind' – and the idea is that the forms exist in the mind of man
as they do in the mind of God. By virtue of the imagination the mind
can create worlds and seas too which have nothing to do with the
world which is reported by the senses. This is the passage which seems
to have caused such trouble to commentators, who look to learned
originals like Plotinus and Ficino for the explanation: but in fact the
Platonism here is dilute and current.

It is a commonplace of Renaissance poetic that God is a poet, and
that the poet has the honour of this comparison only because of the
creative force of fancy or imagination. Nor is the power exclusive to
poets. The mind, which 'all effects into their causes brings',[12] can
through the imagination alone devise new and rare things: as Puttenham says, 'the phantasticall part of man (if it be not disordered) is a
representer of the best, most comely and bewtifull images or appar-
ences of thinges to the soule and according to their very truth' (p. 19).
Puttenham shuns 'disordered phantasies . . . monstruous imaginations
or conceits' as being alien to the truth of imagination, but it is conceiv-
able that Marvell, in his suggestion of the mind's ability to create, refers

to a more modern psychology and poetic, with its roots in the Renaissance, but with a new emphasis. Thus Cowley in his Pindaric 'The Muse' says that the coach of poetry can go anywhere:

> And all's an *open Road* to *thee.*
> Whatever *God* did say,
> Is all thy plain and smooth, uninterrupted *Way.*
> Nay, ev'n beyond his *Works* thy *Voyages* are known,
> Thou hast a thousand *Worlds* too of thine *own.*
> Thou speak'st, great *Queen,* in the same *Stile* as *he,*
> And *a new World* leaps forth, when *thou* say'st, *Let it be.*

And in a note he obligingly explains this:

> The meaning is, that *Poetry* treats not only of all Things that are, or can be, but makes *Creatures* of her own, as *Centaurs, Satyrs, Fairies,* &c., makes *Persons* and *Actions* of her own ... makes *Beasts, Trees, Waters,* and other irrational and insensible Things to act above the Possibility of their Natures as to *understand* and *speak*; nay makes what *Gods* it pleases too without *Idolatry,* and varies all these into innumerable *Systemes,* or *Worlds* of Invention.

These other worlds are thoughts in the mind of man as the world is a thought in the mind of God. Empson is probably right in his guess that *streight* means 'packed together' as well as 'at once'. The whole idea is illuminated by a passage of extraordinary interest in Leigh (who was imbued with that passion for optics which later became common among poets) in which the reduced images of the eye are contrasted with the illimitable visions of the mind. The mind contains everything undiminished by the deficiencies of sense.[13] The mental activity which Marvell is describing is clear; it is the working of the imagination, which, psychologically, follows sense and precedes intellection, and is therefore the means of rejecting the voluptuous suggestions of sense; and which 'performs its function when the sensible object is rejected or even removed'.[14] The mind's newly created worlds are, in the strict sense, phantasms, and without substance: and since they have the same mental status as the created world, it is fair to say that 'all that's made' is being annihilated, reduced to a thought.

But a green thought? This is a great bogey; but surely the thought is green because the solitude is green, which means that it is also the antithesis of voluptuousness? Here the normative signification of green in the poem is in accord with what is after all a common enough notion – green for innocence, Thus, in 'Aramantha' Lovelace asks:

> Can trees be green, and to the Ay'r
> Thus prostitute their flowing Hayr? (*Poems*, p. 112)

But I cannot think the green has any more extensive symbolic intention. Green is still opposed to red and white; all this is possible only when women are absent and the senses innocently engaged.

The stanza thus alludes to the favourable conditions which enable the mind to apply itself to contemplation. The process is wittily described and the psychology requires no explanation in terms of any doctrinaire Platonism, whether pseudo-Dionysian, Plotinian, or Florentine.

The seventh stanza is also subject to much ingenious comment. The poet allows his mind to contemplate the ideas, and his soul begins a Platonic ascent. Here there are obvious parallels in the English mystics, in Plotinus, in medieval and Florentine Platonism; but we must see this stanza as we see the rest of the poem, in relation to the genre. Failing to do this we shall be involved in an endless strife between rival symbolisms, as we are if we try to find an external significance for *green*. As it is, there is no need to be over-curious about the fountain; its obvious symbolic quality may have an interesting history, but it is primarily an easily accessible emblem of purity. As for the use of the bird as an emblem of the soul, that is an image popularized by Castiglione,[15] and used by Spenser of the early stages of the ascent:

> Beginning then below, with th'easie vew
> Of this base world, subiect to fleshly eye,
> From thence to mount aloft by order dew,
> To contemplation of th'immortall sky,
> Of that soare faulcon so I learne to fly,
> That flags awhile her fluttering wings beneath,
> Till she her selfe for stronger flight can breath.
> ('Hymne of Heavenly Beauty')

Spenser has just passed from the consideration of woman's love and beauty to the heavenly love and beauty. The bird which prepares its wings for flight is evidently a symbol with as settled a meaning as the dew, which Marvell also shared with many other poets.

The hungry soul, deceived with false beauties, may have 'after vain deceiptfull shadowes sought' – but at last it looks 'up to that soveraine light, From whose pure beams al perfect beauty springs' ('HHB'). Marvell's bird 'Waves in its Plumes the various Light'. Once more we might spring to Ebreo or Plotinus or even Haydocke, but we shall do better to note how this same image is used in literature more closely related to Marvell.

> Les oyseaux, d'un joyeux ramage,
> En chantant semblent adorer
> La lumière qui vient dorer
> Leur cabinet et leur plumage –

thus Théophile, in his Ode, 'Le Matin'.[16] In *Partheneia Sacra* Hawkins uses the dove as other poets use the dew or the rainbow –

> Being of what coulour soever, her neck being opposed to the Sun will diversify into a thousand coulours, more various then the Iris it-self, or that Bird of *Juno* in al her pride; as scarlet, cerulean, flame-coulour, and yealding a flash like the Carbuncle, with vermilion, ash-coulour, and manie others besides. . . . (p. 202)

Marvell's use of the Platonic light-symbolism is therefore not technical, as it might be in Chapman, but generalized, as in Quarles or Vaughan, and affected by imagery associated with the garden genres. We are thus reminded that the point about the ascent towards the pure source of light is not that it can be achieved, but that it can be a product of *Solitude* rather than of *Jouissance* and that it is an alternative to libertine behaviour in gardens. It is the ecstasy not of beauty but of heavenly beauty.

The eighth stanza at last makes this theme explicit. This is a special solitude, which can only exist in the absence of women, the agents of the most powerful voluptuous temptation. This has been implied throughout, but it is now wittily stated in the first clear reference to Eden. The notion that Adam would have been happy without a mate is not, of course, novel; St Ambrose believed it. Here it is another way of putting the case that woman offers the wrong beauty, the wrong love, the red and white instead of the green. Eve deprived Adam of solitude, and gave him instead an inferior joy. Indeed she was his punishment for being mortal (rather than pure Intelligence?). Her absence would be equivalent to the gift of a paradise (since her presence means the loss of the only one there is). This is easy enough, and a good example of how naturally we read references to the more familiar conceptions of theology and philosophy as part of the play of wit within the limited range of a genre.

In the last stanza the temperate quiet of the garden is once more asserted, by way of conclusion. (The Earthly Paradise is always in the temperate zone.) The time, for us as for the bee (a pun on 'thyme'), is sweet and rewarding; hours of innocence are told by a dial of pure herbs and flowers. The sun is 'milder' because in this zodiac of flowers fragrance is substituted for heat; Miss Bradbrook and Miss Lloyd Thomas have some good observations here. The time computed is likewise spent in fragrant rather than hot pursuits. This is the *Solitude*, not the *Jouissance*; the garden of the *solitaire* whose soul rises towards divine beauty, not that of the voluptuary who voluntarily surrenders to the delights of the senses.

This ends the attempt to read 'The Garden' as a poem of a definite historical kind and to explore its delicate allusions to a genre of which the 'norms' are within limits ascertainable. Although it is very improbable that such an attempt can avoid errors of both sophistication and simplification, one may reaonably claim for it that in substituting poetry for metaphysics it does no violence to the richness and subtlety of its subject.

SOURCE: *Essays in Criticism II* (1952).

NOTES

1. 'The Mode of Existence of a Literary Work of Art', in *Critiques and Essays in Criticism, 1920–1948*, ed. R. W. Stallman (New York, 1949) pp. 210–23.

2. M. C. Bradbrook, 'Marvell and the Poetry of Rural Solitude' in *Review of English Studies*, XVII (Jan 1941) 37–46; M. C. Bradbrook and M. G. Lloyd Thomas, *Andrew Marvell* (1940).

3. Montaigne, *Essayes*, translated by John Florio (Everyman Edition) III 316.

4. See F. A. Yates, *The French Academies of the Sixteenth Century* (1947) pp. 128ff. From Plato (*Symposium* 202A, *Republic* 477 et seq.) through the Pléiade to Sidney there ran the argument that poets were not competent to make philosophical statements; they affirm nothing.

5. Frank Kermode, 'Two Notes on Marvell', in *Notes and Queries*, CXCVII (March 1952) 136–8.

6. *Poems*, ed. G. Thorn-Drury (1929) p. 110.

7. *Poems*, ed. C. H. Wilkinson (1930) p. 147.

8. *De Constantia, Of Constancie*, translated by Sir J. Stradling, ed. R. Kirk and C. M. Hall (1939) pp. 132ff.

9. *Partheneia Sacra*, ed. Iain Fletcher (1950) (reprint of 1633), p. 2.

10. Proposed by A. H. King, 'Some Notes on Marvell's Garden', in *English Studies*, XX (1938) 118–21.

11. *Œuvres Completes*, ed. Ch.-L. Livet (1855) I 119.

12. Sir John Davies, *Nosce Teipsum* ('The Intellectual Powers of the Soul', stanza 5).

13. *Poems*, ed. Hugh Macdonald (1947) pp. 36ff.

14. Gianfrancesco Pico della Mirandola, *De Imaginatione*, edited and translated by H. Caplan (1930) p. 29.

15. *The Book of the Courtier*, translated by Thomas Hoby (Everyman Edition) p. 338.

16. *Œuvres Complètes*, ed. M. Alleaume (1856) I 174-5.

JOSEPH H. SUMMERS

Marvell's 'Nature' (1953)

THE similarities between the verse of Marvell and that of many modern poets are seductive. A number of Marvell's poems have been cited as evidence to support the critical assumption, based largely on modern poetic practice, that the most mature and rich works of literature are necessarily ironical. One can disagree with the assumption and still recognize that irony, not a of a paralyzing variety, is central to most of Marvell's poems. Marvell's surfaces, moreover, are close to one modern ideal. The tones of the typical modern *personae* echo the sensuous richness of Marvell more often than the logical violence of Donne – that poet who wrote 'To Mr Samuel Brooke', boastfully yet accurately, 'I sing not Siren like to tempt; for I / Am harsh'. The 'speakers' of Marvell's poems are farther removed from immediate embroilment in action than are Donne's. They approach their situations from some distance, with a wider and a clearer view. Their speech is closer to that of meditation or of a quiet colloquy in a garden than to the raised voice, the immediate and passionate argument. And the verse which they speak shows a concern for euphony, a delicate manipulation of sound patterns suggesting Campion's songs – or much of the verse of Eliot and MacLeish and many younger poets.

The differences between Marvell and the moderns, however, are equally noteworthy, and failure to perceive them has resulted in strange readings of a number of Marvell's poems. To prevent misreadings, to define any specific poem, we need to achieve some sense of the body of Marvell's work. And here is the difficulty, for our sense of that work is likely to be an impression of dazzling fragments, each brilliant and disparate. The reader may feel that the sixth stanza of 'The Gallery', the poem in which the poet invites Chlora to view her portraits in his soul as 'an inhumane murtheress', Aurora, 'an enchantress', Venus, and 'a tender shepherdess', applies more justly to the poet than to Chlora:

> These Pictures and a thousand more,
> Of Thee, my Gallery do store;
> In all the Forms thou can'st invent
> Either to please me, or torment.

Yet the poem assures us that Chlora is one, however numerous her pictures; and the poet who could take various and even contradictory positions on the claims of the active and contemplative lives, of the body and the soul, of the time-honored plea to 'seize the day', of gardens ('These Pictures and a thousand more') is equally one poet. The attempts to bring intellectual order out of the apparent confusion by means of a hypothetical biographical development of the poet have been unconvincing. The development or rather break in his poetic practice after 1660 is clear. Before that time, the single poem 'Upon Appleton House' indicates that Marvell was an extraordinarily sophisticated poet, capable of employing numerous traditions and multiple attitudes as occasions or moments demanded. Among the few attitudes which I have been unable to discover in Marvell's poetry, however, are those expressed in two of the modern poems which owe most to Marvell. Archibald MacLeish's 'You, Andrew Marvell' concludes with the lines,

> And here face downward in the sun
> To feel swift how secretly
> The shadow of the night comes on . . .

Robert Penn Warren's 'Bearded Oaks' includes the following stanza:

> Upon the floor of light, and time,
> Unmurmuring, of polyp made,
> We rest; we are, as light withdraws,
> Twin atolls on a shelf of shade.

In Marvell's verse man is neither an atoll nor an island, and if night is anticipated, so is light.

An examination of Marvell's uses of 'Nature', the world of the flowers and fruits and the green grass, provides a sketch not only of the virtuosity and multiple intellectual and moral stances within the poems, but also of the central vision which occurs most frequently in the most successful poems. Occasionally Marvell used nature as an image of

classical order, an artfully contrived realization of the mean which man
is to imitate – or, more properly, which a specific man has imitated.
Jonson had shown in his ode 'To the Memory of Sir Lucius Cary and
Sir Henry Morison' that nature conceived as an ordered mean was a
most effective source of hyperbolical compliment. In 'Upon the Hill
and Grove at Bill-borow', Fairfax too is at one with nature. After his
active life (in which he had 'thunder'd' 'Through Groves of Pikes',
'And Mountains rais'd of dying Men'), Fairfax has returned to the
retirement of the hill and grove; the humanized landscape is both his
ward and his image:

> See how the arched Earth does here
> Rise in a perfect Hemisphere!
> The stiffest Compass could not strike
> A Line more circular and like;
> Nor softest Pensel draw a Brow
> So equal as this Hill does bow.
> It seems as for a Model laid,
> And that the World by it was made. (st. 1)
>
> . . .
>
> See what a soft access and wide
> Lyes open to its grassy side;
> Nor with the rugged path deterrs
> The feet of breathless Travellers.
> See then how courteous it ascends,
> And all the way it rises bends;
> Nor for it self the height does gain,
> But only strives to raise the Plain. (st. III)

After this delightfully artificial description of landscape as Republican
gentleman, we are not surprised that these Roman oaks should speak
oracles of praise for Fairfax. In the opening lines of 'Upon Appleton
House', an ordered and properly proportioned nature is again the symbol for Fairfax and his dwelling, particularly in contrast to the 'unpro-
portion'd dwellings' which the ambitious have constructed with the
aid of 'Forrain' architects: 'But all things are composed here, Like
Nature, orderly and near.' Nature is also near and extraordinarily
'orderly' when a natural object, 'A Drop of Dew' for example, is
examined as an emblem. Here we are close to Herbert, but in Marvell
we are chiefly compelled by the ingenuity with which the natural is
made to reflect the conceptual.

More often nature is nearer if not so orderly when it is conceived as the lost garden, whether Eden or the Hesperides or England:

> O Thou, that dear and happy Isle
> The Garden of the World ere while,
> Thou *Paradise* of four Seas,
> Which *Heaven* planted us to please,
> But, to exclude the World, did guard
> With watry if not flaming Sword:
> What luckless Apple did we tast,
> To make us Mortal, and The Wast?
>
> ('Upon Appleton House', st. XLI)

The lost garden represents not measure but perfect fulfilment; its memory is an occasion for ecstasy:

> And Ivy, with familiar trails,
> Me licks, and clasps, and curles, and hales.
> Under this *antick Cope* I move
> Like some great *Prelate of the Grove*,
> Then, Languishing with ease, I toss
> On Pallets swoln of Velvet Moss.
>
> ('Upon Appleton House', st. LXXIV–LXXV)

> What wond'rous Life in this I lead!
> Ripe Apples drop about my head;
> The Luscious Clusters of the Vine
> Upon my Mouth do crush their Wine;
> The Nectaren, and curious Peach,
> Into my hands themselves do reach;
> Stumbling on Melons, as I pass,
> Insnar'd with Flow'rs, I fall on Grass.
>
> ('The Garden', st. V)

It is in this vein that Marvell occasionally gives a sensuous particularity to his descriptions of natural objects which may remind us of Vaughan's 'those faint beams in which this hill is drest, / After the Sun's remove' ('They are all gone into the world of light!'), and which has led some readers to consider him a romantic born too early. And yet the 'gelid *Strawberryes*' and 'The hatching *Thrastles* shining Eye' of 'Upon Appleton House' contribute to a complicated vision of nature which is finally unlike the nineteenth-century's; the *'Hewel's* wonders' (the activities of the woodpecker) teach the *'easie Philosopher'* who 'Hath read in *Natures mystick Book'* the just relationships between sin and death:

> Who could have thought the *tallest Oak*
> Should fall by such a *feeble Strok'*!
>
> Nor would it, had the Tree not fed
> A *Traitor-worm*, within it bred.
> (As first our *Flesh* corrupt within
> Tempts impotent and bashful *Sin*.)
> And yet that *Worm* triumphs not long.
> But serves to feed the *Hewels young*.
> While the Oake seems to fall content,
> Viewing the Treason's Punishment.
>
> ('Upon Appleton House', st. LXIX–LXX)

In 'The Garden', too, identification with nature is neither complete nor simple. The famous fifth stanza which I have quoted above, expertly 'imitates' the bodily ecstasy, and the following stanzas systematically portray the higher ecstasies of the mind and the soul; all, moreover, are framed with witty and civilized reversals of the ordinary civilized values, of classic myth, of the biblical account of the creation of woman, and of the idea that sexual relations are 'natural'. To read 'The Garden' and 'The Mower against Gardens' in succession is to realize that in Marvell's poetry the man-made garden and the 'natural' meadows are significant not intrinsically but instrumentally. Both poems are ultimately concerned with lost perfection. 'The Garden' presents a fictional and momentary attempt to recapture what has been lost. In 'The Mower against Gardens', the garden itself is an image of the sophisticated corruption responsible for the loss of 'A wild and fragrant Innocence'. Marvell's image of the lost garden is as much an occasion for the recognition of man's alienation from nature as it is for remembered ecstasy.

The degree to which Marvell both followed and modified conventional practice can be seen most clearly in the 'pastoral' poems in in which he substituted the mower for the traditional shepherd. The life of the shepherds had imaged the pre-agricultural golden age, the paradisiacal simplicity ideally if not actually associated with the simple country life, away from cities and civilizations, wars and corruptions. When love was concerned, the passion was usually direct, uncontaminated by worldly considerations, and not much affected by age, even if the lover was unhappy or the mistress proved untrue. The good shepherd and his sheep could imply the ideal political relation between the ruler and the ruled, and the Christian poets explored the rich possibilities of the Good Shepherd and his flock and the large pastoral inheritance of the Psalms. Milton, who retained the shepherd image in 'Lycidas', kept the humanist emphasis on higher man (the poet, the pastor) as the guide of less perceptive humanity through the labyrinth of nature to an ultimate goal. The shepherd followed Christ, and he also led his own sheep into the true fold. Marvell used some of this material in a direct if not very distinguished fashion in 'Clorinda and Damon', and although the participants are oarsmen rather than shepherds, the spirit of the tradition is present in 'Bermudas'. He gave up most of these associations, however, when he chose the figure of the mower as his central image. That figure, of course, had its own traditions. As 'Damon the Mower' mentions, the mower's craft had long served to picture man's greatest mystery and fear:

> Only for him no Cure is found,
> Whom *Julianas* Eyes do wound.
> 'Tis death alone that this must do:
> For Death thou art a Mower too.

The mower who cut down the living grass was a natural symbol for death. Because of the seasonal nature of his activities, he was also a symbol for time. Marvell's mower does not lead; he destroys. However simple his character or sincere his love, he cuts down for human ends what nature has produced. He symbolizes man's alienation from nature:

> With whistling Sithe, and Elbow strong,
> These Massacre the Grass along:
> While one, unknowing, carves the *Rail*,
> Whose yet unfeather'd Quils her fail.
> The Edge all bloody from its Breast
> He draws, and does his stroke detest:
> Fearing the Flesh untimely mow'd
> To him a Fate as black forebode.
>
> ('Upon Appleton House', st. L)

'The Mower's Song' is a playful and elaborately artificial lament of a lover, but it is more than that. The refrain insists that the mower-lover's relation to nature exactly parallels his cruel mistress's relation to him:

> For *Juliana* comes, and She
> What I do to the Grass, does to my Thoughts and Me.

Greenness in this poem, as so often in Marvell's verse, represents hope and vitality and virility, the fertile promise of life which man desires and destroys. The mower, angry that there is no true sympathy between man and nature, 'fictionally' determines to destroy nature to make the symbolism more complete:

> Unthankful Medows, could you so
> A fellowship so true forego,
> And in your gawdy May-games meet,
> While I lay trodden under feet?
> When *Juliana* came, and She
> What I do to the Grass, does to my Thoughts and Me.

> But what you in Compassion ought,
> Shall now by my Revenge be wrought:
> And Flow'rs, and Grass, and I and all,
> Will in one common Ruine fall.
> For *Juliana* comes, and She
> What I do to the Grass, does to my Thoughts and Me.

The Mower poems conveniently define the crucial terms of Marvell's most frequent poetic use of nature. Marvell did not discover an impulse from the vernal wood which spoke unambiguously to the human heart and which offered a possibility for man's at-oneness with all. Nor did he, like George Herbert, usually see in nature patterns of a distinguishable and logical divine will, the *paysage moralisé* which offered a way to the understanding and imitation of God. Human moral criteria do not apply to most of Marvell's landscapes. In his poems nature apart from man is usually 'green', vital, fecund, and triumphant. Since it affirms life it is, as part of the divine plan, 'good', but its goodness is neither available nor quite comprehensible to man. Man is barred from long or continuous spiritual communion, and his intellect cannot comprehend the natural language. Since his alienation with the departure from Eden, man can only live in nature either as its observer or its destroyer; since he partially partakes of nature, he is, if he acts at all, also his own destroyer. His capacity for self-destruction is clearly implied by the contrast between nature's fecundity and man's harassed and frustrated attempts at love. Faced with unrequited love, man the mower only sharpens his scythe for the destruction of the grass and sharpens the 'Woes' which destroy himself:

> How happy might I still have mow'd,
> Had not Love here his Thistles sow'd!
> But now I all the day complain,
> Joyning my Labour to my Pain;
> And with my Sythe cut down the Grass,
> Yet still my Grief is where it was:
> But, when the Iron blunter grows,
> Sighing I whet my Sythe and Woes.
>
> ('Damon the Mower')

But man destroys the natural and dies not only because he is inferior but also because, suspended between the natural and divine, he is superior to the green world. In 'A Dialogue between the Soul and the Body' each of the protagonists charges wittily and convincingly that the other is the source of human misery; of the first 40 lines, each speaks 20, and points are made and capped so expertly as to produce a forensic stalemate. But the Body wins and ironically resolves the argument with its final additional four lines:

> What but a Soul could have the wit
> To build me up for Sin so fit?
> So Architects do square and hew,
> Green Trees that in the Forest grew.

Without the soul the body would be truly a part of nature and could not sin. Yet architecture, whether external or internal, is the product and desire of a higher part of man, even though many 'Green trees' may be destroyed for it. Whether the building is used for good or ill, man's capacities for reason, for structure, for creation outside the carnal, are not natural but Godlike. Man's distinctive gifts are as destructive within the post-Eden garden as are his weaknesses and his corruption.

It is, moreover, exactly man's superiority to the vegetative world which allows him to recognize his alienation. Nature does not possess the capacity for man's choices between the active and contemplative lives: it can only act. The rival claims of those two chief modes of man's life are ever present in Marvell's poetry, and they are closely related to his themes of nature and time. Man must act and he must contemplate, and he must do each in accordance with the demands of time. Yet the contemplative life is usually the more desirable way – at least for the poet. The poet surpasses most men in the degree and consistency of his recognition of man's alienation, for he is chiefly concerned with the contemplation of the condition of man. In Marvell's poetry, significantly, natural beauty is usually described and appreciated as if it were an imitation of the works of man. The fort and artillery of the garden in 'Upon Appleton House' are not simply factual or fanciful. In 'The Mower to the Glo-Worms' nature is the gracious and kindly courtier to man, so lost in love 'That I shall never find my home'. In one of the most memorable descriptions in 'Bermudas' God Himself is the manlike decorator:

> He hangs in shades the Orange bright,
> Like golden Lamps in a green Night.
> And does in the Pomgranates close,
> Jewels more rich than *Ormus* show's.

It is the artifacts, the 'golden Lamps' and the 'Jewels more rich than *Ormus* show's', which contribute most of the sensuous richness to the passage. In relation to the garden man is the judge and the measure as well as the accused.

Whatever the immediate resolutions, man is usually suspended between the greenness and God at the conclusions as well as at the beginnings of Marvell's poems. Within 'A Dialogue Between The Resolved Soul, and Created Pleasure', the Soul deftly propounds the orthodox thesis that the sensuous and worldly pleasures are only appearances, that the soul possesses the quintessence of all pleasures in his resolution. Yet the tensions are still felt, and the soul's conclusions, while 'true', are also partial. At the moment of death 'The rest' (both the ease and the remainder of all the pleasures) *does* 'lie beyond the Pole, / And is thine everlasting Store'. But before that moment, Marvell and most of his contemporaries believed that no man enjoyed fully and continuously either the flesh or the spirit, that the battle was constantly renewed so long as a living spirit inhabited a living body. This did not imply that the battle lacked interest nor that decisions and momentary achievements were impossible. Such decisions and such achievements were, in fact, the poet's subjects, not only in 'A Dialogue' but also 'To his Coy Mistress'. The speaker of the latter poem seems to resolve clearly for sensuality: *Carpe diem* appears to be all. The image of the 'birds of prey', however, makes us realize the costs of a resolution to 'devour' time, to choose destructive brevity of life since eternity cannot be sensually chosen.

The reader's awareness of Marvell's complex use of nature should cast light on almost any one of the poems. Within such light, the presentation of Cromwell in 'An Horatian Ode' as a force of nature seems not perplexing but inevitable. 'Upon Appleton House' is Marvell's most ambitious and in many respects his most interesting poem. A full consideration of it would require another essay, and I only wish to suggest here that it is a mistake to read it as an artificial 'public' poem interesting chiefly for a few 'personal' passages. Similarly, 'The Picture of little T. C. in a Prospect of Flowers' is not a graceful trifle which somehow goes wrong. It is a fine poem, and it elucidates Marvell's central vision of man and nature:

I

See with what simplicity
This Nimph begins her golden daies!
In the green Grass she loves to lie,
And there with her fair Aspect tames
The Wilder flow'rs, and gives them names:
But only with the Roses playes;
            And them does tell
What Colour best becomes them, and what Smell.

II

Who can foretel for what high cause
This Darling of the Gods was born!
Yet this is She whose chaster Laws
The wanton Love shall one day fear,
And, under her command severe,
See his Bow broke and Ensigns torn.
            Happy, who can
Appease this virtuous Enemy of Man!

III

O then let me in time compound,
And parly with those conquering Eyes:
Ere they have try'd their force to wound,

Ere, with their glancing wheels, they drive
In Triumph over Hearts that strive,
And them that yield but more despise.
      Let me be laid,
Where I may see thy Glories from some shade.

IV

Mean time, whilst every verdant thing
It self does at thy Beauty charm,
Reform the errours of the Spring;
Make that the Tulips may have share
Of sweetness, seeing they are fair;
And Roses of their thorns disarm:
      But most procure
That Violets may a longer Age endure.

V

But O young beauty of the Woods,
Whom Nature courts with fruits and flow'rs,
Gather the Flow'rs, but spare the Buds;
Lest *Flora* angry at thy crime,
To kill her Infants in their prime,
Do quickly make th' Example Yours;
      And, ere we see,
Nip in the blossome all our hopes and Thee.

The opening stanza of the poem tells us of the child's alienation from and superiority to nature, as well as of her delight in it. Her apparently successful imposition of her own order and value on nature raises inevitably the question of the prospect of time, and we see prophetically in the second stanza her future triumph over 'wanton Love' – and over man. Not a combatant, the speaker of the poem resolves to observe the dazzling scene from the shade which allows vision, for the god-like glories cannot be viewed immediately by profane man. If he is to admire her triumph, it must be from a distance where there is no fear of its destructiveness. With the 'Mean time' of the fourth stanza we are back at the present prospect, and the observer from his advantageous point of view advises the present T. C. At the golden moment when 'every verdant thing' charms itself at her beauty, she is instructed to prepare for her future career by reforming the 'errours of the Spring'.

At first it seems, or perhaps would seem to a child, an almost possible command. With the talismanic power of her 'fair Aspect' she already 'tames / The Wilder flow'rs, and gives them names', and she tells the roses 'What Colour best becomes them, and what Smell'. At least within the circle of her immediate view she may, perhaps, by a judicious bouquet arrangement cause the tulips to share in sweetness, and it is possible to disarm roses of their thorns with assiduous labor. But the thing which should be 'most' procured is impossible for the human orderer even within his small area. And all of it is, of course, impossible if all the 'errours of the Spring' are in question. For, in comparison either with the triumph of T. C. or the vision of Eden, Spring is full of errors; the decorative details suggest exactly how far nature fails to sustain human visions of propriety, delight, and immortality. T. C. and the idealizing aspect of man wish delight and beauty and goodness to be single, but they cannot find such singleness within the promising verdancy of nature; if they desire it they must impose it on nature or must seek it in an 'unnatural' or supernatural world. The tulips show how improperly the delights of the senses are separated in this world; the roses with their thorns traditionally indicate the conjunction of pain and pleasure, the hidden hurts lying under the delights of the senses; and the transience of the violets is a perpetual reminder of the mortality of life and innocence and beauty. The description of the preceding triumph is placed in a doubtful light. If T. C.'s reformation of floral errors is so doomed, how much real hope or fear can there be of her reformation of the errors of that higher order, man? Is the former description a fantasy, ideal yet frightening, of what might happen if the superhuman power as well as the superhuman virtue were granted, a fantasy proceeding from the observer's sharing for one moment the simplicity of the nymph?

In the exclamatory warning of the final stanza the observer and the reader see the picture of little T. C. in the full prospect of time which the flowers have furnished. At the present moment 'Nature courts' her 'with fruits and flow'rs' as a superior being; she represents the promise of an order higher than we have known. But she is also the 'young beauty of the Woods', and she is a 'Bud'. The child of nature as well as its potential orderer, she shares the mortality as well as the beauty of the flowers; her own being, in the light of the absolute, is as 'improper' as are the tulips or the roses. The former vision of her triumph implied full recognition of only one half of her relationship to the fruits and

flowers. The introduction of Flora reminds us more sharply than anything else in the poem of the entire relationship. However lacking in the
ideal, Flora has her own laws which man violates at the peril of self-
destruction. Flora decrees that life shall continue: the infants shall not
be killed 'in their prime' – either in their moment of ideal promise or in
their first moment of conception. The sexual concerns which have been
suggested throughout the poem are made explicit in the final stanza.
The picture in the central stanzas of the complete triumph of T. C., the
absolute rule of human notions of propriety, has inevitably meant that
'wanton Love's' bow will be broken, his ensigns torn: there will be no
more marriages. With a recognition of mortality and of the power of
Flora, we recognize also the doom of such a triumph, for both the ideal
and the reality will soon die, and there is no prospect of renewal in
future 'T. C.'s' The conclusion, however, is neither a Renaissance nor a
modern 'naturalism'. Because perfect fulfilment is impossible, man is
not therefore to abandon his attempts at perfection. T. C. is allowed
and even commanded to 'Gather the Flow'rs', to expend her present
and her future energies in ordering the natural nearer to the ideal
pattern – so long as she spares the buds. The qualification is all important. Man must beware of attempting to anticipate heaven by
imposing the ideal absolutely on earth. The killing of the infants in
their prime is not only a crime against Flora but against all the gods, for
man is never free to commit either murder or suicide in the pursuit of
the abstract ideal. The human triumph must function within and wait
upon the fulness of time. It must recognize the real and individual as
well as the ideal and the general or it becomes a horror. The ending of
the poem revalues everything which has gone before. 'Ere we see' may
mean something equivalent to 'in the twinkling of an eye'; it certainly
means, 'Before we see what will become of you and the vision of a new
and higher order.' What will be nipped 'in the blossom', in the first
full flowering, unless the warning is heeded will be not only 'all our
hopes' (our hopes of the idealized child and of a possible new order, our
hopes of love and of a new generation), but also 'Thee', the living
child.

'The Picture of little T. C. in a Prospect of Flowers' is characteristic
of Marvell's poetry both in its complexity and in its subtle use of superficially 'romantic' or decorative detail. It may remind us of modern
poetry, but ultimately Marvell is both more complex and more assured
of his meanings than are most of the moderns. Marvell does not present

a *persona* simply and finally torn between this world and the next, distracted by the sensuous while attempting to achieve a spiritual vision. For Marvell, as for most Rennaissance poets, the perception of a dilemma was not considered a sufficient occasion for a poem. Marvell made precise the differences between the values of time and of eternity. He recognized that man exists and discovers his values largely within time; he also believed that those values could be ultimately fulfilled only outside time. The recognition and the belief did not constitute a paralyzing dilemma. Each of his early poems implies the realization that any action or decision costs something; yet each presents a precise stance, an unique position and a decision taken at one moment with a full consciousness of all the costs. The costs are counted, but not mourned; the position is taken, the poem is written, with gaiety.

When we have understood what the 'prospect of flowers' implies, 'The Coronet' does not seem a churchly recantation of all that Marvell valued, but an artful recognition of the ultimate issues. Here the decision is taken in the full light of eternity, and, as in George Herbert's 'A Wreath' (which Marvell probably remembered), the intricate and lovely form of the poem provides an index to the joy. The speaker of the poem describes his attempt to create a coronet for Christ. He dismantles 'all the fragrant Towers / That once adorn'd my Shepherdesses head' to gather the necessary flowers, but he discovers that the Serpent has entwined himself into the proposed offering, 'With wreaths of Fame and Interest'. The poet prays that Christ would untie the Serpent's 'slipp'ry knots',

> Or shatter too with him my curious frame:
> And let these wither, so that he may die,
> Though set with Skill and chosen out with Care.
> That they, while Thou on both their Spoils dost tread,
> May crown thy Feet, that could not crown thy Head.

The poem is moving as well as orthodox in its expression of willingness to sacrifice man's sensuous and aesthetic structures to a divine necessity. But Marvell's most Miltonic line, 'Though set with Skill and chosen out with Care', ruefully insists that, whatever his vision of ultimate value, the living poet also values the structures of time.

SOURCE: *Journal of English Literary History,* XX (June 1953).

J. V. CUNNINGHAM

Logic and Lyric:
'To his Coy Mistress' (1953)

IN this essay I shall propose the question: May the principal structure of a poem be of a logical rather than of an alogical sort? For example, to confine ouselves to the Old Logic: May a lyric be solely or predominantly the exposition of a syllogism? and may the propositions of the lyric, one by one, be of the sort to be found in a logical syllogism?

The incautious romantic will deny the possibility, and with a repugnance of feeling that would preclude any further discussion. For logic and lyric are generally regarded as opposites, if not as contradictory terms. 'It is a commonplace', says a recent writer on logic, 'that poetry and logic have nothing to do with each other, that they are even opposed to one another.'[1] You will find this explicitly stated, sometimes with the substitution of 'science' for 'logic', in most of the school handbooks on the study of literature, in most of the introductions to poetry. 'The peculiar quality of poetry', we read in one of these, 'can be distinguished from that of prose if one thinks of the creative mind as normally expressing itself in a variety of literary forms ranged along a graduated scale between the two contrasted extremes of scientific exposition and lyrical verse.' And, a little later, '[Poetry] strives for a conviction begotten of the emotions rather than of the reason.' Consequently, we are told, 'The approach of poetry is indirect. It proceeds by means of suggestion, implication, reflection. Its method is largely symbolical. It is more interested in connotations than in denotations.'[2] This is common doctrine. Poetry is in some way concerned with emotion rather than with reason, and its method is imaginative, indirect, implicit rather than explicit, symbolical rather than discursive, concerned with what its terms suggest rather than with what they state. The kind of poetry which most fully possesses and exhibits these concerns, methods, and qualities is generally thought to be the lyric, and hence the lyric, of all poetry, is regarded as the most antithetical to reason, logic, and science.

This was not always the case. In the eighth century, for example, a scholiast of the school of Alcuin regarded not only grammar and rhetoric but dialectic or logic also as the disciplines that nourish and form a poet. In the medieval and Renaissance traditions of commentary on Aristotle's logic, poetic is sometimes regarded as a part, a sub-division, of logic – as, indeed, I consider it myself. So late as the eighteenth century, David Hume writes in an essay 'Of the Standard of Taste': 'Besides, every kind of composition, even the most poetical, is nothing but a chain of propositions and reasonings; not always indeed the justest and most exact, but still plausible and specious, however disguised by the coloring of the imagination.' And even today the writer on logic whom I quoted earlier asserts, in denial of the commonplace: 'Every poem, except in rare extreme cases, contains judgements and implicit propositions, and thus becomes subject to logical analysis.'[3]

But may the chain of propositions and reasonings be not merely plausible and specious but even sufficiently just and exact? May the poem be not merely subject to logical analysis but logical in form? May, to return to our point, the subject and structure of a poem be conceived and expressed syllogistically? Anyone at all acquainted with modern criticism and the poems that are currently in fashion will think in this connection of Marvell's 'To his Coy Mistress'. The apparent structure of that poem is an argumentative syllogism, explicitly stated. 'Had we but world enough, and time,' the poet says,

> This coyness, Lady, were no crime . . .
>
> But at my back I always hear
> Time's winged chariot hurrying near . . .
>
> Now, therefore . . .
> . . . let us sport us while we may.

If we had all the space and time in the world, we could delay consummation. But we do not. Therefore. The structure is formal. The poet offers to the lady a practical syllogism, and if she assents to it, the appropriate consequence, he hopes, will follow:

> Had we but world enough, and time,
> This coyness, Lady, were no crime;
> We would sit down and think which way

To walk and pass our long love's day.
Thou by the Indian Ganges side
Shouldst rubies find; I by the tide
Of Humber would complain. I would
Love you ten years before the Flood,
And you should, if you please, refuse
Till the conversion of the Jews.
My vegetable love should grow
Vaster than empires, and more slow.
An hundred years should go to praise
Thine eyes and on thy forehead gaze;
Two hundred to adore each breast;
But thirty thousand to the rest;
An age at least to every part,
And the last age should show your heart;
For, Lady, you deserve this state,
Nor would I love at lower rate.
    But at my back I always hear
Time's winged chariot hurrying near;
And yonder all before us lie
Deserts of vast eternity.
Thy beauty shall no more be found,
Nor in thy marble vault shall sound
My echoing song; then worms shall try
That long preserved virginity,
And your quaint honour turn to dust,
And into ashes all my lust:
The grave's a fine and private place,
But none, I think, do there embrace.

    Now, therefore, while the youthful hue
Sits on thy skin like morning dew,
And while thy willing soul transpires
At every pore with instant fires,
Now let us sport us while we may,
And now, like amorous birds of prey,
Rather at once our time devour
Than languish in his slow-chapt power.
Let us roll all our strength and all
Our sweetness up into one ball,
And tear our pleasures with rough strife
Thorough the iron gates of life:

> Thus, though we cannot make our sun
> Stand still, yet we will make him run.[4]

The logical nature of the argument here has been generally recognized, though often with a certain timidity. Mr Eliot hazards: 'the three strophes of Marvell's poem have something like a syllogistic relation to each other'. And in a recent scholarly work we read: 'The dialectic of the poem lies not only or chiefly in the formal demonstration explicit in its three stanzas, but in all the contrasts evoked by its images and in the play between the immediately sensed and the intellectually apprehended.'[5] That is, the logic is recognized, but minimized, and our attention is quickly distracted to something more reputable in a poem, the images or the characteristic tension of metaphysical poetry. For Mr Eliot the more important element in this case is a principle of order common in modern poetry and often employed in his own poems. He points out that the theme of Marvell's poem is 'one of the great traditional commonplaces of European literature . . . the theme of . . . "Gather ye rosebuds", of "Go, lovely rose," ' 'Where the wit of Marvell', he continues, 'renews the theme is in the variety and order of the images'. The dominant principle of order in the poem, then, is an implicit one rather than the explicit principle of the syllogism, and implicit in the succession of images.

Mr Eliot explains the implicit principle of order in this fashion:

> In the first of the three paragraphs Marvell plays with a fancy which begins by pleasing and leads to astonishment. . . . We notice the high speed, the succession of concentrated images, each magnifying the original fancy. When this process has been carried to the end and summed up, the poem turns suddenly with that surprise which has been one of the most important means of poetic effect since Homer:

> > But at my back I alwaies hear
> > Times winged Charriot hurrying near;
> > And yonder all before us lye
> > Desarts of vast Eternity.

A whole civilization resides in these lines:

> Pallida Mors æquo pulsat pede pauperum tabernas
> Regumque turres . . .

A modern poet, had he reached the height, would very likely have closed on this moral reflection.

What is meant by this last observation becomes clear a little later, where it is said that the wit of the poem 'forms the crescendo and diminuendo of a scale of great imaginative power'.[6] The structure of the poem, then, is this: It consists of a succession of images increasing in imaginative power to the sudden turn and surprise of the image of time, and then decreasing to the conclusion. But is there any sudden turn and surprise in the image of time? and does the poem consist of a succession of images?

This talk of images is a little odd, since there seem to be relatively few in the poem if one means by 'image' what people usually do – a descriptive phrase that invites the reader to project a sensory construction. The looming imminence of Time's winged chariot is, no doubt, an image, though not a full-blown one, since there is nothing in the phrasing that properly invites any elaboration of sensory detail. But when Mr Eliot refers to 'successive images' and cites 'my *vegetable* love', with *vegetable* italicized, and 'Till the conversion of the Jews', one suspects that he is provoking images where they do not textually exist. There is about as much of an image in 'Till the conversion of the Jews' as there would be in 'till the cows come home', and it would be a psychiatrically sensitive reader who would immediately visualize the lowing herd winding slowly o'er the lea. But 'my *vegetable* love' will make the point. I have no doubt that Mr Eliot and subsequent readers do find an image here. They envisage some monstrous and expanding cabbage, but they do so in ignorance. *Vegetable* is no vegetable but an abstract and philosophical term, known as such to the educated man of Marvell's day. Its context is the doctrine of the three souls: the rational, which in man subsumes the other two; the sensitive, which men and animals have in common and which is the principle of motion and perception; and, finally, the lowest of the three, the vegetable soul, which is the only one that plants possess and which is the principle of generation and corruption, of augmentation and decay. Marvell says, then, my love, denied the exercise of sense but possessing the power of augmentation, will increase 'Vaster than empires'. It is an intellectual image, and hence no image at all but a conceit. For if one calls any sort of particularity or detail in a poem an 'image', the use of the wrong word will invite the reader to misconstrue his experience in terms of images, to invent sensory constructions and to project them on the poem.

A conceit is not an image. It is a piece of wit. It is, in the tradition in

which Marvell was writing, among other possibilities, the discovery of
a proposition referring to one field of experience in terms of an intellectual structure derived from another field, and often enough a field of
learning, as is the case in 'my vegetable love'. This tradition, though it
goes back to the poetry of John Donne, and years before that, was current in Marvell's day. The fashionable poetry at the time he was writing
this poem, the poetry comparable to that of Eliot or of Auden in the
last two decades, was the poetry of John Cleveland, and the fashionable
manner was generally known as 'Clevelandizing'. It consisted in the
invention of a series of witty hyperbolical conceits, sometimes inter-
spersed with images, and containing a certain amount of roughage in
the form of conventional erotic statements:

> Thy beauty shall no more be found,
> Nor in thy marble vault shall sound
> My echoing song. . . .

It was commonly expressed in the octosyllabic couplet. Cleveland, for
example, writes 'Upon Phillis Walking in a Morning before Sun-
rising':

> The trees, (like yeomen of the guard,
> Serving more for pomp than ward). . . .

The comparison here does not invite visualization. It would be inappropriate to summon up the colors and serried ranks of the guard.
The comparison is made solely with respect to the idea: the trees, like
the guard, serve more for pomp than ward. Again:

> The flowers, called out of their beds,
> Start and raise up their drowsy heads,
> And he that for their colour seeks
> May find it vaulting to her cheeks,
> Where roses mix,—no civil war
> Between her York and Lancaster.[7]

One does not here picture in panorama the Wars of the Roses. One
sees rather the aptness and the wit of York and Lancaster, the white
rose and the red, reconciled in her cheeks, or one rejects it as forced and
far-fetched. This is a matter of taste.

But if the poem is not a succession of images, does it exhibit that other principle which Mr Eliot ascribes to it – the turn and surprise which he finds in the abrupt introduction of Time's chariot and which forms a sort of fulcrum on which the poem turns? Subsequent critics have certainly felt that it has. In a current textbook we read:

> The poem begins as a conventional love poem in which the lover tries to persuade his mistress to give in to his entreaties. But with the introduction of the image of the chariot in l. 21, the poet becomes obsessed by the terrible onrush of time, and the love theme becomes scarcely more than an illustration of the effect which time has upon human life.

And the leading scholar in the field, a man who is generally quite unhappy with Mr Eliot's criticism, nevertheless says:

> the poet sees the whole world of space and time as the setting for two lovers. But wit cannot sustain the pretence that youth and beauty and love are immortal, and with a quick change of tone – like Catullus' *nobis cum semel occidit brevis lux* or Horace's *sed Timor et Minae* – the theme of time and death is developed with serious and soaring directness.[8]

These, I believe, are not so much accounts of the poem as accounts of Mr Eliot's reading of the poem. Let us question the fact. Does the idea of time and death come as any surprise in this context? The poem began, 'Had we but world enough and time'. That is, it began with an explicit condition contrary to fact, which, by all grammatical rules, amounts to the assertion that we do not have world enough and time. There is no surprise whatever when the proposition is explicitly made in line 21. It would rather have been surprising if it had not been made. Indeed, the only question we have in this respect, after we have read the first line, is: How many couplets will the poet expend on the ornamental reiteration of the initial proposition before he comes to the expected *but*? The only turn in the poem is the turn which the structure of the syllogism had led us to await.

Mr Eliot compares the turn and surprise which he finds in this poem to a similar turn in an ode of Horace, and the scholars seem to corroborate the comparison. This is the fourth ode of the first book:

> solvitur acris hiems grata vice veris et Favoni,
>   trahuntque siccas machinae carinas.

The poem begins with a picture of spring and proceeds by a succession of images, images of the external world and mythological images:

Sharp winter relaxes with the welcome change to spring and the west wind, and the cables haul the dry keels of ships. The herd no longer takes pleasure in its stalls or the farmer in his fire, and the pastures no longer whiten with hoar frost. Cytherean Venus leads her dancers beneath the overhanging moon, and the beautiful graces and nymphs strike the ground with alternate foot, while blazing Vulcan visits the grim forges of the Cyclops. Now is the time to wind your bright hair with green myrtle or with the flowers that the thawed earth yields. Now is the time to sacrifice to Faunus in the shadowed woods, whether it be a lamb he asks or a kid:

> pallida mores æquo pulsat pede pauperum tabernas
>   regumque turres.

Pallid death with indifferent foot strikes the poor man's hut and the palaces of kings. Now, fortunate Sestius, the brief sum of life forbids our opening a long account with hope. Night will soon hem you in, and the fabled ghosts, and Pluto's meager house.[9]

Death occurs in this poem with that suddenness and lack of preparation with which it sometimes occurs in life. The structure of the poem is an imitation of the structure of such experiences in life. And as we often draw a generalization from such experiences, so Horace, on the sudden realization of the abruptness and impartiality of death, reflects:

> vitae summa brevis spem nos vetat incohare longam.
> [The brief sum of life forbids our opening a long account with hope.]

But the proposition is subsequent to the experience; it does not rule and direct the poem from the outset. And the experience in Horace *is* surprising and furnishes the fulcrum on which the poem turns. It has, in fact, the characteristics which are ascribed to Marvell's poem but which Marvell's poem does not have. The two are two distinct kinds of poetry, located in distinct and almost antithetical traditions; both are valuable and valid methods, but one is not to be construed in terms of the other.

In brief, the general structure of Marvell's poem is syllogistic, and it is located in the Renaissance tradition of formal logic and of rhetoric. The structure exists in its own right and as a kind of expandable filing system. It is a way of disposing of, of making a place for, elements of a different order: in this case, Clevelandizing conceits and erotic propositions in the tradition of Jonson and Herrick. These reiterate the propositions of the syllogism. They do not develop the syllogism, and they are not required by the syllogism; they are free and extra. There could be more or less of them, since there is nothing in the structure that determines the number of interpolated couplets. It is a matter of tact and a matter of the appetite of the writer and the reader.

The use of a structure as a kind of expandable filing system is common enough in the Renaissance. The narrative structure of a Shakespearean play can be regarded as a structure of this order. It exists in its own right, of course, but it is also a method for disposing various kinds of material of other orders – a set speech or passion here, an interpolated comic routine in another place. The structure offers a series of hooks upon which different things can be hung. Whether the totality will then form a whole, a unity, is a question of interpretation and a question of value. It is a question, for example, of what sort of unity is demanded and whether there are various sorts.

In Marvell's poem, only the general structure is syllogistic; the detail and development are of another order, and critics have been diligent in assigning the poetic quality of the whole to the non-syllogistic elements. Is it possible, then, to write a lyric that will be wholly or almost wholly syllogistic? It is. There is such a lyric in the *Oxford Book of English Verse*, a lyric of somewhat lesser repute than Marvell's, but still universally praised and universally conceded to possess the true lyrical power. It is Dunbar's 'Lament for the Makaris'.[10]

SOURCE: *Modern Philology*, LI (August 1953).

NOTES

1. Richard von Mises, *Positivism* (Cambridge, Mass., 1951) p. 289.

2. Harold R. Walley and J. Harold Wilson, *The Anatomy of Literature* (New York, 1934) pp. 143, 144.

3. Scholiast cited in Otto Bird, 'The Seven Liberal Arts', in *Dictionary of World Literature*, ed. Joseph T. Shipley (New York, 1943) p. 55; J. E. Spingarn, *A History of Literary Criticism in the Renaissance*, 2nd ed. (New York, 1908) pp. 24–7; David Hume, *Philosophical Works* (Boston and Edinburgh, 1854) III 264; von Mises, loc. cit.

4. Modernized from *The Poems and Letters of Andrew Marvell*, ed. H. M. Margoliouth (Oxford, 1927).

5. T. S. Eliot, in the essay (1921) reprinted in this volume, this extract appearing on p. 48.

6. Eliot, op. cit. p. 48.

7. *The Poems*, ed. John M. Berdan (New Haven, 1911) pp. 80–1.

8. *Reading Poems*, ed. Wright Thomas and Stuart Gerry Brown (New York, 1941) p. 702; Douglas Bush, *English Literature in the Earlier Seventeenth Century* (Oxford, 1945) p. 163.

9. My translation, except for 'the brief sum of life forbids our opening a long account with hope', which is Gildersleeve's; see Shorey and Gordon J. Laing, *Odes and Epodes*, ed. Paul Shorey, revised ed. (Chicago, 1910) *ad loc.*

10. [Editor's note.] In reply see Frank Towne, 'Logic, Lyric, and Drama', in *Modern Philology*, ʟɪ (May 1954) 265–8; also Bruce E. Miller, 'Logic in Marvell's "To his Coy Mistress" ', in *North Dakota Quarterly*, xxx (1962) 48–9.

F. W. BATESON and F. R. LEAVIS

'A Dialogue between the Soul and Body': a debate (1953)

I: F. W. BATESON

A LITERARY context must be distinguished, of course, from a literary background. The latter is best limited, I think, to the constituents of a literary work before and after their momentary synthesis in it. An author's biography, the social history of his age, an account of earlier treatments of his subject-matter – these are all background topics and have only, on this basis, a limited critical relevance. Context, however, is the framework of reference within which the work achieves meaning. To read a poem and ignore its context is, in fact, to misread it. A similar ignorance of its background may make a poem a little more difficult to understand but can do no positive harm. Background, in short, is extrinsic, context is intrinsic.

The implications and ramifications of context can be best demonstrated by a concrete example. A good one can be found on page 74 of *Revaluation*, where Leavis has printed side by side four lines by Marvell (from 'A Dialogue between the Soul and Body'):

> A Soul hung up, as 'twere, in Chains
> Of Nerves, and Arteries, and Veins.
> Tortur'd, besides each other part,
> In a vain Head, and double Heart.

and four lines by Pope (*Dunciad* IV 501–4):

> First slave to Words, then vassal to a Name,
> Then dupe to Party; child and man the same;
> Bounded by Nature, narrow'd still by Art,
> A trifling head, and a contracted heart.

Leavis's point is the 'affinities' between the two passages. It is part of his case that Pope's 'wit' represents a continuation of the Metaphysical tradition. Whatever the merits of the general thesis, it receives no support from these lines, since the 'affinities' only exist within a verbal context of meaning. The verbal similarity between the last line of each passage is, of course, striking and obvious. But Leavis makes the collocation in order to establish a resemblance between Marvell's and Pope's poetic styles, and once the matter is raised to a stylistic context the 'affinities' disappear. In terms of literary tradition the meanings of 'head' and 'heart' are demonstrably quite different in the two passages. In Marvell's lines the vivid images of the first couplet almost compel the reader to visualize the torture-chambers of the 'vain Head, and double Heart'. It is the kind of allegory that was popularized in the early seventeenth century by the Emblem Books, in which a more or less conventional concept is dressed up in some striking new clothes, the new clothes being the real *raison d'être*. In Pope's last line, however, the abstract or quasi-abstract words which lead up to it make it almost impossible to *see* either the 'trifling head' or the 'contracted heart'. Obviously Pope's 'head' and 'heart' belong to the same order of reality as his 'Nature' and 'Art'. They are simply items in his psychological terminology, one the antithetical opposite of the other, and their modern equivalents would, I suppose, be the intellect and the emotions. Nothing could be further removed than these grey abstractions from Marvell's picture-language.

So far the analysis of the two passages has been verbal and stylistic. The apparent verbal identity is, as I have shown, contradicted by the very different figures of speech and stylistic conventions employed by the two poets. In Marvell's lines the image has run away with the antithesis (it doesn't really matter whether the torture-chamber is in the head or the heart or some other part of the body), whereas in Pope's lines the concept has almost killed the imagery, the progress being towards a mathematical purity with the sensuous elements segregated into a separate compartment of their own. And there is a still further contradiction. The most interesting feature in the lines is that the Metaphysical style in which he was writing has *forced* Marvell to say what he cannot have wanted to say. And Pope's Augustan style has forced his hand in the same way.

Marvell's poem is a thoroughly serious affair, but the vividness of the imagery has resulted in a blurring of the argument by making it impossible for the reader not to equate – or, indeed, in terms of the poetic impact, *subordinate* – the immoral head and heart with such relatively innocent and secondary members as the nerves, arteries and veins. So gross a breach of the poem's logic cannot possibly have been intended by Marvell. The passage from the *Dunciad* raises a similar problem. How is it Pope, a master of language if ever there was one, has used his concrete terms with so little precision? In these lines 'slave', 'vassal' and 'dupe' are virtually interchangeable. And so are 'Bounded', 'narrow'd' and 'contracted'. These tautologies can't have been *meant* by Pope.

To understand what lies behind these contradictions between what Marvell and Pope would like to have written and what they actually wrote it is necessary to invoke a wider context – that of the 'climate of opinion', or the thought-patterns current in their time. There is an obvious connection between Marvell's metaphors and the analogical thinking of the Tudor and Stuart divines. (Hooker, for example, uses the regularity of the motions of the heavenly bodies as an argument for imposing ecclesiastical law upon the Puritans.) And the abstract character of Pope's diction can be related without difficulty to the philosophies of Hobbes, Locke, Berkeley and Hume. But this intellectual context, important though it certainly is for understanding Marvell and Pope, does not seem to provide the ultimate framework of reference within which their poems need to be read. Behind the intellectual context lies a complex of religious, political and economic factors that can be called the social context. As this level of meaning seems to be the final context of which the critical reader of literature must retain an awareness, it will be worth while trying to summarize, however baldly, the social contexts implicit in these two passages.

Marvell's 'A Dialogue between the Soul and Body' seems to have been written in the late 1640s, when he was still a Royalist, if a Puritan Royalist. The language and ideas used in the poem were the expression of a way of life shared by most cultivated Englishmen who had grown up in the half-century preceding the Civil War. The basis of that way of life was a confidence in physical appearances, which were held to be symbolic or anagrammatic of the ultimate realities. With the partial discrediting of medieval hierarchies and values in the transition to a money-economy, physical appearances had come to assume a new importance in the sixteenth century. (The wealth that now conferred status, instead of birth or office, was invisible and could only be inferred, therefore, from a 'brave' appearance.)[1] It is perhaps significant that this was the period when portrait-painting established itself in England. In

Court circles, in particular, where the *jus et norma loquendi* determined the English literary language, a man tended to be assessed by his looks, manners, clothes, jewels and physical accomplishments (dancing, jousting, duelling, etc.). On the highest levels the competition for the Prince's favour was largely a matter of banquets, pageants and masques, and the degree of a favourite's success was measured by the number and magnificence of his retainers and 'clients'. This world of appearances came to a disastrous end, of course, in the 1640s, and a certain *grotesquerie*, bordering at times on farce, in Marvell's 'Dialogue' can be taken as a half-realization that his medium was on its last legs and could no longer be taken with complete seriousness.

Pope's language, style and mode of thought, on the other hand, are those of a governing class that had learnt the lesson of the Civil War. The conscious reconstruction of almost every aspect of English upper-class life that began in the 1650s – and in which Marvell incidentally took part, though at the cost of writing no more poetry – was directed by 'common sense', i.e. the rational faculty which enables all human beings to communicate on matters of common interest. And 'common sense' inevitably left its rationalist imprint on the language and the literary tradition from which Pope's poetry was created. It is true that by his infusion of the Picturesque (the object of most of his thefts from the Metaphysical poets) Pope was able to mitigate to some extent the abstractness of his medium. But by his time the pressure towards social conformity that followed the Restoration had noticeably relaxed. A new upper middle class was in process of formation that was serving as a sort of cushion between the Tory and Whig extremists, and it is in Pope's position as an intermediary between this class and the aristocracy that his personal significance lies.

II: F. R. LEAVIS

I do not like, let me say at this point (it seems a fitting one), the way in which scholarship is commonly set over against criticism, as a thing separate and distinct from this, its distinctive nature being to cultivate the virtue of accuracy – it is a way I had occasion to object to in an exchange with Mr Bateson some eighteen years ago. Accuracy is a matter of relevance, and how in the literary field, in any delicate issue, can one hope to be duly relevant – can one hope to achieve the due pointedness and precision of relevance – without being intelligent about literature? Again, how does one acquire the necessary scholarly knowledge? Some of the most essential can be got only through much intelligent reading of the literary-critical kind, the kind trained in 'practical criticism': in the interpretation and judgement, that is, of poems (say) where it can be assumed that the text, duly pondered, will yield its meaning and value to an adequate intelligence and sensibility. Such intelligent reading, directed upon the poetry of the seventeenth century, cannot fail to be aware of period peculiarities of idiom, linguistic usage, convention, and so on, and of the need, here, there and elsewhere, for special knowledge.

The most important kind of knowledge will be acquired in the cultivation of the poetry of the period, and of other periods, with the literary critic's intelligence. Miss Tuve's insistence on an immense apparatus of scholarship before one can read intelligently or judge is characteristic of the academic over-emphasis on scholarly knowledge; it accompanies a clear lack of acquaintance with intelligent critical reading. And of so extravagant an elaboration of 'contextual' procedures as Mr Bateson commits himself to one would even without the conclusive exemplifying he does for us, have ventured, with some confidence, that the 'contextual' critic would not only intrude a vast deal of critical irrelevance on his poem; he would show a marked lack of concern for the most essential kinds of knowledge.

The astonishing manifestations of irresponsibility (to take over the offered word from Mr Bateson) that he actually achieves, however, could hardly have been divined. I will deal with the instances in which he undertakes to correct myself. And I start by noting what I had to note when I had my first exchange with him all those years ago, and have had to note again in the interval: in framing his charges of default of the scholar's trained and delicate scruple he displays something strikingly other than scrupulousness in presenting the alleged defaulter.

The implications and ramifications of context can be best demonstrated by a concrete example. A good one can be found on p. 74 of *Revaluation*, where Leavis has printed side by side four lines by Marvell (from 'A Dialogue between the Soul and Body'):

> A Soul hung up, as 'twere, in Chains
> Of Nerves, and Arteries, and Veins.
> Tortur'd, besides each other part,
> In a vain Head, and double Heart

and four lines by Pope (*Dunciad* IV 501-4):

> First slave to Words, then vassal to a Name,
> Then dupe to Party; child and man the same;
> Bounded by Nature, narrow'd still by Art,
> A trifling head, and a contracted heart.

Leavis's point is the 'affinities' between the two passages. It is part of his case that Pope's 'wit' represents a continuation of the Metaphysical tradition. Whatever the merits of the general thesis, it receives no support from these lines, since the 'affinities' only exist within a verbal context of meaning. The verbal similarity between the last line of each passage is, of course, striking and obvious. But Leavis makes the collocation in order to establish a resemblance between Marvell's and Pope's poetic styles, and once the matter is raised to a stylistic context the 'affinities' disappear.

It turns out that once a matter is raised to a stylistic context by Mr Bateson most of the things that concern a literary critic are likely to disappear; but perhaps it is worth my pointing out that the 'resemblance' discussed in those pages of *Revaluation* is a very different matter from what Mr Bateson suggests: I take some trouble to make plain that it is a matter neither of the Metaphysical tradition nor of the verbal similarity between the last lines of the passages from Marvell and Pope. If the reader looks at page 74 of *Revaluation* he will find, immediately after the piece of Pope reproduced by Mr Bateson, this:

> But such particularity of resemblance may hinder as much as help; it may be better to adduce something as insistently unlike anything Pope could have written as King's

> 'Tis true, with shame and grief I yield,
> Thou like the Vann first took'st the field
> And gotten hast the victory
> In thus adventuring to dy
> Before me, whose more years might crave
> A just precedence in the grave.

A certain crisp precision of statement, a poised urbanity of movement and tone, that relates this passage to the other two becomes very apparent in the last line. The effect is as of an implicit reference, even here in King where personal feeling is so indubitably strong, of the immediate feeling and emotion to a considered scale of values – a kind of critical 'placing', as it were.

That last sentence, with its carefully related words and phrases, associating mode of 'statement' with 'movement' and 'tone', defines well enough, I think, in relation to the *three* quoted passages, the qualities upon which I wanted to focus attention. What, in fact, I am doing is to develop the proposition that immediately precedes, in *Revaluation* (see the bottom of page 73), the passage quoted from Marvell: 'It is, then, plain enough that Pope's reconciliation of Metaphysical wit with the Polite has antecedents.'

I am indicating the way back from Pope to Ben Jonson, and if Mr Bateson had thought the whole presented case worth attending to he might have been led to observe in Marvell some marked antecedents of the Augustan to which 'the implications and ramifications of context' leave him blind.

It is depressing when one's immense pains to be precise in observation and delicately firm in thought go so unrewarded, but in justice to Mr Bateson I have to admit that what I complain of is as nothing, measured by the treatment he accords Marvell and Pope. It is at their expense that he confounds me. This is the way in which he demonstrates how completely wrong I am:

> In terms of literary tradition the meanings of 'head' and 'heart' are demonstrably quite different in the two passages. In Marvell's lines the vivid images of the first couplet almost compel the reader to visualize the torture-chambers of the 'vain Head, and double Heart'. It is the kind of allegory that was popularized in the early seventeenth century by the Emblem Books, in which a more or less conventional concept is dressed up in some striking new clothes, the new clothes being the real *raison d'être*. In Pope's last line, however, the abstract or quasi-abstract words which lead up to it make it almost impossible to *see* either the 'trifling head' or the 'contracted heart'. Obviously Pope's 'head' and 'heart' belong to the same order of reality as his 'Nature' and 'Art'. They are simply items in his psychological terminology, one the antithetical opposite of the other, and their modern equivalents would, I suppose, be the intellect and the emotions. Nothing could be further removed than these grey abstractions from Marvell's picture-language.
>
> So far the analysis of the two passages has been verbal and stylistic. The apparent verbal identity is, as I have shown, contradicted by the very different figures of speech and stylistic conventions employed by the two poets.

But Mr Bateson has shown nothing at all. What he has asserted about the 'very different figures of speech and stylistic conventions employed by the two poets' he has merely asserted; and it can, by anyone who *reads* Marvell's poem (to take that first), immediately be seen to be in great part false. Here is the whole first speech of *A Dialogue between the Soul and Body*:

> O who shall, from this Dungeon, raise
> A Soul inslav'd so many wayes?
> With bolts of Bones, that fetter'd stands
> In Feet; and manacled in Hands.
> Here blinded with an Eye; and there
> Deaf with the drumming of an Ear.
> A Soul hung up, as 'twere, in Chains
> Of Nerves, and Arteries, and Veins.
> Tortur'd, besides each other part,
> In a vain Head, and double Heart.

There is undoubtedly some 'vivid', that is (to avoid the visual suggestion) potent, imagery here; but can Mr Bateson describe what he *sees* in response to Marvell's 'picture-language'? Can he, in fact, give any account of the poem that will begin to make the expression, 'picture-language', anything but disconcertingly inappropriate? Can he suggest what picture *could* be drawn of the Soul 'inslav'd' in the dungeon of the body in *any* of the 'many ways' against which it protests?

None *could* be that bore any relation to Marvell's poem, which is an utterly different thing from what Mr Bateson says it is. Of its very nature it eludes, defies and transcends visualization. So one is surprised to be told, by a scholar (who should know these things), that it is 'the kind of allegory that was popularized in the early seventeenth century by the Emblem Books'. To call it an allegory at all can only mislead, and to say, as Mr Bateson does, that it 'dresses up' a 'more or less conventional concept' in some 'new clothes' (these being the 'real *raison d'être*') is to convey the opposite of the truth about it. For it is a profoundly critical and inquiring poem, devoted to some subtle exploratory thinking, and to the *questioning* of 'conventional concepts' and current habits of mind.

The paradoxes with which it opens may not be unrelated to convention, but that undoubted force which so strikes Mr Bateson (though he hasn't bothered with significance) is not in the least a matter of their compelling us to *visualize* anything; it is that they are paradoxes the essence of which is to elude or defy visualization.

> With bolts of Bones, that fetter'd stands
> In Feet; and manacled in Hands.

– How do we see the Soul? What visual images correspond to 'fetter'd'
and 'manacled'? We certainly don't see manacles on the Soul's hands
and fetters on its feet: the Soul's hands and feet are the Body's, and it is
the fact that they *are* the Body's that makes them 'manacles' and
'fetters'. No doubt there is in every reader's response to those words
some kind of visual element; but the reader for whom the response is
in any major way a matter of *seeing* manacles and fetters has not adjusted himself to the poem. Reading this rightly, we feel, as something
more than stated, the Soul's protest (paradoxically in part physical –
this is where 'imagery' comes in) against the so intimately and inescap-
ably associated matter: the introductory 'with bolts of Bones' makes
the antithesis, Soul and Body, seem clear and sharp.

In the next couplet Mr Bateson himself can hardly have explained
the effect as a matter of our being made to visualize:

> Here blinded with an Eye; and there
> Deaf with the drumming of an Ear.

The Soul is protesting against the conditions and limitations of life
in a world of sense-experience. And the eye is a physical organism – it
can be pulled out; and a diagram can be drawn of the ear. But the
antithesis, Soul and Body, has lost some of the sharpness it had when
the Body was represented by 'bolts of bones'. This development is
confirmed by what follows. The comment on

> A Soul hung up, as 'twere, in Chains
> Of Nerves, and Arteries, and Veins

is made by the Body when it, in turn, speaks. The effect of these lines
is immediate, and it is one concerning which we can say that we
certainly do not *see* the Soul hanging in its 'Chains'. And when we
come to the 'vain Head' and 'double Heart' it takes the wit of 'double'
to remind us that the heart (and the head too) can be thought of as a
mere physical part of the material body. We don't, with that reminder,
see them, or think of them, as 'torture-chambers'; it is not in them as
'torture-chambers' that the Soul is tortured, and Mr Bateson's criticism

derives from a striking failure of attention: 'In Marvell's lines the image has run away with the antithesis (it doesn't really matter whether the torture-chamber is the head or the heart or some other part of the body) . . .'

The poem offers no such simple scheme as he supposes. It is devoted to exploring a sense of the relation between 'soul' and 'body' that couldn't have been expressed in any simple scheme – emblematic, allegorical, diagrammatic, or what. The 'vain Head' and the 'double Heart', though they stand here for the Body, are clearly not just the physical part and the muscular organ. And this is not inadvertence, or slackness of grasp, in Marvell, whatever Mr Bateson may be inclined to suggest (he writes of a 'half-realization [in Marvell's 'Dialogue'] that his medium was on its last legs and could no longer be taken with complete seriousness'). When the Body speaks we have this:

> O who shall me deliver whole
> From bonds of this Tyrannic Soul?
> Which, stretcht upright, impales me so,
> That mine own Precipice I go . . .

Will Mr Bateson say that he finds himself compelled to visualize the Soul 'stretcht upright' and 'impaling' the Body? Hardly. What is conveyed with such power here is the Body's sense of the perilous game that, in its erect posture, it plays with gravity.[2] The passage answers (concave to convex, as it were) to that in which the Soul speaks of being hung up in chains – a passage that expresses a sense of the inseparable, indistinguishable, implication of life in 'nerves and arteries and veins'. It wouldn't, the comment came as one read, have been 'hung up' if life had not informed the nerves and arteries and veins, and made them more than a material network. And now, as one reads, the comment comes that the conditions against which the Body protests are those which make it a body. It is a comment that is insisted on by what follows:

> And warms and moves this needless Frame:
> (A Fever could but do the same).

A Frame that has lost its warmth, its power of motion and its needs is on the way to becoming a 'kneaded clod'.

> And, wanting where its spight to try,
> Has made me live to let me dye.

– The Body (as Claudio testifies), having acquired its needs and become a body, cannot want to become 'needless'.

> A Body that could never rest,
> Since this ill Spirit it possest.

– To 'rest' would be to die, which the Body, of its very nature, cannot wish to do. What it rebels against is the state, entailed in its state of being a body, of needing to fear death: 'mine own Precipice I go' – the point is now made with fuller significance.

A body that fears to die, and has to fear to die because it has been made to live by the Soul, is not so readily to be set over against the soul, as something clearly distinguished, as the title of the poem seems to imply. And that is the point of the poem. The succeeding speech of the Soul develops it:

> What Magick could me thus confine
> Within another's Grief to pine?
> Where whatsoever it complain,
> I feel, that cannot feel, the pain
> And all my Care its self employes,
> That to preserve, which me destroys:
> Constrain'd not only to indure
> Diseases, but, whats worse, the Cure:
> And ready oft the Port to gain,
> Am Shipwrackt into Health again.

The Body's ills may be the Body's, but 'I feel, that cannot feel, the pain': the other's 'Grief' is equally the Soul's, for all the distinction that has been stated as an antithesis. I need not comment on the rest of the speech – except, perhaps, to ask how much picture-language Mr Bateson finds even in the closing couplet of it. The Body's counterpart of this speech concludes the poem:

> But Physick yet could never reach
> The Maladies Thou me dost teach;
> Whom first the Cramp of Hope does Tear:
> And then the Palsie Shakes of Fear.
> The Pestilence of Love does heat:
> Or Hatred's hidden Ulcer eat.

Joy's chearful Madness does perplex:
Or Sorrow's other Madness vex.
Which Knowledge forces me to know;
And Memory will not forego.
What but a Soul could have the wit
To build me up for Sin so fit?
So Architects do square and hew,
Green Trees that in the Forest grew.

The maladies of the Soul – described as that because they are of the kind that Physick cannot reach – are equally the Body's. The Body is exposed, it says, to suffering them by Knowledge and Memory, which it speaks of as belonging to the Soul, but which are nevertheless sufficiently of the Body to involve the Body in maladies.

I am not suggesting that Marvell rejected the distinction between the soul and the body. But, plainly, this poem has for theme the *difficulty* of the distinction – its elusiveness; it explores with remarkable originality and power the perplexities and problems that, for one bent on distinguishing, must, in concrete experience, be found to lie behind the distinction as conventionally assumed – as assumed, for instance, by an allegorical or emblematic writer. I will not here go into the significance of the closing couplet (I confess, indeed, that I have not wholly convinced myself with any account of the development that, with its curiously satisfying effect as of a resolution, it gives to the theme). The poem is among Marvell's supreme things, profoundly original and a proof of genius; and my notes on its not unobvious (I should have thought) characteristics are enough to bring out the remarkable nature of Mr Bateson's feat. Of this poem he can say: 'It is the kind of allegory that was popularized in the early seventeenth century by the Emblem Books, in which a more or less conventional concept is dressed up in some striking new clothes, the new clothes being the *raison d'être*.' With his eyes (presumably) on it he can tell us:

> There is an obvious connection between Marvell's metaphors and the analogical thinking of the Tudor and Stuart divines. (Hooker, for example, uses the regularity of the motions of the heavenly bodies as an argument for imposing ecclesiastical law upon the Puritans.)

How can we explain such a performance? Can it be said that the critic who can tell us, with this serene assurance, these things about such a poem has, in any serious sense of the verb, *read* it? And Mr Bateson tells us them in a considered pronunciatory essay in which he offers to expose the irresponsibility of other critics, and to show us how we may achieve precision, and a certitude of correctness, in analysis, interpretation and judgement. What makes the performance the more astonishing is that he circulated the essay, he tells us, among his editorial colleagues (the note on the Editorial Board in front of *Essays in Criticism* lists eight) before publishing it. Is it possible that none of them made any remark on the extraordinary aberrations I have adduced?

But the essay contains much more, of various kinds, that is equally matter for wonder, and seems equally to have escaped remark from Mr Bateson's colleagues. He treats Pope, for instance, with as confident and dumbfounding an arbitrariness as that which Marvell suffers:

> In Marvell's lines the image has run away with the antithesis (it doesn't really matter whether the torture-chamber is in the head or the heart or some other part of the body), whereas in Pope's lines the concept has almost killed the imagery, the progress being towards a mathematical purity with the sensuous elements segregated into a separate compartment of their own. And there is a still further contradiction. The most interesting feature in the lines is that the Metaphysical style in which he was writing has *forced* Marvell to say what he cannot have wanted to say. And Pope's Augustan style has forced his hand in the same way.
>
> Marvell's poem is a thoroughly serious affair, but the vividness of the imagery has resulted in a blurring of the argument by making it impossible for the reader not to equate – or, indeed, in terms of the poetic impact, *subordinate* – the immoral head and heart with such relatively innocent and secondary members as the nerves, arteries and veins. So gross a breach of the poem's logic cannot possibly have been intended by Marvell. The passage from the *Dunciad* raises a similar problem. How is it Pope, a master of language if ever there was one, has used his concrete terms with so little precision? In these lines 'slave', 'vassal' and 'dupe' are virtually interchangeable. And so are 'Bounded', 'narrow'd' and 'contracted'. These tautologies can't have been *meant* by Pope.

Mr Bateson's ability to believe, and judicially to pronounce, that Marvell has been guilty of a 'breach of the poem's logic' such as 'cannot possibly have been intended' goes, we have seen, with his decision that Marvell shall have intended what, on the unequivocal and final evidence of the poem itself, he clearly didn't – the poem offers not the faintest ghost of a ground for the belief, which wholly denatures it.

III: F. W. BATESON

Dr Leavis devotes nearly half his article to a minute and sometimes rather niggling examination of some brief comments of mine on two passages from Marvell and Pope which he had originally juxtaposed in *Revaluation*. The Marvell lines –

> A Soul hung up, as 'twere, in Chains
> Of Nerves, and Arteries, and Veins.
> Tortur'd, besides each other part,
> In a vain Head, and double Heart.

receive the following comment in *Revaluation*: 'The familiar turn of that close, a turn not confined to Marvell, of whom, however, the supreme representative of seventeenth-century urbanity, it is most characteristic, surely has affinities with a characteristic effect of Pope's longer couplet'. Four lines were then quoted from *The Dunciad*:

> First slave to words, then vassal to a Name,
> Then dupe to Party; child and man the same;
> Bounded by Nature, narrow'd still by Art,
> A trifling head, and a contracted heart.

After which Dr Leavis inserted a reservation – 'But such particularity of resemblance may hinder as well as help' – before passing on to discuss some lines from Henry King's *Exequy*. It was all as clear as houses. If words mean anything at all Dr Leavis's point in making this collocation in *Revaluation* was to suggest that the resemblances in the last line of each of the passages quoted *typified* in some way the affinities between Marvell's poetry and Pope's. If he hadn't meant that, what can his object have been in selecting these particular passages for quotation? Of course the passages also possess other qualities which may or may not have been shared by the two poets, but in 1936 at any rate Dr Leavis obviously expected the 'particularity of resemblance' to 'help' the reader to take his point, if on reflection he also realized it might 'hinder'. I cannot understand, therefore, why he should now berate me (page 170)* for attributing to him an interest in 'the verbal similarity between the last lines of the passages from Marvell and Pope'. That he was wrong in finding the similarity significant, as he now seems to admit, does not alter the fact that he did once make this mistake –

---

* Page references have been amended to those of this volume.

which in any case is not of any great importance. My reason for citing it in my article was not to catch out *Revaluation*, a book for which I have considerable respect, but to show in a striking example how the same words tend to assume different meanings in Metaphysical and Augustan poetry. Dr Leavis had simply saved me the trouble, as I thought of hunting out an example for myself of the difference between purely verbal and 'stylistic' levels of meaning.

In themselves Dr Leavis's expansions and elaborations of his earlier comments on the two passages are persuasive and often acute. But instead of refuting my thesis he tends to talk round it. I had argued (i) that, as Marvell used the words *head* and *heart*, the sense-impression predominated, whereas for Pope the words were primarily conceptual, and (ii) that the general linguistic trend represented by these passages had resulted here in a distortion or enfeeblement of the poetic argument. Dr Leavis seems to think that he has disposed of my first point by showing that there are non-sensuous elements in Marvell's poems. Of course there are. There are non-sensuous elements in the Emblem Books. If Dr Leavis will turn to Emblem VIII in the fifth Book of Quarles's *Emblemes*, he will find a crude exemplification of the convention in which Marvell was writing – a skeleton lolling in a sitting posture (the Body) with a kneeling figure inside it (the Soul). The essence of the paradoxical relationship was that the idea of the mutual dependence of body and soul could only be explored in physical terms. 'How do we see the Soul?', Dr Leavis asks. '. . . we certainly do not *see* the Soul hanging in its "Chains" ' (p. 170). Well, Quarles saw his Soul. And if, as is surely the case, the comparison of the network of human nerves, arteries and veins with the chains fastened round a dead criminal's body (in order that it might not disintegrate) is a visual metaphor, how can the reader fail to complete the metaphor by *seeing* the soul in the corpse on the gallows? I suspect that Dr Leavis has missed the full force of the allusion.

My second point depended upon the hierarchical pre-eminence of the head and the heart in Marvell's time. A poem in which the feet, the hands, the eyes, the ears, and the nerves, arteries and veins receive more memorable treatment than the head and the heart would have puzzled and disturbed a seventeenth-century reader. Dr Leavis's insistence on reading everything written in English as though it was written yesterday has in this instance accidentally improved Marvell's poem for him.

IV: F. R. LEAVIS

[Mr Bateson] asserts again that superiority in scholarship the pretension to which I had noted as the distinctive mark of *Essays in Criticism*, and he demonstrates again with a truly remarkable conclusiveness that what he conceives to be a use of scholarship can only promote an incapacity to read poetry. That superior scholarship of his feeds its confidence on misconception. With what aplomb he tells me that I insist on 'reading everything in English as though it was written yesterday'! The fact that his formulation points to is that *I* have read Marvell's poem, whereas he insisted – and still insists – on busying himself with his apparatus of interpretation instead. Let me tell him that I have also read other poems of Marvell, and read them a great deal, and that I have read a great deal of other seventeenth-century poetry. I have even heard of Quarles, and have even read him. And it seems to me that Mr Bateson might well have been better qualified to read Marvell's poem if *he* had not read Quarles, and had not turned to Emblem VIII in the fifth Book. He tells us that the picture he describes is a 'crude exemplification of the tradition in which Marvell was *writing*' (my italics). That odd proposition might have passed if it had led to Mr Bateson's showing us how utterly different a thing from an attempt to present such an Emblem in words Marvell's poem is. But what Mr Bateson in his essay actually told us about the 'Dialogue' was: 'It is the kind of allegory that was popularized in the early seventeenth century by the Emblem Books, in which a more or less conventional concept is dressed up in some striking new clothes, the new clothes being the real *raison d'être*.'

So convinced is he that Marvell's poem *must* be *this* that he could talk, in his essay, of 'Marvell's picture-language', a description the disastrous falsity of which I still suppose myself to have demonstrated; for he produces no reason for believing otherwise. And to my careful ('niggling') account of the 'Dialogue' as a superlatively successful poem of an extremely original kind (and not, as Mr Bateson judges, one that betrays a 'half-realization' in Marvell that 'his medium was on its last legs, and could no longer be taken with complete seriousness'), Mr Bateson replies, in effect, that I must be wrong, because in my ignorance (having missed, he 'suspects', the 'full force of the allusion'), I can't see that the 'Dialogue' asks us to control and limit our response with a visualization of Quarles's Emblem. For this belief about the poem he gives no grounds, except his conviction that it clearly *must* be so, because Marvell is writing in that convention. I demonstrate that it is *not* so, by giving a detailed analysis of what the poem actually does, and Mr Bateson replies that my ignorance 'has in this instance accidentally improved Marvell's poem for him'.

But for that 'accidentally' I should have supposed Mr Bateson to be intending irony. As it is I can only take him to mean that, by some freak of chance, my analysis has the convincing effect of applying to the poem, so that, if you read this without keeping your mind on Quarles, you find yourself reading the remarkably subtle and successful poem I analyse – which only shows (that appears to be Mr Bateson's moral) how important it is to hold firmly on to your scholarship. He doesn't dispute that, if you read the text 'as if it had been written yesterday' (*his* phrase, of course, not mine), you have the poem that I establish in analysis. But it is an illicit poem, illicitly better than the one that Marvell actually wrote, and it must be rejected by the responsible critic.

SOURCE: This debate is abstracted from a larger discussion between Mr Bateson and Dr Leavis: F. W. Bateson, 'The Function of Criticism at the Present Time', in *Essays in Criticism*, III (Jan 1953), F. R. Leavis, 'The Responsible Critic: or the function of criticism at any time', in *Scrutiny*, XIX (Jan 1953) 162–83; and the 'Correspondence: The Responsible Critic' in *Scrutiny* XIX (Oct 1953), from F. W. Bateson, pp. 317–21, and from F. R. Leavis, pp. 321–8. (These page numbers cover the whole discussion.) F. W. Bateson's original article is reprinted in his *English Poetry: a critical introduction*, 2nd ed. (1966) pp. 175–94.

NOTES

1. The history of the word *brave*, in the sense of 'well-dressed' or 'admirable' provides linguistic evidence of the duration of this dominance of physical appearances. According to the *O.E.D.* it was first used in this sense in 1568 and it had already become archaic in the eighteenth century.

2. After he was stretch'd to such an height in his own fancy, that he could not look down from top to toe but his eyes dazled at the Precipice of his Stature' – *Rehearsal Transpros'd* I 64 (quoted in the Commentary to the Poems, edited by Margoliouth).

A. ALVAREZ

Marvell and the Poetry of Judgement (1960)

IN all the diverse talent of the School of Donne, Richard Crashaw and
Andrew Marvell are the two poets most wholly opposed. With
Crashaw the recurrent question is why, given that power and fertility,
he was not a greater poet. It is as though he had in him the essential
stuff of great poetry, but frittered it away. Marvell, on the other hand,
produced some of the most perfect poems in the language and yet is,
for all that, somehow not a 'major poet'. Dr Leavis once wrote of
Dryden: 'He may be a greater poet than Marvell, but he did not write
any poetry as indubitably great as Marvell's best.' The corollary is also
true: Marvell may have written a few great poems but he was not a
great poet.

He has done very well in this century. Eliot, Leavis and Empson,
for example, have been prompted by him to some of their finest
criticism. So his excellence is firmly established. I merely want to
suggest here why, for all the subtlety and accomplishment of his
writing, Marvell was essentially one of the last products of a school,
but still too much part of it to be quite able to go forward to the next.

He is, in a way, the School of Donne in miniature, working in all the
variations of the style: in 'To his Coy Mistress', 'The Definition of
Love' and, in another way, 'On a Drop of Dew', he writes like Donne;
in 'The Coronet' and 'Eyes and Tears' he is largely a follower of
Herbert; 'The Match', 'The Fair Singer' and 'The Picture of little
T. C.' are like Carew and Lovelace; 'Upon Appleton House' is heavily
influenced by Cleveland; 'A Dialogue between the Resolved Soul,
and Created Pleasure' has something of the formal stance of Cowley;
his pastoral poems have behind them an Elizabethan and continental
tradition which descended through poets like Aurelian Townshend;
'The Nymph complaining for the death of her Faun' sounds like a kind

of pastoral-classical Crashaw; he went on to write political satires in rhymed couplets. In none of these poems was he a mere imitator; he always rehandled his themes and styles in a peculiarly original way. But the variety and varied perfection of his work show that, despite his correct, almost sedate, career – gentleman tutor, government official, M.P. – he was, in terms of technical accomplishment, the most professional of that extraordinary group of amateurs that made up the School of Donne. He was, in short, 'literary' where Crashaw, with his religious-heroic style, his inventive enthusiasm and his Baroque principle of sensuous substitution, was the most 'rhetorical'. The difference is between a poet whose intelligence worked *on* literature, critically and analytically, and a poet who needed a great deal of artifice in order to express his intelligence at all.

The main element in Marvell's poetry is its balance, its pervading sense of intelligent proportion. He is, I think, the foremost poet of judgement in the English language, and 'An Horatian Ode' is his foremost poem. By *judgement* I mean a quality which presents, balances and evaluates a whole situation, seeing all the implications and never attempting to simplify them. The poet's whole effort is directed towards a full and delicate sanity, so that what he finally achieves is a kind of personal impersonality. For example:

> 'Tis Madness to resist or blame
> The force of angry Heavens flame:
> And, if we would speak true,
> Much to the Man is due.

The poem gets its effect by the certainty with which it balances the large religious and political context – in the first couplet – against a personal judgment, so that both appear necessary parts of a whole understanding of the situation.

Again:

> [Who] Could by industrious Valour climbe
> To ruine the great Work of Time,
> And cast the Kingdome old
> Into another Mold.
> Though Justice against Fate complain,
> And plead the antient Rights in vain:
> But those do hold or break
> As Men are strong or weak.

> Nature that hateth emptiness,
> Allows of penetration less:
>   And therefore must make room
>   Where greater Spirits come.

I have seen the lines used as an example of political slipperiness, as though Marvell were praising Cromwell whilst fundamentally supporting the King. But what in fact is so impressive in the poem is the sureness with which the poet separates out the various threads so that he can proceed without disorder in the full knowledge of what his feelings on the subject really are. Personal preferences and natural sanity hold each other in check. His distaste for that kind of hard-working ambition, particularly when it sets itself up against the tested sanctities of tradition, sway the balance one way. His acknowledgement of the natural and rational laws of power sway it back the other. This manner of opposing two ways of thinking and feeling is, of course, typical of a good deal of Metaphysical poetry. But elsewhere, in, say, Herbert's 'The Collar' or 'Affliction(I)', the turnabout always follows some peculiarly intricate dialectic by which the poet argues himself into accepting his full responsibilities. He presents the whole process of understanding: the knot, the gradual untying and the final ordering of the threads. In Marvell's poetry, on the other hand, the personal balance is already achieved before the poem begins. He approaches his subjects fully aware of his personal bias. The result is that he always has the air of a man dealing with something outside him, rather than with what at least began as an unresolved complex of emotions. It is this impression of the mind detachedly at play over a number of possible choices that earns Marvell the title of poet of judgement. Another way of putting it would be to call him a political poet. Certainly, 'An Horatian Ode' is one of the two finest political poems in the language; the other is *Coriolanus*. As a political poet he works analytically, resolving at every point personal choice into a larger context of general or social responsibilities. In this sense, Marvell is closer to Dryden and Pope than he is to Donne.

This habit of always leaving himself the elbow-room of impersonality – whether it is called judgement, a political trick of the mind, or a peculiar intensity of civilization – has saved him from the excesses of his interpreters. There is, for example, an aura of suggestiveness about a great deal of his work than can, with a little effort, be translated into symbolism of a kind. But the fact that Marvell disliked violence – which we know from comments not in his poems – appreciated the peace and quiet of gardens as a relief from the turbulence of the Civil War, and so wrote eloquently, in one disguise or another, on the subject of Eden, does not make him a Quietist, nor does it illuminate his poetry with flashes of mystical insight *à propos* of God or Nature. The strangeness of a poem like 'The Nymph complaining for the death of her Faun', or of that unexpected couplet in 'Bermudas':

> But Apples plants of such a price,
> No tree could ever bear them twice

is no evidence of any specific, extendable religious symbolism in Marvell's verse, nor of any plan to take his readers in by writing charmingly about what was really very serious. Marvell's use of religion seems to be much the same as his classicism. The subtlety of some of the nymph's complaints for her faun:

> Had it liv'd long, it would have been
> Lillies without, Roses within

or

> There is not such another in
> The World, to offer for their Sin

is no greater nor less than that of:

> The brotherless *Heliades*
> Melt in such Amber Tears as these.

Empson once wrote of this last couplet: 'It is tactful, when making an obscure reference, to arrange that the verse should be intelligible even when the verse is not understood . . . If you had forgotten, as I had myself, who their brother was, and look it up, the poetry will scarcely seem more beautiful; such of the myth as is wanted is implied.' The Biblical echoes are tantalizing and evocative in precisely the same way: they lend the poem weight and seriousness. But they do not restrict the area of its action to their own special realm. The Bible came more naturally to the seventeenth century than to our day; it did not demand any peculiarly specialized effort of attention. For Marvell, as for every

other educated man of his time, the Bible, like the classics, was a
dimension of his extraordinarily civilized sensibility, and was controlled
by it.

It is this that makes him such a deliberate, literary and decorous poet,
particularly in his conceits. *Pace* Eliot, I cannot see that Marvell was
ever carried away by his ingenuity with metaphors. But he came, as
I said, at the end of the School of Donne and so could judge the
technical means both for its vitality and in its corruption. And the
corrupt conceit had effects very different from Donne's. In short,
Marvell had read and taken good account of Cleveland; which meant he
knew how to play the game of wit when it suited him. It was this
element that Eliot missed when he accused Marvell's figure of the
'*Antipodes* in Shoes' of being one of those 'images which are over-
developed or distracting; which support nothing but their own
misshapen bodies'. There is a side to Marvell's wit less serious than the
one Eliot wished to emphasize. You can see it directly the conceit is
put in its full context:

> But now the *Salmon-Fishers* moist
> Their *Leathern Boats* begin to hoist;
> And, like *Antipodes* in Shoes,
> Have shod their *Heads* in their *Canoos*.
> How *Tortoise like*, but not so slow,
> These rational *Amphibii* go?
> Let's in: for the dark *Hemisphere*
> Does now like one of them appear.

Marvell's concept of wit was flexible enough to include the kind of
deliberate playfulness that is found only in light verse, and, if Eliot's
Old Possum poems are typical, not often in that. The '*Antipodes* in
Shoes', in fact, is not so much a conceit as a joke. And Marvell works
for it deliberately. There is a preparatory pun in the preceding line –
'*Leathern Boats*' suggests 'boots' and so makes way for the 'shoes' – a
solemn pedantry in the couplet following and a final piece of absurdity
– the comparison of the dark coming down over the hemisphere with
the coracles over the heads of the fishermen. They all have the same
effect, and the effect is deliberately comic. 'Deliberately', since it is
unlikely that a poet as skilful as Marvell would have lapsed so absurdly
at the end of a long poem without knowing why. I suggest he has two

reasons: the first has to do with the occasion of the poem, the second with its literary means.

The absurd solemnity of that closing stanza may be more extreme than anything that has gone before in the poem but it is the same in kind. The poem is dedicated to Lord Fairfax, whose child, Mary, Marvell was then tutoring. All through the poem Marvell has treated the conventional occasions for conventionally exaggerated praise with a polite mock-seriousness, using conceits that are too conceited, too extreme. This does not hinder him from being very serious indeed in praising what he really admires in Fairfax, the political moderation and the firm desire for peace. But he writes with such delicate control that he can change from the fanciful to the profound without any clashing of gears. The whole effort presumes on a kind of formal intimacy between the poet and his audience: Marvell can be witty with his conventional praise because it is understood that his patron has qualities rarer and finer. In that sense it is a family poem; it would not be in good taste to be fulsome where fulsomeness is to be expected from everyone.

It is also a family poem in that the fancy is supposed to be amusing. And not only, I suggest, to Lord Fairfax. Compare, for example, those infamous Antipodes with a far more successful passage:

> And now to the Abbyss I pass
> Of that unfathomable Grass,
> Where Men like Grashoppers appear,
> But Grashoppers are Gyants there:
> They, in their squeking Laugh, contemn
> Us as we walk more low then them:
> And, from the Precipices tall
> Of the green spir's, to us do call.

This is a conceit, but it is hardly Metaphysical. It is, instead, nearer the wit of Lewis Carroll. The conceit, that is, is a matter of sharply refocusing the scene until it is adjusted to a child's vision: the hay tall enough to drown in and the grasshoppers gigantic, threatening presences. There was nothing in the detached elegance of the wit at Marvell's command which barred him from writing vivid, adult poetry which might also amuse a child. The tradition of an exclusively patronizing children's verse did not seem to have existed in the seventeenth century; perhaps it did not begin until Isaac Watts stooped to conquer. Marvell's conceit is no less successful because, like the elaborate pedantry of the '*Antipodes* in Shoes', it has behind it a faint nonsense air.

I am far from accusing Marvell of quaintness or suggesting that his poetry was, in any way, kid's stuff. On the contrary, Marvell's ability to blend this kind of fanciful exaggeration with a far more serious wit, and to give both an equivalent, if not an equal, subtlety, is a measure of his sophistication. It is pre-eminently a literary sophistication. Far from being victimized by the style, the poet seems perfectly aware of what the exaggerated conceit is and is not good for. It is, in fact, possible that by using this kind of witty playfulness to amuse the daughter of the house he is even taking the measure of the corrupt Metaphysical style. The most elaborate conceits begin when Mary Fairfax enters the poem, and this coincides with an obvious and deliberate echo of Cleveland. Marvell has:

> See how the Flow'rs, as at *Parade*,
> Under their *Colours* stand displaid:
> Each *Regiment* in order grows,
> That of the Tulip Pinke and Rose . . .

Cleveland wrote:

> The trees, like yeomen of her guard,
> Serving more for pomp than ward,
> Ranked on each side, with loyal duty
> Weave branches to enclose her beauty . . .

I am not pretending that Marvell's poem is really an elaborate critical parody of Cleveland; but it does seem that when he played Cleveland's game of wit to amuse his patron and his pupil, he was showing that he knew its precise range and value. Instead of being occasionally the victim of false wit, Marvell used it for his own ends.

I have defended at length some not very distinguished lines in order to point up a vital aspect of the poetry of judgement: its peculiarly literary control in the choice and manipulation of special effects. If these are an index of poetic achievement, then Marvell is a master. But when compared with Donne, it seems that what Marvell gained in control he lost in pressure. He rarely, if at all, lapses as Donne did at times. But then he hasn't the excuse. He was never as original; his poetic discoveries were within already charted poetic forms. His first desire in verse was, I think, to do it perfectly. And he gained this perfection by keeping away from insistently personal situations and absorbing all his energies in the literary form and process. He rarely has that air of creative improvisation, of having to invent a new form for a unique occasion. Instead, each poem seems to start from a peculiarly sensitive critical analysis of the particular genre.

Consider, for instance, 'The Definition of Love':

I

My Love is of a birth as rare
As 'tis for object strange and high:
It was begotten by despair
Upon Impossibility.

II

Magnanimous Despair alone
Could show me so divine a thing,
Where feeble Hope could ne'er have flown
But vainly flapt its Tinsel Wing.

III

And yet I quickly might arrive
Where my extended Soul is fixt,
But Fate does Iron wedges drive,
And alwaies crouds it self betwixt.

IV

For Fate with jealous Eye does see
Two perfect Loves; nor lets them close:
Their unione would her ruine be,
And her Tyrannick pow'r depose.

V

And therefore her Decrees of Steel
Us as the distant Poles have plac'd,
(Though Loves whole World on us doth wheel)
Not by themselves to be embrac'd.

VI

Unless the giddy Heaven fall,
And Earth some new Convulsion tear;
And, us to joyn, the World should all
Be cramp'd into a *Planisphere*.

VII

As Lines so Loves *oblique* may well
Themselves in every Angle greet:
But ours so truly *Paralel*,
Though infinite can never meet.

VIII

Therefore the Love which us doth bind,
But ours so truly *Paralel*,
Is the Conjunction of the Mind,
And Opposition of the Stars.

It is based on a single aspect of some of Donne's love poems: his habit
of bolstering up a feeling with abstract and scientific imagery until it
can bear the weight of his complex logic. But Marvell presses this
logical abstraction so hard that the feeling which justifies it seems to
refine away to nothing. This is apparent in the imagery. The poem
begins with three-dimensional allegorical figures – Despair, Hope,
Fate – with tinsel wings, iron wedges and decrees of steel, who control
'Loves whole World'. It is all hard, solid and definite. The substantial
globe, however, is then reduced to a two-dimensional model, the
planisphere, and that, in turn, is reduced to the mere lines of a geometrical figure. Marvell's conclusion about the abstract refinement of
their love – 'the Conjunction of the Mind' – is borne out by the steady
abstraction of the imagery. The poem is less of a love poem than an
essay in abstraction. The poet, presumably, meant something of this
kind when he called it 'The Definition of Love'. He is not to be
criticized for failing to write a poem he never intended. But perhaps
the piece is more formally perfect and neat than most of Donne's
because Marvell has only the formal aspects to bother about. His stake
in the thing seems first and foremost craftsmanly.

Marvell's practice in 'The Definition of Love' is the rule for his work,
not the exception. There is not one of his love poems which, when set
next to any of Donne's, seems more than an exercise in the poetic kind.
This holds even for one of his most perfect poems, 'To his Coy Mistress'. I cannot believe that, in terms of the poem – the biography, in
these matters, being neither here nor there – the mistress ever existed.
She is merely part of the poem's traditional occasion. She is of course
wooed with wit and some admirable ironical flourishes. But the irony
is largely at Marvell's own expense:

> Thou by the *Indian Ganges* side
> Should'st Rubies find: I by the Tide
> Of *Humber* would complain . . .

She is to do exotic things in exotic surroundings, while he is left to scribble away at his complaints on the dreary banks of the Humber, which flows through his native city, Hull. Even the brilliant conceit of his 'vegetable Love' gains an extra dimension of irony when you remember his 'green thought in a green shade' and all those innocent, Eden-like gardens to which Marvell wrote so many love poems of another kind. As for his mistress and his ideal love-making:

> An hundred years should go to praise
> Thine Eyes, and on thy Forehead Gaze . . .

That, and such physical detail as appears, is, as the editors have pointed out, founded on a turn of wit that Marvell took from Cowley. But the tone of the verse deepens and the rhythm becomes more charged when in the section beginning 'But at my back I alwaies hear . . . ' the subject changes from the girl to death. It is this sudden quickening of the witty detachment into something distinctly more sharply felt that makes me certain that Marvell is addressing himself rather than any supposed mistress. The real and moving poem is about time, death, waste and the *need* to love, rather than about love itself. Whatever of its power does not come from this source comes from the perfection of the performance: from the inevitable syllogistic progression (by which, incidentally, Marvell argues himself into accepting images of violence and war that go flatly against the current of all his other poetry), and, as Eliot said, from the weight behind the verse of the whole tradition of European love poetry.

One of the main differences between Marvell and Donne was not in the sophistication of their wit, which was where most of the other late Metaphysicals fell down, but in the uses their wit was put to. Donne's was exploratory; it brought whole and unexpected areas of awareness into the service of his single, immediate situation; and in doing so he changed the whole language of poetry. By accommodating it to the extraordinary range of his intelligence and to the kind of sceptical intensity of feeling of which he was master, he introduced into poetry a wholly new standard of realism. Marvell's wit, on the other hand,

worked in literary forms already to hand and perfected them; it was a
force that restrained, controlled and impersonalized.

But there are moments, admittedly rare, when this emphasis on
civilized control and artistic impersonality lapses into what might, in a
poet less skilled, be vulgar indifference:

> How wide they dream! The *Indian* Slaves
> That sink for Pearl through Seas profound,
> Would find her Tears yet deeper Waves
> And not of one the bottom sound.
>
> I yet my silent Judgement keep,
> Disputing not what they believe:
> But sure as oft as Women weep,
> It is to be suppos'd they grieve.

The first stanza is one of the most allusive Marvell ever wrote, and he
always wrote well on tears. Rhythmically, I think, it is based on
Donne:

> O wrangling schooles, that search what fire
> Shall burne this world, had none the wit
> Unto this knowledge to aspire,
> That this her feaver might be it?

But Marvell's stanza has undergone a distancing typical of his work;
it is something more than merely changing 'wrangling' to 'dreaming'.
The slight roughness of Donne's verse has wholly disappeared: for
example, the repetition of 'That' and 'this' so close together, which
gives the lines their colloquial directness and which depends upon the
personal cadence of the speaking voice to carry them off. Gone, too, is
the reference to a lively contemporary issue – the Schoolmen at that
time were very much under attack. The essence of Marvell's conceit
is a certain exoticism; he uses all the technical skill he can muster to
build up the strangeness and grandeur of the weeping woman: the
alliteration of consonants and vowels, for example, which makes the
second and third lines echo on themselves. But having built up his
effects with such imaginative strength, Marvell seems able to reassert
his 'silent Judgement' only by a final gesture of lame cynicism. Admittedly, the last stanza is more in keeping with the tone of the rest of

the poem than is that oddly rich conceit; but the renewed cynicism is so sudden and extreme that it makes me suspect that that beautiful detachment of Marvell's was, at times, defensive. If Donne is also guilty at times of sudden lapses into cynicism, the occasions are always a matter of too much assertion, never of too delicate a withdrawal.

With the exception of George Herbert, Marvell is the most considerable of Donne's followers. But his strength is quite different. He is, as I suggested, far more carefully and absorbedly a craftsman in poetry; and this went with a different poetic stance. It matters not a jot that his love poems are thin in comparison with Donne's; there is, after all, little outside Shakespeare's sonnets that can stand that comparison. The difference is between kinds of poets: between the poet whose first concern is to judge and the poet who, above all, synthesizes. The vitality of Donne's poetry depends on his knack of taking on everything that comes with the same immediacy, accuracy and full, tough intelligence. At the end of any of Donne's poems the forces have been resolved and ordered in such a way as to make you believe that a similar readjustment of the feelings have taken place in the poet himself. It is, in a sense, a poetry of action. Marvell, however, is always a little further outside his subjects. His extraordinarily civilized sophistication is a fixed quantity. With it he weighs and judges his material with such dispassionate fairness as to leave you, as a final and lasting taste, with the mature subtlety of his judgement. Unlike Donne and Herbert, he never writes a poem which shows him in the process of attaining this maturity. It is, rather, a quality without which he would not have been able to begin to write. Marvell's detached and sophisticated wit may be infinitely more subtle and less stereotyped than that of the Augustan Man of Sense, but it is of essentially the same kind. In achievement, if not chronologically, he is the last of the School of Donne.

SOURCE: *Hudson Review*, XIII (1960); reprinted as chapter 5 of *The School of Donne* (1961).

J. B. LEISHMAN

Some Themes and Variations in the Poetry of Andrew Marvell (1961)

THE small collection of Marvell's pre-Restoration poetry, most of which was probably seen by only a few of his intimate friends and which has reached us almost by accident, is perhaps the most remarkable example we have of the interaction between what Mr Eliot, in a famous phrase, called Tradition and the Individual Talent. For, although Marvell's poetry is highly original and, at its best, unmistakably his own and no one else's, he is almost always acting upon hints and suggestions provided by earlier poets, and almost never writing entirely, as children would say, out of his own head. When he returned from his foreign travels in (as is probable) 1646, he seems to have bought and read attentively many of those notable volumes of verse by living or recently deceased poets which, from 1640 onwards, appeared in such rapid succession, often from the press of that most enterprising of publishers Humphrey Moseley. Particular borrowings or imitations prove that he had read (I mention them in order of publication) Carew's *Poems* (1640, 1642, 1651), Waller's *Poems* (1645), *The Poems of Mr John Milton* (1645), Crashaw's *Steps to the Temple* (1646, 1648), Cowley's *The Mistress* (1647), Cleveland's *Poems* (1647 and 1651), Lovelace's *Lucasta* (1649), and Davenant's *Gondibert* (1651). These and other poets, including the Ancients, were continually suggesting to Marvell new and amusing things to do. And how remarkable, considering the comparatively small number of his poems, is their variety! There is something in almost every one of them that recalls some other seventeenth-century poet, and yet perhaps no single one of them is really like a poem by anyone else. Marvell, in fact, is the most representative of all those fine amateur poets of the earlier seventeenth century who wrote mainly for their own pleasure and that of a few friends. It would be going too far to say that whatever any other seventeenth-century poet has done well Marvell has done better. In the art of making the purest poetry out of almost pure abstractions not even Donne has surpassed Marvell's 'Definition of Love', but Marvell has nothing comparable with that tenderness which is no less characteristic of Donne's poetry than its wit: nothing like

> I wonder by my troth, what thou and I
> Did, till we lov'd?

or

> All other things, to their destruction draw,
>   Only our love hath no decay;

or

> So, so breake off this last lamenting kisse.

Marvell's moralizing 'On a Drop of Dew' is no less beautiful than Vaughan's moralizing on 'The Water-fall', but he has nothing comparable with the intense vision of 'The World' or the white ecstasy of 'The Retreate'. Some of Marvell's descriptions and images have both the colour and the crystalline purity of Crashaw's, but, although he is free from Crashaw's not infrequent mawkishness and sentimentality, he also lacks both Crashaw's child-like tenderness and his rapture. And, although he often equals George Herbert in structure, he has none of his passionate personal drama. Nevertheless, although Marvell cannot equal any of the poets I have mentioned in their special intensities, he can surpass each and all of them in variety and breadth. This is partly because he is, in comparison with them, singularly uncommitted. His poetry is, so to speak, the poetry of a temperament rather than of any urgent personal experience, but of a temperament in which nearly all the most attractive virtues of the earlier seventeenth century seem to be combined.

To attempt to review, with something more than superficiality, all Marvell's most notable poems would be impossible in a single lecture; one would have to take account of so many other seventeenth-century poets and poems that such a 'project' (as our American friends call it)

could only be realized in a sizable book, such as that on which I have
myself been for several years intermittently engaged. All I am now
going to attempt is to suggest something of the ways in which tradition
and originality are combined in a few representative poems, with, I
hope, not more illustrative detail than can be comfortably assimilated
from a spoken discourse.

How did Marvell begin? There are a few commendatory, elegiac,
satirical, and political poems, all of them, except the great Cromwell
ode, in the heroic couplet, and all of them, except for that ode, of
small intrinsic importance, which can be assigned, because of their
allusions to public events, to various dates between 1646 and 1650.
When, though, we come to the unpublic, the lyrical, reflective, or
descriptive poems, we have almost no external evidence to help us. A
recently discovered manuscript proves that the pastoral 'Dialogue
between Thyrsis and Dorinda' must have been written before September 1645, and therefore probably before Marvell set out on his foreign
travels in or about 1642. It is impossible not to suppose that the poems
'Upon the Hill and Grove at Bill-borow' and 'Upon Appleton House',
both dedicated 'To the Lord Fairfax', and 'Musicks Empire', in which
Fairfax is evoked in the last stanza, were written during the two years,
1651 to 1653, which Marvell spent with the retired Lord General at his
estate of Nun-Appleton in Yorkshire, as tutor to his young daughter
Mary. And it seems reasonable to suppose that the poem 'Bermudas'
was written some time after July 1653, when Marvell, together with
his pupil, Cromwell's ward William Dutton, began his residence with
John Oxenbridge, Fellow of Eton College, who had twice visited those
islands. These, I think, are the only private poems for whose dates
there is any kind of external evidence. I myself am inclined to believe
that nearly all the best of what it seems convenient to call Marvell's
private poems were written during those two years at Nun-Appleton,
when he had infinite leisure and the society of a friend and patron who
was both a lover of poetry and, in a small way, a poet himself. The
affinity between 'The Garden' and the poem on Appleton House is
obvious, and it is difficult not to associate the predominantly pastoral or
descriptive element in many other poems with Marvell's residence at
Nun-Appleton: more important, though, as a common characteristic
is that maturity and security which is equally apparent in poems
otherwise so different as the Cromwell ode, 'The Definition of Love',
'To his Coy Mistress', 'The Picture of little T.C. in a Prospect of

Flowers', the Mower poems, 'On a Drop of Dew'. I need not prolong the list: apart from certain careless amateurishnesses – an excessive use of inversion for the sake of rhyme, and excessive use of expletives such as 'do', 'did', and 'doth' to supply syllables – of which he never rid himself, one feels that in all these poems, and in those which seem to belong with them, Marvell knew exactly what he wanted to say before he began to write, and that in each poem he has completely realized his intention. I myself seem to be aware almost of a difference in kind between their assuredness, their maturity and security, and what, in comparison, seem the uncertainty, inequality, and sometimes laboured ingenuity of six poems which stand rather apart from the rest. Three of these – 'The Match', 'The Unfortunate Lover', 'The Gallery' – are predominantly and sometimes grotesquely emblematical or allegorical, and three of them – 'Mourning', 'Eyes and Tears', 'The Fair Singer' – have a more obvious affinity with certain kinds of Renaissance Latin epigram than we find in Marvell's more characteristic poems. Were these Marvell's earliest surviving poems, his beginnings, or were they simply lapses – experiments, contemporary with the more character-istic poems, of a kind which he decided not to pursue? Three of them, I said, were predominantly allegorical, but then so too is 'Musicks Empire', which must have been written at Nun Appleton, since it concludes with a compliment to the Lord General. It is not, indeed, like 'The Match' and 'The Unfortunate Lover', grotesquely allegorical, and it contains the unforgettable phrase, a phrase one might have expected to find rather in Rilke than in Marvell, 'Musick, the Mosaique of the Air'; nevertheless, if one examines it carefully, one finds that the correspondence between the literal and the metaphorical (so exquisitely preserved in 'On a Drop of Dew') is continually breaking down.

'On a Drop of Dew': my parenthetical mention of this, one of Marvell's most perfect poems, may remind us of the fact that, even after he had achieved stylistic assurance, he never lost his taste for allegory in the medieval sense of extended metaphor, for the elaborate comparison or series of comparisons, running through an entire poem, and that this kind of writing is (despite popular notions to the contrary) quite un-characteristic of Donne. If, then, which is by no means certain, 'The Match' and 'The Unfortunate Lover'[1] are early poems, they are not like Donne, and Marvell did not begin as a disciple of Donne. It would be more possible to maintain that he began as a disciple of Crashaw and of those neo-Latin epigrammatists whom Crashaw often imitated.

Consider for a moment the poem 'Eyes and Tears'. It was almost certainly suggested by Crashaw's 'The Weeper', and the fourteen stanzas into which its fifty-six octosyllabic couplets are divided are as loosely connected and as transposable as those of Crashaw's poem, each of them developing, more cerebrally and definingly and less pictorially than Crashaw, some ingenious metaphor or simile to express the superiority of tears to any other terrestrial sight and of sorrow to any other human emotion: laughter turns to tears; the sun, after distilling the world all day, is left with nothing but moisture, which he rains back in pity; stars appear beautiful only as the tears of light, and so on. The eighth stanza,

> So *Magdalen*, in Tears more wise
> Dissolv'd those captivating Eyes,
> Whose liquid Chaines could flowing meet
> To fetter her Redeemers feet,

might almost be regarded as a complimentary allusion to Crashaw's weeping Magdalene, and at the end of his poem Marvell has added a translation of this stanza into Latin elegiacs which would not have been out of place in *Epigrammata Sacra*, the little collection of Latin epigrams on sacred subjects which Crashaw published in 1634. The poem 'Mourning', which, in nine octosyllabic quatrains, attempts to say, by means of ingenious similes and metaphors, what Chlora's tears are, recalls, more immediately than do any of Marvell's more individual and characteristic poems, various things in the enormous and enormously popular collections of Renaissance Latin epigrams. Étienne Pasquier (1529–1615), for example, has a poem entitled 'De Amœna Vidua', 'On Amœna,* having lost her husband', which contains the lines:

> His tamen in lachrimis nihil est ornatius illa,
>   Perpetuusque subest eius in ore nitor.
> Siccine, defunctum quae deperit orba maritum,
>   Semper aget viduo fœmina mæsta thoro?
> Quae flet culta, suum non luget, Amœna, maritum;
>   Quid facit ergo? alium quaerit Amœna virum.

('Yet, amid these tears, nothing could be handsomer than she, and there lurks a perpetual brightness in her face. Will she, who pines in her bereavement for

---

* Pasquier is using the adjective *amœna* ('lovely', 'charming') as a proper noun.

her dead husband, always be thus enacting the mourner on a widowed bed? One, Amœna, who weeps with elegance is not mourning her husband. What, then, is she doing? Amœna, she's looking for another.')[2]

It was at any rate somewhat in this manner, if not actually with these lines in his memory, that Marvell wrote:

> Her Eyes, confus'd and doubled ore
> With Tears suspended ere they flow,
> Seem bending upwards, to restore
> To Heaven, whence it came, their Woe,
>
> When, molding of the watry Sphears,
> Slow drops unty themselves away;
> As if she, with those precious Tears,
> Would strow the ground where *Strephon* lay.
>
> Yet some affirm, pretending Art,
> Her Eyes have so her Bosome drown'd,
> Only to soften near her Heart
> A place to fix another Wound;
>
> And, while vain Pomp does her restrain
> Within her solitary Bowr,
> She courts her self in am'rous Rain,
> Her self both *Danae* and the Showr.
>
> Nay others, bolder, hence esteem
> Joy now so much her Master grown,
> That whatsoever does but seem
> Like Grief, is from her Windows thrown;
>
> Nor that she payes, while she survives,
> To her dead Love this Tribute due,
> But casts abroad these Donatives★
> At the installing of a new . . .
>
> I yet my silent Judgment keep,
> Disputing not what they believe:
> But sure as oft as Women weep,
> It is to be suppos'd they grieve.[3]

★ 'A donation, gift, present; *esp.* one given formally or officially, as a largess or bounty' (O.E.D.).

The cynical notion of grief as something deliberately assumed by a woman in order to increase her attractiveness is the sort of thing we scarcely find in English poetry before about 1630. Such notions, such 'conceits', had for long been 'thought up' by continental Latin poets, searching for subjects on which they could write wittily and antithetically, but when the English poets at last 'got around' to them, they often, as Marvell has done here, treated them with far greater subtlety and elaboration; and it is this, I suppose, that has led us to acquiesce too readily in the application of the term 'metaphysical' to their development of such conceits. I hasten to assure you that I am not now proposing to argue about that term. Professor Robert Ellrodt of the Sorbonne has recently argued at length, and, on the whole, convincingly, that Donne and George Herbert are the only poets who are metaphysical; if, then, to write metaphysically means to write like Donne, Marvell here is not being metaphysical, for he is certainly not writing like Donne. Also entirely within the tradition of the neo-classical epigram, although – I think one can say it without fearing any accusation of insularity – with characteristically English pre-eminence, is that beautiful poem 'The Fair Singer'. Characteristically English, but less individually Marvellian, less unmistakably his own, than are most of Marvell's best poems; for, if none of his contemporaries wrote one quite so good as this, several of them wrote charming epigrammatic poems on similar themes, although, since it is easier to describe sights than sounds, they generally performed some variation on the theme of 'Seeing her Walking' (in the Snow, in the Rain, on the Grass, in the Park, &c.).

> I could have fled from One but singly fair:
> My dis-intangled Soul it self might save,
> Breaking the curled trammels of her hair.
> But how should I avoid to be her Slave,
> Whose subtile Art invisibly can wreath
> My Fetters of the very Air I breath?

It would not have been at all surprising had Marvell appended a translation of this exquisite second stanza into Latin elegiacs. One recalls (although their wit is of a different and less pleasing kind) the three Latin epigrams 'Ad Leonoram Romae canentem' which Milton, during his stay in Rome in the winter of 1638–9, addressed to the famous singer Leonora Baroni. To Donne such a topic would have seemed far too established and conventional, too little of his own choosing and devising, too much of an initial advantage, too much a topic on which some far lesser intellect might conceivably write a not wholly despicable poem. It was not for the likes of him to be just one more encomiast of some Leonora Baroni.

Is Marvell ever really like Donne? His 'Definition of Love',[4] although its last stanza, almost certainly the germ from which the whole poem sprang, was suggested by the third stanza of a not very good poem in Cowley's *The Mistress* entitled 'Impossibilities' – his 'Definition of Love' is, as many readers must have felt, more like Donne's 'A Valediction: forbidding mourning' than perhaps any other single seventeenth-century poem is like any one of Donne's *Songs and Sonets*: 'like', not as a deliberate and inferior imitation, as are so many of the poems in Cowley's *Mistress*, but like with the likeness of a peer. Certainly, without the example of Donne's 'Valediction' I doubt whether Marvell's poem could have been what it is. In what might be called (though I do not much like the phrase) its concrete intellectuality, the way in which it intellectualizes feeling or sensation into conceptions, into more or less abstract ideas, which still retain the vividness of perceptions, the style of Marvell's poem strikingly resembles Donne's; and yet, below the surface, is there not a fundamental difference? Let us place three stanzas from each poem side by side.

> Dull sublunary lovers love
> (Whose soule is sense) cannot admit
> Absence, because it doth remove
> Those things which elemented it.
>
> But we by a love, so much refin'd,
> That our selves know not what it is,
> Inter-assured of the mind,
> Care lesse, eyes, lips, and hands to misse.
>
> Our two soules therefore, which are one,
> Though I must goe, endure not yet
> A breach, but an expansion,
> Like gold to ayery thinnesse beate.

Donne, as in nearly all the more serious of the *Songs and Sonets*, is here analysing his immediate experience of a particular situation, real or

imagined, and developing the paradox that for true lovers absence is
not incompatible with presence. Now listen to Marvell:

> For Fate with jealous Eyes does see
> Two perfect Loves; nor lets them close:
> Their union would her ruine be,
> And her Tyrannick pow'r depose.
>
> And therefore her Decrees of Steel
> Us as the distant Poles have plac'd,
> (Though Loves whole World on us doth wheel)
> Not by themselves to be embrac'd,
>
> Unless the giddy Heaven fall,
> And Earth some new Convulsion tear;
> And, us to joyn, the World should all
> Be cramp'd into a *Planisphere*.*

Marvell is not starting from the immediate experience of a particular
situation, is not really being analytic and psychological and paradoxical
like Donne, but is simply performing, with characteristically seventeenth-century intellectuality, ingenuity, hyperbole, and antithesis, an
elaborate series of variations on the ancient theme of star-crossed
lovers. While Donne, not merely in the stanzas I quoted but throughout his poem, is developing an argument ('Even though physically
parted, we can remain spiritually united'), Marvell is simply saying over
and over again, in various ingenious ways, 'we can never meet'. He
is not really, like Donne, being paradoxical: what at first sight looks like
paradox appears, when we examine it more closely, to be merely
antithesis:

> Their union would her ruine be,
> And her Tyrannick pow'r depose.

And that characteristically exhilarating piece of semi-burlesque hyperbole, that the poles-apart lovers could only be joined if the world were
'cramp'd into a *Planisphere*' – what is it but our old friend the catalogue

---

* A map or chart formed by the projection of a sphere, or part of one, on a plane.
O.E.D. quotes from Thomas Blundeville's *Exercises* (1594): 'Astrolabe . . . is called of
some a Planispheare, because it is both flat and round, representing the Globe or Spheare,
having both his Poles clapt flat together.'

of impossibilities, ἀδύνατα ('till oaks sweat honey', 'till fish scale the mountains', &c.), so familiar in Greek and Roman poetry, brought up to date? This is one of the great differences between Donne and Marvell: while Donne, one might almost say, devised entirely new ways of saying entirely new things, Marvell assimilated, recombined, and perfected from his contemporaries various new ways of saying old ones.

In what, after the Cromwell ode, is perhaps Marvell's finest single poem, 'To his Coy Mistress', it can be shown that throughout he is doing very old and traditional things in a new way, and that he is only being very superficially like Donne. The poem is indeed, like many of Donne's and unlike 'The Definition of Love', a continuous argument, and even a more rigidly syllogistic argument than I think we shall find in any of the more serious of the *Songs and Sonets*, where Donne is usually concerned with analysis rather than with demonstration.

> If we had infinite time, I should be happy to court you at leisure;
>   But our life lasts only for a moment:
> Therefore, in order to live, we must seize the moment as it flies.

It is only, I think, in such fundamentally unserious poems as 'The Will' that we shall find Donne being as neatly syllogistic as this. Where this poem most resembles Donne, and is perhaps more fundamentally indebted to his example than any other of Marvell's poems, is in its essentially dramatic tone (more dramatic than in any other of Marvell's poems), in the way in which it makes us feel that we are overhearing one of the speakers in a dialogue. But, before proceeding, let us make sure that we have the poem vividly in our minds:

> Had we but World enough, and Time,
> This coyness Lady were no crime.
> We would sit down, and think which way
> To walk, and pass our long Loves Day.
> Thou by the *Indian Ganges* side
> Should'st Rubies find: I by the Tide
> Of *Humber* would complain. I would
> Love you ten years before the Flood:
> And you should if you please refuse
> Till the Conversion of the *Jews*.
> My vegetable Love should grow
> Vaster than Empires, and more slow.

An hundred years should go to praise
Thine Eyes, and on thy Forehead Gaze.
Two hundred to adore each Breast:
But thirty thousand to the rest.
An Age at least to every part,
And the last Age should show your Heart.
For Lady you deserve this State;
Nor would I love at lower rate.
    But at my back I alwaies hear
Times winged Charriot hurrying near:
And yonder all before us lye
Desarts of vast Eternity.
Thy Beauty shall no more be found;
Nor, in thy marble Vault, shall sound
My ecchoing Song: then Worms shall try
That long preserv'd Virginity:
And your quaint Honour turn to dust;
And into ashes all my Lust.
The Grave's a fine and private place,
But none I think do there embrace.
    Now therefore –

and Marvell reaches the conclusion of his semi-syllogistic argument, and, after some lines which are poetically rather below the general level of his poem, magnificently concludes:

Let us roll all our Strength, and all
Our sweetness, up into one Ball:
And tear our Pleasures with rough strife,
Thorough the Iron gates of Life.
Thus, though we cannot make our Sun
Stand still, yet we will make him run.

The tempo, *allegro molto* at least, is much faster than that of any of the more serious of Donne's *Songs and Sonets*, and, both in its speed, its mock-serious argument and its witty hyperbole, the poem might seem to have some affinity with Donne's tone and manner in some of his more exuberant elegies. The hyperbole, though – often, like that in 'A Definition of Love', approaching burlesque – is not, as I shall try to show later, really like Donne's, and the argument, although I have called it 'mock-serious', is really more serious, less paradoxical, than the sort of argument Donne conducts in the Elegies. It is also, I think, an argument which Donne would have regarded as too traditional and literary – the argument of Catullus'

> Vivamus, mea Lesbia, atque amemus . . .
> Soles occidere et redire possunt:
> nobis cum semel occidit brevis lux,
> nox est perpetua una dormienda,

which Ben Jonson so delightfully paraphrased as:

> Come my CELIA, let us proue,
> While we may, the sports of loue;
> Time will not be ours for euer:
> He, at length, our good will seuer.
>
> Spend not then his guifts in vaine.
> Sunnes, that set, may rise againe:
> But if once we loose this light,
> 'Tis, with vs, perpetuall night.

On this ancient theme Marvell has executed a series of brilliant seventeenth-century variations, which were partly suggested to him by the last stanza of a poem in Cowley's *The Mistress* entitled 'My Dyet', a stanza from which Marvell has borrowed and made unforgettable the phrase 'vast Eternity':[5]

> On 'a *Sigh* of Pity I a year can live,
>   One *Tear* will keep me twenty 'at least,
>   Fifty a gentle *Look* will give:
> An hundred years on one *kind word* I'll feast:
>   A thousand more will added be,
> If you an *Inclination* have for me;
> And all beyond is vast *Eternitie*.

Cowley was by no means the first to introduce arithmetic into love-poetry, but he has here exploited its possibilities in a way that seems to be original. The earliest of these arithmetical amorists, so far as I know, was an anonymous Alexandrian imitator of Anacreon, who, anticipating Leporello's catalogue of his master's conquests in Mozart's *Don Giovanni*, wrote a poem which begins: 'If you can count the leaves of all trees and the waves of the whole ocean, then I will make you sole reckoner of my loves. First set down twenty from Athens and add to them fifteen. Then set down whole chains of loves from Corinth, for it is in Achaea, where women are beautiful.'[6] Catullus, at the conclusion of 'Vivamus mea Lesbia', seems to have been the first poet to write arithmetically of kisses:

> Da mi basia mille, deinde centum,
> dein mille altera, dein secunda centum –

in Ben Jonson's paraphrase:

> Kisse againe: no creature comes.
> Kisse, and score up wealthy summes
> On my lips, thus hardly sundred,
> While you breath. First giue a hundred,
> Then a thousand, then another
> Hundred, then vnto the tother
> Adde a thousand, and so more:
> Till you equall with the store,
> All the grasse that *Rumney* yields
> Or the sands in *Chelsey* fields,
> Or the drops in siluer *Thames*,
> Or the starres, that guild his streames.

Like Johannes Secundus[7] before him, the French Renaissance Latin poet Étienne Pasquier, whom I have already quoted on the subject of a lovely widow, combined, in a poem 'Ad Sabinam', this osculatory arithmetic, or arithmetical osculation, with one of the most popular themes of classical and Renaissance love-poetry, the catalogue of a mistress's charms, declaring that he would print a thousand kisses on every part of Sabina's body:

> Quid reniteris? obstinatiora
> Carpo basia mille singulatim.
> Labris millia, millia en ocellis,
> Genis millia, millia en papillis,
> Obsignabo, licet puella nolit.[8]

('Why do you resist? I snatch my kisses all the more resolutely, a thousand at a time. Thousands on lips, thousands on eyes, thousands on cheeks, thousands on breasts I will implant – unwilling though the girl may be.')

Throughout the first twenty lines of his poem Marvell is making a brilliantly original use of the time-measuring arithmetic in that stanza of Cowley's from which he borrowed the phrase 'vast Eternity'. In the passage beginning

> An hundred years should go to praise
> Thine Eyes, and on thy Forehead Gaze,

he has applied it to that traditional and popular topic, the catalogue of a mistress's charms – a novel combination, I think, although it may have been suggested to him by Pasquier's combination of that traditional catalogue with the osculatory arithmetic of Catullus. In the exuberant hyperbole and antithesis of his opening lines, declaring that, had they but world enough and time, he would be willing to court her and be refused by her from ten years before the Flood until the conversion of the Jews, Marvell is not only being original, but writing in a manner in which no poets except those of the English seventeenth century ever wrote. When ancient poets handled the topics of *carpe diem* and *carpe florem*, when they pointed to the contrast between the returning anise and parsley, the returning seasons, the returning sun and moon and the unreturning lives of men, or when they exhorted some unresponsive girl or boy to learn a lesson from the withering and neglected rose, they nearly always wrote with an undiluted pathos and seriousness and even solemnity; or, if any trace of a smile was there, it was a sad one. And the Renaissance Italian and French poets, when they handled these topics, nearly always preserved a similar tone. It was only certain English poets of the earlier seventeenth century who expanded and varied these and other traditional topics with the witty, elaborate, and sometimes positively hilarious ingenuity of Marvell in this poem.

This does not mean that Marvell's poem is, in comparison, slight or unserious or superficial, for in its central section it sounds notes as deep as those of any ancient poetry on the topics of *carpe diem* and *carpe florem*.

> But at my back I alwaies hear
> Times winged Charriot hurrying near:
> And yonder all before us lye
> Desarts of vast Eternity.
> Thy Beauty shall no more be found;
> Nor, in thy marble Vault, shall sound

My ecchoing Song: then Worms shall try
That long preserv'd Virginity:
And your quaint Honour turn to dust;
And into ashes all my Lust.
The Grave's a fine and private place,
But none I think do there embrace.

'Your quaint Honour': that indeed is a characteristically post-classical conception, with a faint echo of the *Roman de la Rose* and a much stronger one of a famous chorus in Tasso's pastoral drama *Aminta*, celebrating that *bel età del oro* when *il gigante Onor* was unknown. But behind the rest of this passage lies, I feel almost sure, either directly or indirectly (for it was imitated by several Renaissance poets, both Latin and vernacular), something much more ancient: an epigram by Asclepiades in the Greek Anthology (v 85):

> Φείδη παρθενίης· καὶ τὶ πλέον; οὐ γὰρ ἐς Ἅδην
> ἐλθοῦσ' εὑρήσεις τὸν φιλέοντα, κόρη.
> ἐν ζωοῖσι τὰ τερπνὰ τὰ Κύπριδος· ἐν δ' Ἀχέροντι
> ὀστέα καὶ σποδιή, παρθένε, κεισόμεθα.

Hoarding your maidenhood – and why? For not when to Hades
 You've gone down shall you find, maiden, the lover you lack.
Only among the alive are the joys of Cypris, and only,
 Maiden, as bones and dust shall we in Acheron lie.

Here, as so often, out of something old Marvell has made something entirely new – or, what amounts to the same thing, something that gives impression of being entirely new.

> ἐν δ' Ἀχέροντι
> ὀστέα καὶ σποδιή, παρθένε, κεισόμεθα

The Grave's a fine and private place,
But none I think do there embrace:

had he not known that epigram of Asclepiades, I doubt whether Marvell would, or perhaps could, have written those lines; and yet their irony, their concentration, their colloquial vigour are absolutely Marvellian and absolutely seventeenth-century: they could have been written at no other period, and probably by no other poet. How pale and thin and unmemorable in comparison (to mention two of the most famous poets of the preceding century) is Johannes Secundus's imitation of this epigram in one of his Elegies (I v) and Ronsard's imitation of Secundus's imitation in his 'Ode à sa maîtresse'![9] While Marvell remains absolutely contemporary, Ronsard brings in Pluto and Charon's skiff:

> Pour qui gardes-tu tes yeux,
> Et ton sein délicieux,
> Ta joue et ta bouche belle?
> En veux-tu baiser Pluton,
> Là-bas, après que Caron
> T'aura mise en sa nacelle?

While Ronsard's lines are no more than an agreeable example of neo-classic imitation, such as any other member of the Pléiade could have produced, what Marvell has given us is not so much an imitation as a transmutation. And, indeed, his whole poem is a superb example of what I meant when I said that his poetry, although in the highest degree original, would have been impossible without the numerous literary sources from which he derived inspiration, stimulation, and suggestion. A stanza of Cowley's, a poem of Catullus, a Greek epigram, possibly a neo-Latin one – we can see how they all played an essential part in the genesis of Marvell's poem, and yet, at the same time, we can also see that he has transmuted them into something unmistakably his own. This is indeed originality, but it is a different kind of originality from that which Donne wanted to achieve.

Nor is it only in what, comparatively speaking, may be called its literariness and traditionality that Marvell's manner in this poem differs from Donne's.

> I would
> Love you ten years before the Flood:
> And you should if you please refuse
> Till the Conversion of the *Jews*.
> My vegetable Love should grow
> Vaster than Empires, and more slow.

Here we have not merely what seems to be an entirely original use of the well-established topic, or trope, of amatory arithmetic; we have also, as in 'The Definition of Love', our old classical friend, the catalogue of impossibilities, ἀδύνατα, brought up to date. But the manner in which it is brought up to date is not, I think, a manner which Marvell

learnt from Donne. Donne, it is true, excelled in witty hyperbole, but
these lines are not merely hyperbolical, they are almost burlesque – or,
at any rate, they have a touch of that burlesque extravagance and hilar-
ity which Marvell, I am convinced, learnt from that enormously
popular contemporary poet John Cleveland and practised extensively
in the Billborough and Appleton House poems and even, to some
extent, in 'The Garden' and the 'Dialogue between the Soul and Body'.
Consider, for example, the third stanza of Cleveland's 'To the State of
Love; or, the Senses' Festival', first printed in the 1651 edition of his
poems:

> My sight took say,* but (thank my charms!)
> I now impale her in my arms;
> (Love's compasses confining you,
> Good angels, to a circle too.)
> Is not the universe strait-laced
> When I can clasp it in the waist?
> My amorous folds about thee hurled,
> Like Drake I girdle in the world;[10]
> I hoop the firmament, and make
> This, my embrace, the zodiac.
>   How would thy centre take my sense
>   When admiration doth commence
>   At the extreme circumference?

It was Cleveland too, who, in his poem 'Upon Phillis Walking in a
Morning before Sun-rising', consummated, in a manner which inspired
many passages in Marvell's 'Appleton House', a characteristic seventeenth-century development of what, since it occurs in pastorals of
Theocritus and Virgil, I have been accustomed to call the 'pastoral
hyperbole', and which in those two poets amounted to little more than
saying that all things flourished in the presence of the beloved and
withered at her (or his) departure. It seems likely that the attention of
our seventeenth-century poets was first directed to the possibilities of
witty elaboration in this topic by that enormously popular poem of
Strode's 'On Chloris walking in the Snow', itself inspired by a poem of
Tasso's,[11] in whose *Rime* there are many elegant variations on this
topic, most of them rather pale and anaemic in comparison with

---

* Made trial: see *O.E.D.*, *say*, sb.[2] (an aphetic form of *assay*), sense 6, 'a trial of food by
taste or smell'. *O.E.D.* quotes Cooper, *Thesaurus* (1565) '*Degusto* . . . to taste: to take a
little saye.'

those of our own poets.[12] Even after the topic had been so often
handled as to excite Suckling to something like parody,[13] Waller seems
to have given a new lease of life to it with one of his Sacharissa poems,
'At Penshurst',[14] first printed in the 1645 edition of his *Poems*, a poem
from which I think it can be shown that both Cleveland and Marvell
took hints. But while Waller and his predecessors, though bolder and
more vigorous than Tasso, had still kept their personifications within
more or less decorous and classical bounds, Cleveland in this poem,
printed in his first volume of 1647, lets himself go with a riotous and
hilarious extravagance that approaches burlesque.

> The sluggish morn as yet undressed,
> My Phillis brake from out her East,
> As if she'd made a match to run
> With Venus, usher to the sun.
> The trees, like yeomen of her guard,
> Serving more for pomp than ward,
> Ranked on each side, with loyal duty
> Weave branches to enclose her beauty.
> The plants, whose luxury was lopped,
> Or age with crutches underpropped,
> Whose wooden carcasses are grown
> To be but coffins of their own,
> Revive, and at her general dole
> Each receives his ancient soul.
> The winged choiristers began
> To chirp their matins, and the fan
> Of whistling winds like organs played,
> Until their voluntaries made
> The wakened East in odours rise
> To be her morning sacrifice.

I have only time to place side by side with this a few lines from that
passage towards the end of 'Appleton House' where Nature pays her
respect to the 'young Maria', but they should be sufficient to demonstrate that this way of writing, which we have come to regard as so
characteristic of him, was suggested to Marvell by Cleveland:

> See how loose Nature, in respect,
> To her, it self doth recollect;
> And every thing so whisht and fine,
> Starts forth with to its *Bonne Mine*.

The *Sun* himself, of *Her* aware,
Seems to descend with greater Care;
And lest *She* see him go to Bed,
In blushing Clouds conceales his Head.

(st. LXXXIII)

'Tis *She* that to these Gardens gave
That wondrous Beauty which they have.

(st. LXXXVII)

Therefore what first *She* on them spent,
They gratefully again present.
The Meadow Carpets where to tread;
The Garden Flow'rs to Crown *Her* Head;
And for a Glass the limpid Brook,
Where *She* may all *her* Beautyes look;
But, since *She* would not have them seen,
The Wood about *her* draws a Skreen.

(st. LXXXVIII)

My time is up, and I have been able to do little more than scratch the surface of this fascinating subject. Except in my incidental allusion to what I have called the 'pastoral hyperbole', I have said nothing about Marvell's happy acquiescence in various characteristic seventeenth-century developments of the pastoral tradition and of what, including therein both Marlowe's 'Passionate Shepherd' and Milton's 'L'Allegro' and 'Il Penseroso', might be called the 'catalogue of delights'. While Donne seems to have scornfully rejected all topics and subjects that might tempt readers to admire him for anything but his sheer poetic skill, anything, such as descriptions of things obviously beautiful or attractive, which stimulated what modern critics have called the 'stock response', Marvell's originality was of a much more tolerant and un-ambitious kind. He was ready, one might almost say, to accept, to exploit, and to recombine, to Marvellize and seventeenth-centurify, anything that had ever made poetry enjoyable.

SOURCE: *Proceedings of the British Academy*, XLVII (1961).

NOTES

1. The first two lines of the last stanza of this poem,

> This is the only *Banneret*
> That ever Love created yet,

were certainly suggested, as H. M. Margoliouth indicated in a note, by two lines in the poem 'Dialogue – Lucasta, Alexis' in Lovelace's *Lucasta* (1649) a volume to which Marvell contributed some commendatory verses:

> Love nee're his Standard when his Hoste he sets,
> Creates alone fresh-bleeding Bannerets.

Lucasta was licensed on 4 February 1647–8, and if lines 21–32 of Marvell's commendatory verses are taken to mean that the book had not yet been licensed, we may assume that Marvell wrote them at some time *before* that date and *after* his return from his travels in 1646 (see *Poems and Letters*, ed. Margoliouth, 1 216). Is it, though, absolutely necessary to suppose that Marvell had read all the poems in the book before he commended it?

2. *Deliciae C[entum] Poetarum Gallorum*, ed. R. Gherus (1609) II 875.

3. I have omitted the first and eighth stanzas and have made various necessary changes in the punctuation.

4. In what I have to say about this poem I am greatly indebted to some remarks by Professor R. Ellrodt, *Les Poètes métaphysiques anglais*, part I, vol. II (1960) 123 and 148.

5. Cowley, too, evidently thought the phrase a good one, for he used it again in the penultimate line of his ode 'Sitting and Drinking in the Chair made out of the Reliques of Sir *Francis Drake's* Ship', first printed in *Verses lately written upon several Occasions* (1663):

> The streits of time too narrow are for thee,
> Launch forth into an indiscovered Sea,
> And steer the endless course of vast Eternity,
> Take for thy Sail this Verse, and for thy Pilot Me.

6. *Anacreontea* 14, Εἰ φύλλα πάντα δένδρων.

7. *Basia*, VII.

8. *Deliciae C[entum] Poetarum Gallorum*, ed. R. Gherus (1609) II 1000.

9. In his *Poèmes* of 1569 Ronsard published an undistinguished translation of this epigram of Asclepiades, beginning 'Dame au gros cœur, pourquoy t'espargnes-tu?,' and a not much more distinguished expansion of it into a sonnet, beginning 'Douce beauté, meudrière de ma vie'.

10. In Geoffrey Whitney's *A Choice of Emblemes and other Devises* (1586) there is an emblem – reproduced in Rosemary Freeman's *English Emblem Books* (1948) p. 56 – representing a freely suspended globe, on the top of which is poised Drake's ship. In the top left-hand corner the hand of Providence, outstretched from a cloud, grasps one end of a girdle which hangs in a loop around the suspended globe, its other end being attached to Drake's ship.

11. *Ritorno di Madonna in tempo di neve* ('La terra si copria d'orrido velo'), in *Rime*, ed. Solerti, II 61. Tasso also has a similar poem entitled *Vista impedita della neve* ('Negro era intorno, e in bianche falde il cielo'), op. cit. 331, together with many less specialized developments of the 'pastoral hyperbole', among the more notable of which are 'Or che riede Madonna al bel soggiorno' (p. 232) and 'Or che l'aura mia dolce altrove spira' (p. 258). See also pp. 216, 222, 224, &c.

12. Strode's poem was first printed in 1632, in W. Porter's *Madrigals and Airs*. Among the 'Excellent Poems ... by other Gentlemen' in Benson's edition of Shakespeare's *Poems* (1640) are 'Lavinia Walking in a frosty Morning' (L6ᵛ) and 'Vpon a Gentlewoman

walking on the Grasse' (M2v). In the same year appeared as no. 126 in the first edition of *Wits Recreations* (Camden Hotten reprint of *Musarum Deliciae*, &c., II 17) a poem, perhaps more obviously inspired by Strode's, beginning 'I saw faire *Flora* take the aire'.

13. In the dialogue-poem between himself ('J. S.') and Carew ('T. C.') 'Vpon my Lady Carliles walking in Hampton-Court garden', which must have been written before Carew's death in 1640 and Suckling's in 1642.

14. 'Had Sacharissa (1645: 'Dorothea') lived when mortals made', in *Poems*, ed. Thorn-Drury (Muses Library, 1891) I 46. Waller seems to have begun paying his addresses to Lady Dorothy Sidney ('Sacharissa') towards the end of 1635, and presumably ceased to address poems to her after her marriage in 1639.

MAREN-SOFIE RØSTVIG

'Upon Appleton House' (1962)

ALTHOUGH little is known of Marvell's intellectual interests, a clue is afforded by his association with Thomas, Lord Fairfax – a man whose intellectual bias is indicated by his attempt to translate the voluminous French commentary on the Hermetic dialogues published by François de Foix in 1579. Today the term 'Hermetic' is only too likely to conjure up associations with gnostic thought, perhaps even with the occult, but the commentary that engaged the attention of Marvell's noble employer displays an attitude typical of the Renaissance: Hermes is presented as an 'ancient theologian' who transmits the same divine revelation that was given to Moses. This was believed to be true of Plato as well, and this syncretistic attitude can be traced back to the early Fathers of our Church; it did not originate with the Renaissance Neoplatonists, although these certainly infused new life into the tradition.

The syncretistic attitude becomes less incomprehensible on considering that Plato and Hermes were made to agree with Moses by submitting their writings to a free allegorical interpretation, a method sanctioned by exegetical practice throughout the centuries that separate Marvell from Augustine. The medieval fourfold method of interpreting the Bible[1] survived into the seventeenth century, notably in the works of that famous Roman Catholic theologian Cornelius à Lapide, but the Protestant revolution by no means entailed a complete break with the tradition of tracing a spiritual level of meaning in the Bible. Even Protestants perforce had to believe in the typological significance of the major Old Testament events, since this was a point of view expressed by St Paul. Both Protestants and Roman Catholics therefore habitually searched for a deeper meaning in the text of the Bible, so that it would have seemed eminently reasonable to submit Moses as well as Hermes and Plato to an allegorical technique of interpretation. The purpose of this exercise was to prove the validity of the Biblical story of creation, the Fall, and the scheme of redemption by showing its virtual omnipresence. Since Hermes, then, was supposed to present *Mosaic mysteries*, Marvell's occasional references to Hermetic concepts – usually in a Christian context – must not be taken as evidence of unusual learning or of unorthodox beliefs. To the owner of Appleton House they would have been a compliment to his theological interests as well as an indication of a profound Christian piety on the part of the poet. Even the most radically Hermetic of Renaissance syncretists – Giordano Bruno, for example, or Robert Fludd – focused squarely on the issue of regeneration, and this is also the concern of Andrew Marvell in his longest poem, 'Upon Appleton House'. Rambling and poorly organised though it may seem on a first reading, this poem on Fairfax's estate is grounded on a single theological or religious concept, to wit the contrast between innocence and corruption. The quest for a moral and spiritual regeneration is pursued through regional history (the history of the religious establishment at Nun Appleton), the history of England (in the allusions to the civil war), and universal history (the allusions to the major events of the Old and the New Testament).[2]

The Biblical allusions are worked into the description of the landscape, a technique employed by Edward Benlowes in his religious epic of the soul, *Theophila* (1652). Since Benlowes finished his poem before Marvell entered the employ of the retired Lord General, the many points of similarity between *Theophila* and 'Upon Appleton House' indicate that Marvell may have read this popular epic, which circulated widely in manuscript before it was printed. On viewing the landscape, both Benlowes and Marvell are reminded of the crossing of the Red Sea and the river Jordan, of the miraculous provision of manna and quails in the desert, of Christ's love sacrifice on the cross, and of the religious devotee's union with Christ in a holy death which murders sense. To this Marvell adds references to the building of the tower of Babel and to Noah and the Ark. Both Benlowes and Marvell can be said to juxtapose the two Books of divine revelation – the Book of God's Word and the Book of His Works; both 'texts' are submitted to a searching, multi-levelled technique of interpretation, as a result of which the same basic truths are made to emerge. Marvell's poem therefore possesses great semantic density. Behind the literal, surface meaning lie both political allegory and a deeper, more spiritual sense. The political allegory has been ably explained by Don Cameron Allen.[3] I shall therefore focus on the purely religious or philosophical aspects.

In the course of his exposition D. C. Allen takes notice of certain parts which may be interpreted typologically or anagogically,[4] but this type of insight symbol is not pursued systematically.

An excellent survey of the traditional interpretation of the main events of the Old Testament is given by Jean Daniélou, S. J., in his book *From Shadows to Reality: studies in the typology of the Fathers* (1960). I have also found Rosemond Tuve's *A Reading of George Herbert* (1952) very useful.[5] The following exposition of some main points in the typology of the Church Fathers is based on the former.

The basic principle of typology is found in the belief that human existence constitutes an imperfect order which prepares for and prefigures an order of perfection. This perfection is achieved when natural man turns into spiritual man. The achievement of this process is the purpose of all the events in the Old Testament and the New. God's scheme for the redemption of the fallen Adam stands reflected in the four fundamental types of the Old Testament: the ark of Noah, the crossing of the Red Sea, the Mosaic Law, and the entry into the promised land. In the words of Jean Daniélou: 'All the outstanding persons and leading events of Scripture are both stages and rough outlines to prepare and prefigure the mystery which is one day to be fulfilled in Christ.'[6] Thus paradise lies in the future as well as in the past; the New Paradise was realised with the coming of Christ, and each Christian becomes a New Adam in his turn through Holy Baptism, 'which is thus revealed as a new creation and a return to Paradise'. Paradise may therefore be realised in the Christian life, as Marvell suggests in his homage to Fairfax, whose garden is a literal Paradise. The ark of Noah is particularly rich in typological significance. The deliverance of Noah and the deliverance of Moses are the two main works of God in the Old Testament, and they are often associated together. Noah and Moses are types of Christ, their actions foreshadowing his. With the Flood is associated the sea beast Leviathan, a type of wickedness, just as in the crossing of the Red Sea Pharaoh and his horsemen represent the devil, or sin. Both are overcome by Christ. The Flood is

> the figure of Christ's triumph over the sea dragon through his descent into Hell: he is the true Noah who has experienced the swelling of the waters of death, and has been delivered by God to be the beginning of a new world; it represents also Baptism wherein the Christian is buried with Christ in the water of death through the symbol of the baptismal waters, figuratively

undergoing the punishment due to sin and being free with Christ and henceforth belonging to the new creation . . .

Baptism therefore is a spiritual version of Noah's deliverance from the
Flood, and also of the deliverance wrought by God through Moses
when he commanded the Red Sea to divide.

A further turn of the interpretative screw is achieved on considering
the interpretation submitted by Philo, whose influence on Origen and
St Ambrose was profound. Philo interpreted Genesis as a Platonic
myth. Thus the creation of Adam represented the creation of mind,
while the creation of Eve represented the creation of sensation, or the
life of the senses. As St Ambrose commented: 'Very rightly is mind
represented by the symbol of man, and feeling by that of woman.'
Marvell's rejection of women in 'The Garden' therefore signifies a
rejection of mere sense; at this point the teachings of Hermes and the
Church Fathers coincide. Similarly Philo interprets the rescue of the
Israelites from the Egyptians as a transition from a state dominated by
the body (the Egyptians representing the bodily passions) to a state
dominated by mind. As we shall soon see, Marvell, too, associates
Pharaoh's horsemen with the physical passions, from which he seeks,
and finds, deliverance in his 'yet green, yet growing Ark'. In this
manner the journey through the desert becomes a type of the soul's
passage through life. The passions must be overcome, and this is
achieved through the progressive enlightenment afforded by the Logos.
Both Benlowes and Marvell are intent on depicting such a spiritual
journey. Both refer to the act of retirement as a retreat into a fortress,
from which the soul wages a pious war against the world, the flesh, and
the devil. And, in so doing, both refer to the five senses as the Cinque
Ports over which the strictest guard must be kept.[7]

We can now turn to the poem itself. As already stated, its main
motif is the quest for redemption and innocence regained, a quest
closely associated with the fortunes of the Fairfax family. Thus the
rescue of the 'Virgin *Thwates*' from her gloomy nunnery was a rescue
from a state dominated by Evil ('I know what Fruit their Gardens
yield, / When they it think by Night conceal'd') to the holy state of
matrimony. In the same manner the retirement of the Lord General
was prompted by the wish to avoid the depravity inherent in the world;
it represents the triumph of conscience over ambition, of mind over
the world of sense. Fairfax's environment reflects the same contrast

between innocence and corruption. Over against his modest house ← BO
appears 'proud *Cawood Castle*' as a visual manifestation of the ambition
of its '*Prelate* great' (stanza XLVI). The beauty and sweetness of his garden makes the poet bewail that 'luckless Apple' which made man mortal
and laid waste 'The Garden of the World' (stanza XLI). The corruption
which thus gained entrance into man, Nature, and the body politic is
allegorised in the stanzas describing how the '*Traitor-worm*' destroys
the oak so that it may be felled by the lightest stroke. The cruel
massacres of the mowers (types of soldiers engaged in civil war)
provide a graphic illustration of that state of war which marks the
postlapsarian state.[8] The chaotic state of the world is again strongly
stressed in the concluding stanzas which denounce it as 'a rude heap
together hurl'd; / All negligently overthrown, / Gulfes, Deserts, Precipices, Stone'. The lesser world of the garden contains the same elements, but in 'more decent Order tame'.

The forces of innocence form a strong contrast to the forces of evil.
In attacking the Nunnery and exposing the '*Wooden Saints*' and
'*Relicks False*' the first Fairfax becomes a type of the Protestant hero,
'whose Offspring fierce / Shall fight through all the *Universe*'. On a
smaller scale he imitates the redemptive action of Christ by rescuing
a human soul from corruption to sanctity. A second strong contrast is
that between the cruel massacres of the mowers and the spiritual warfare conducted by the Lord General against the world and his own five
senses. The concluding section focuses on Mary Fairfax as the symbol of
innocence. She is seen as the archetype of that beauty and innocence
which marks the garden of Nun Appleton. By virtue of the sanctity of
its residents, Fairfax's estate becomes '*Heaven's Center, Nature's Lap,* /
And Paradice's only Map'. The internal and external worlds are inter-
dependent in the familiar manner of the Renaissance. When redeemed
from vice, pride, and ambition, man bestows the same redemption
upon Nature, just as conversely the corruption of Adam and Eve once
had brought death and decay into the world.

Mary
Nature

Once it is seen that Marvell's poem is organised in this manner, its
unity becomes apparent. The historical episode concerning the abduc-
tion from the nunnery becomes relevant, and so does the political
allegory, and the various compliments to Fairfax and his daughter.
The individual, the Church, the body politic, and Nature must under-
go the same process of purgation. As in 'The Garden' the method
employed involves a contemplative retirement into rural scenes and a

focusing of all the powers of the mind on God. To the contemplating mind the chief events in the universal history of man yield up their inner, spiritual significance, at the same time that deeper insights are gained from a close study of the Book of God's Work.

After these preliminary remarks we can now examine the poem in more detail.

Stanzas I–IX describe Fairfax and his house. The building is a reflection of the man who lives in it, and accommodates itself to him, like a living organism. While the more extravagant buildings of the age reflect the vanity which once spurred on the builders of Babel (the 'first Builders' of line 24), Fairfax's house is composed 'Like Nature, orderly and near', thus reflecting a more 'sober Age and Mind'. The fact that a man like Fairfax is content to live in 'dwarfish Confines' proves that 'Things greater are in less contained' (line 44). Indeed, so dwarfish is the house that it is compared to '*Romulus* his Bee-like Cell' (line 40). (While considering the 'body politic' of bees Benlowes had commented that 'Great souls' may be confined 'in small breasts' – *Theophila* XII 76.) Because of this disproportion between the outer structure and its inhabitant, the house 'scarce indures the *Master* great' (line 50), and sweats and swells to accommodate him. It takes but little effort to realise that the description forms a conscious analogue to the soul-body relationship. The body labours to support the heavy weight of the mind. The statement that 'the *Square* grows *Spherical*' (line 52) is a piece of literal description, since the great hall was topped by a dome, but the spiritual sense is the most important one. Both the house and man's body are mortal, temporal and imperfect and hence associated with that well-known symbol of the world, the square. Man's soul or mind, however, is divine, immortal and perfect and hence symbolised by the circle. These are the '*holy Mathematics*' that can turn a square into a circle.[9] One may in this manner trace no less than four levels of meaning: Marvell's description of the house conveys literal truth, moral truth (the importance of humility), allegorical truth (the house is but an inn, a temporary dwelling-place in the long pilgrimage of the soul), and ultimate truth (the house-master relationship is a type of the relationship between body and soul, time and eternity).

Stanzas XI–XXXV trace the progress of 'this Houses Fate'. It is a neat paradox that the nunnery stands for a corrupt worldliness, while, after the Protestant reform, it turns into a proper religious house: ''Twas no *Religious House* till now' (line 280). The nunnery was like an enchanted castle; the 'glad Youth' acts to break the evil spell, and so the 'Castle vanishes or rends' (line 270).

Fairfax's career clearly prompted the use of military terms employed in the subsequent description of Fairfax himself and his estate (stanzas XXXVI–XLVI). However, these terms were also surely intended to provoke associations with the traditional picture of the true Christian as a soldier armed with the weapons of his faith.[10] Fairfax's garden reflects his own innocence and piety, and thus forms a suitable setting, like the house. The very stars, flowers, and bees combine to form vigilant patrols to protect this New Paradise. The poet's complaint that man lost his 'Garden of the World' through the 'luckless Apple' carries the argument one step further. After the Fall, man did indeed turn into a soldier, but in a different sense, since war is a symptom of the fallen state. For this reason war and the implements of war have overgrown the innocent magazines and forts of Nature. Instead of flowers, man 'plants' ordnance (artillery)[11] and 'sows' powder. Therefore, what the world (and particularly England) needs more than anything else, is the cultivation of 'that Heaven-nursed Plant', conscience. Its flowers are eternal and shine in 'the Crowns of Saints'.

Stanza XLVII opens that long mid-section where the poet traces the universal history of man in the surrounding landscape. Can it be mere coincidence that this landscape possesses all the features subsequently attributed to the world in the last stanza but one, to wit 'Gulfes, Deserts, Precipices, Stone'? Thus Marvell discovers veritable gulfs in the 'abyss' of the 'unfathomable Grass'; when the mowers cross the field, they remind him of the Israelites in the desert; the green 'spires' of the grass resemble 'Precipices tall' from which giant grasshoppers squeak out their contempt for man, while the haystacks on the level meadow appear like rocks above a calm sea. The poetic vision seems to transform the landscape into a complete map of the world against which all major events in the history of man are acted out.

Marvell has already alluded to the Garden of Eden and the Fall, and to the tower of Babel. The giant grasshoppers of stanza XLVII may therefor be an allusion to that race of giants which peopled the earth between the expulsion from the garden and the Flood. If so, they represent forces of evil. A similar interpretation follows, if one associates the grasshoppers with the events narrated in Numbers 13 : 33 or Nahum 3 : 17, passages which provide useful clues to an understanding of the political allegory.[12] According to the former passage, spies sent by the

Israelites to investigate Canaan bring back false reports which cause the chosen people to lose confidence in God and in Moses. The spies allege that the Promised Land is peopled by giants, 'and we were in our own sight as grasshoppers, and so we were in their sight'. In theological expositions the seven hostile tribes of Canaan were taken to represent the Seven Deadly Sins. Just as Israel, after crossing the Red Sea, had to overcome these tribes in battle, the Christian, after Baptism, must rout the forces of evil. For the time being the giants seem the superior force, pouring out their contempt on men 'as we walk more low than them'. They cannot be overcome until after Baptism, i.e. after the crossing of the Red Sea. This event follows in stanza XLIX. It is possible that the reference to the 'green Sea' and to the 'yet green, yet growing Ark' in line 484 may bear a Hermetic connotation; if it does, then the meaning which it conveys is related to the Christian concept of baptism. Since the *benedicta viriditas* was supposed to represent the spiritual essence of the vegetable world, the crossing of the green sea could be taken to convey a penetration into the divine essence. If so, then Baptism must be defined as a transition into the sphere of the Deity, which is the purpose of the regenerative process as described by Hermes and his Renaissance commentators. A further Hermetic concept is encountered in stanza LXIII, where Marvell emphasises the darkness and closeness of the forest by stating: 'There the huge Bulk takes place, as ment / To thrust up a *Fifth Element.*' An exposition of this concept is given in *The Book of Quinte Essence*,[13] a manuscript treatise dating from 1460–70, professing to be a summary of 'the book of quintis essenciis in latyn, that hermys the prophete and kyng of Egipt, after the flood of Noe fadir of philosophris, had by reuelacioun of an aungel of god to him sende'. The effect of this fifth element or essence is to purify or preserve that which otherwise would have been subject to corruption, and in its working the heaven and the sun combine to influence man 'in as miche as it is possible in deedly nature'. When Marvell therefore retreats into the forest, 'this yet green, yet growing Ark', he enters as it were a Holy Temple penetrated by forces which preserve from corruption.

The retreat into the forest is an escape from the flood. On the political level the flood undoubtedly symbolises civil war, as suggested by D. C. Allen. On the spiritual level, it stands for the kind of confusion which existed in Chaos. Sea monsters were popularly supposed to usurp the dwellings of men at the time of the Deluge,[14] just as a serpent was believed to inhabit the primeval sea of Chaos. The Ark itself was given varying interpretations. It stood for the Church (the saving agency), or it was viewed as a type of the tomb of Christ. Christ stayed in the tomb, as Noah did in the Ark, to put an end to the deluge of foulness.[15] According to St Justin the mystery of man's salvation is implicit in the Flood. Noah once marked a new era in the history of man, thus fore-shadowing the new era brought by Christ. 'Now Christ . . . is become the head . . . of a new race, which has been regenerated by him through water, faith and wood, which embraces the mystery of the cross, as Noah, together with his family, was saved by the wood of the ark carried on the waters.'[16] Marvell's reference to Noah as the 'first Carpenter' may be an allusion to the typological significance of Noah as a type of Christ, the 'second carpenter'. Just as Noah constructed his Ark to serve as an instrument for the deliverance of mankind, Christ saved mankind through the agency of the wood of the cross.

Marvell's flood is caused by the river Denton, and in the Bible it is the Holy Ark of the Tabernacle which is associated with flooded rivers, since it was this holy vessel which, when carried in front of the Israel-ites, caused the river Jordan to dry out (Joshua 3 : 13). The river Denton, like the Jordan, was apt to overflow at harvest-time, and the Jordan was so flooded at the time of the crossing into Canaan. The statement that in the Ark 'all Creatures might have shares, / Although in Armies, not in Paires' can be interpreted on two levels. As applied to the Ark of Noah, the couplet suggests that vast numbers are capable of finding accommodation there. However, since the creatures taken aboard by Noah notoriously arrived in pairs, the negation seems curious. The paradox is explained if we apply the phrase, not to the Ark of Noah, but to the Ark of the Tabernacle as a symbol of God. It is also explained if we interpret the Ark of Noah as the typological symbol of Christ. In Platonic and Hermetic philosophy, God, as pure mind, contains within Himself the archetypes of all created things and of everything yet to be created. Hence 'all Creatures' are encompassed by the sphere of the divinity. The rejection of creatures 'in Paires' is most likely yet another reference to the Hermetic doctrine of the androgynous creation as one in which mind has complete control of matter. After the division into two sexes, man lost this complete com-mand and became mortal and subject to the reign of brute matter unless he succeeded in subjecting his body to his mind. Both 'The Garden' and 'Upon Appleton House' are, in effect, sermons on the necessity of liberating the mind, couched in language understood only by the initiated; the square must be transformed into a circle. If, then, it is the mortal aspect of creatures which is reflected by their living together in pairs, they shed their sexuality together with their mortality on entering the Ark, i.e. the sphere of Christ, or the divinity, which is pure mind.

The attribution, to the forest, of a Fifth Element, serves to stress the purity and immortality of the place. Its holy associations are further strengthened by the subsequent comparison, in stanza LXIV, between the forest and the Holy Temple. At this point Marvell again shares a poetical motif with Benlowes.[17] The trunks form 'Corinthean Porti-coes', the arching boughs the 'columnes of the Temple green', while the birds act as 'winged Quires' which 'echo about their tuned Fires'. Stanzas LXVIII–LXXI focus attention on the single tree. If the Holy Temple of the forest represents the Church, each individual tree would represent one member of this spiritual body. The 'inverted Tree' of line 568 recalls Plato, who compares man both to an inverted plant and an inverted tree. Thus the Phaedrus states that man is a tree 'whose nervie root Springs in his top'. And Timaeus, section 9, places 'the most sovereign form of soul in us' in 'the summit of our body'. This soul 'lifts us from earth towards our celestial affinity, like a plant whose roots are not in earth, but in the heavens. And this is most true, for it is to the heavens whence the soul first came to birth, that the divine part attaches the head or root of us and keeps the whole body upright.'

The manner in which Marvell, in stanzas LXXI–LXXVI, identifies him-self with his environment, merging his own identity with trees and birds, suggests the contemplative technique of Plotinus, according to which the advanced stages of contemplation are marked by an intimate union between the contemplator and the object of his contemplation.[18] A similar intimate union had marked the prelapsarian relationship between God and man, and man and the res creatae. The statement that the poet begins to understand the language of the birds therefore sug-gests that his contemplation is leading to a re-establishment of man's ancient innocence and of his effortless communion with all created things. According to Genesis 2 : 20 the first man had control over the animals, while Ezekiel 34 : 28 prophesies that in the Messianic era he will have such dominion again. This era will also be marked by com-plete harmony and peace (Isaiah 11 : 6). In other words, the effect of the Fall is annulled when the poet begins to speak in the language of the birds; the Messianic era is at hand. Marvell is in complete accordance with Biblical tradition when he proceeds to describe this new creation in terms of a new Paradise. Ezekiel describes the new Jerusalem in terms of a new Paradise, and so do the non-canonical Jewish apocalypses.[19] Christ is the New Adam, but so is each Christian. This New Adam is born through Holy Baptism (the entry into the Ark of Noah), which is, in fact, a return to Paradise and a new creation. The poet's communion with all created things is so intimate that he begins to grasp the occult significance of that which he reads in 'Natures mystick Book'. He reads all secrets of life in a 'light Mosaic'. The literal sense (that the light, falling through the branches and the leaves, forms a design in mosaic) should be supplemented by interpreting the phrase as a reference to 'the Light that Moses, also brooding in the wilderness, saw in the blazing bush'.[20] Mosaic may also be taken in a wider sense as referring to all accounts of the mysteries of creation. Thus Ficino refers to the Hermetic account of creation as Mosaica mysteria.

Stanzas LXXIV–LXXVIII form the central part of the poem. Marvell begins by depicting himself as a priest whose 'antick Cope' consists of oak leaves, caterpillars, and the 'familiar trails of ivy', which enclose him like a mistress. The breezes and the mossy banks similarly court the poet, offering soft beds and cooling air. Stanzas LXXIV–LXXV recall the fifth stanza of 'The Garden' and indubitably have the same background in Hermetic lore. The vegetable part of creation loves man for the sake of the image of God in man, and so man becomes a lover-priest, mediating between the res creatae and God.

Marvell's reference to 'Chaff' in stanza LXXV supports the theory that he is thinking of the Ark as a type of the Church. The image of the winnowing of chaff is one of Augustine's favourite metaphors for the Church; he uses it over and over again in his sermons on the Psalms. During this life the winnowing is done by the wind of trials and tribulations, but the process is necessarily incomplete; the final separation will occur only on the Last Day and so, until then, we must be content to suffer the presence of sinners as well as saints within the confines of the Ark of the Church. Marvell's wish that his head be winnowed from the chaff is therefore a clear expression of the desire to be saved rather than sentenced to eternal damnation.

Stanza LXXVI may refer to the apocalyptic horsemen, as suggested by D. C. Allen, but it seems to me to make better sense to associate the horsemen with Pharaoh and his hosts, in theological exposition the traditional symbol of the devil and his forces, or according to Plato and Philo, of the bodily desires. Exodus 14 refers so frequently to 'Pharaoh's horses, his chariots, and his horsemen' that the phrase is hammered home like a refrain. The poet, then, has 'incamp'd' his mind behind the trees (the symbol of the Ark and of spiritual baptism) so that he is as invulnerable in relation to 'the World' as the encamped Israelites were in relation to Pharaoh and his horsemen.[21] When attacked, the Israelites are rescued when Moses, lifting up his rod, divides the Red Sea. An allusion to this action also occurs in stanza LXXVIII, where the *trees* are said to *divide* before their Lord. The Lord in question is Fairfax, who is thus presented as a new Moses, leading a recalcitrant nation through the desert. It is in this lane, protected by the rod of Moses–Fairfax that Marvell wishes to remain fixed or staked down.

Stanzas LXXVII–LXXVIII employ phrases which suggest that the lover-priest turns into a sacrifice in imitation of the Passion of Christ. It has already been stated that Christ on the Cross was viewed as the New Adam, bringing about a return to a New Paradise, and that each Christian, through Baptism, similarly became a New Adam. St Paul's Epistle to the Romans, chapter 6, is the best possible commentary on stanzas LXXVII–LXXVIII, the gist of this chapter being that the old Adam must be crucified with Christ; 'we are buried with him by baptism into death', so that similarly 'we also should walk in newness of life'. I take stanza LXXVIII to mean that through baptism (i.e. by being placed in the lane which divides before its Lord) the poet, in the words of St Paul, is baptised 'into his [Christ's] death' so that his 'old man' is 'crucified with him, that the body of sin might be destroyed'. It will easily be seen how this spiritual baptism closely parallels that release of the mind from the passions of the body which forms the core of Platonic and Hermetic doctrines. Benlowes, too, describes Christ's entrance into man as a crucifixion of the old man and the birth of a totally new being. Thus he states that Christ 'binds when he embraceth us', he 'kills us into life'. That which dies on the cross are our carnal affections, and as soon as this has been achieved, 'the soul becomes a living sacrifice, holy and acceptable unto God'.[22] Stanza LXXVII reads like a paraphrase of Benlowes's statement: 'In the cords of love he leads us captives.' The woodbines and the vines are traditional symbols of love, the twining vine often symbolising the mystic wedding of the soul to Christ. Benlowes frequently refers to Christ as the vine, and he describes the mystic union in those sexual terms which derive from the accepted spiritual interpretation of *Canticles.* Thus he exclaims: 'Loving, I'm lov'd! While with my Spouse I twine!'[23]

Several points support the theory that the purpose of the sacrifice described in stanzas LXXVII–LXXVIII is to establish the reign of mind over body. The initial description of Fairfax and his house had stressed the view that the mind should command the body, that the mind should turn the square of the body into a circle, i.e. into that which is eternal and immortal. And in the stanza just preceding the symbolical crucifixion, Marvell had stressed how completely his *mind* has encamped itself behind the trees, and how securely he 'gauls' the horsemen of the world. My interpretation therefore depends not only upon the descriptive terms ('*Brambles,* chain me too', 'courteous *Briars* nail me through', and 'stake me down'), but upon the entire context. While 'stake me down' and 'tye my Chain' might be taken as simply suggesting that Marvell is comparing himself to an animal chained to a stake, I cannot see that 'nail me through' fits into such a context. Surely the briars are chosen for their resemblance to the crown of thorns? And when one considers the sequence of events leading up to this stanza – the reference to the first Garden of Eden, the tower of Babel, the Fall, the race of giants begotten by devils on the descendants of Cain, the Flood, the exodus from Egypt, the crossing of the Red Sea and the defeat of Pharaoh and his horsemen – when one considers this sequence of events and their typological significances, one is led to conclude that stanzas LXXVII–LXXVIII must present an imitation of the crucial moment in the universal history of man – the crucifixion – as symbolically imitated by each Christian.

The lane where Marvell desires to be staked down is compared not only to the crossing of the Red Sea, but also to 'a long and equal Thread' leading 'Betwixt two *Labyrinths*'. The lane in other words represents that narrow path on which the Christian must pass through the wilderness of this world. The final staking down must occur 'where the Floods did lately drown'. The next stanza (LXXIX) explains the reason why. Now that the Flood has receded, 'No *Serpent* new nor *Crocodile* / Remains behind our little *Nile*'. The reference must be to Ezekiel 29 : 3. In chapter 23 God promises deliverance to the 'house of Israel' while chapter 29 denounces the king of Egypt (referring to him as 'the great dragon that lieth in the midst of his rivers . . .'). This must be the basis for the typological interpretation of Pharaoh as sin, or the devil, an interpretation followed by Milton in *Paradise Lost,* XII 190–6.

Milton is also clearly following the typological technique when, in lines 312–14, he concludes that on the killing of 'the adversarie Serpent' 'long wandered man' is finally brought 'Safe to eternal Paradise of rest'. This is also what happens in Marvell's poem. The serpent of the Nile has been killed, Chaos has been overcome, and the result is a new creation and a new Paradise, whose grass 'Seems as green Silke but newly washt'.

The most conspicuous feature of the new creation is the 'Chrystal Mirrour slick' of the river, 'Where all things gaze themselves, and doubt / If they be in it or without' (stanza LXXX). And, like Narcissus, the sun pines for its own reflection in the water. These lines are clearly charged with allusions to Platonic and Hermetic ideas. Ficino states flatly that the mind is the mirror of God: *Mens est Dei speculum*. If the river, then, symbolises the mind of man (that which reflects God), the purity of the river suggests a corresponding purity in the mind of man. The crucifixion of the old Adam has brought about a purification of the mind so that it reflects things truly. Lines 636–8 should be compared to lines 43–4 of 'The Garden', where Marvell compares the mind to an ocean where each kind 'Does streight its own resemblance find'. As an emanation of the Divinity, the mind must – like the river – reflect all things within itself. Which is true reality – the *res creatae*, or their archetypal forms in the mind of God? The fact that the river now holds the meadow in 'wanton harmless fold', licking 'its yet muddy back', suggests a new relationship between all created things in general and perhaps between mind and matter in particular. Conflict has been superseded by mutual love and harmony.

The comparison between the sun and Narcissus becomes meaningful when interpreted in the light of the Hermetic account of creation: pure mind, on seeing its own reflection in the waters of the earth, falls in love with it and desires to cohabit with it, and in the course of this process man's physical body is created. In Marvell's lines it is the sun which views its own reflection in the waters, yearning for it like Narcissus for his own image. The physical sun was usually viewed as the shadow of God, and Marvell refers to it in this manner in 'The Garden', when he characterises our great luminary as that 'milder sun'. Ficino had written: 'What is the light of the sun? The shadow of God. What, then, is God? God is the sun of the sun, the light of the sun is God in earthly form.'[24] If God, then, is the sun of the sun, we get a series of diminishing reflections of the divine mind: in the visible sun, and in the reflection of the visible sun in the river. Although the image of the sun in the river is a reflection of a reflection, the reflecting medium is so pure that there is little loss in power or quality. This then, is what happens when the serpent is expelled and the world made over anew. The image of God (the sun) is reflected in the mind of man (the river) without distortion and is attracted to it.

The descriptive terms of stanza LXXXI further underline the identification between the mind and the river, the body and the muddy bank. Thus the poet's temples are said to be 'hedged' with 'heavy sedge', while his 'lazy Side' is 'Stretcht as a Bank unto the Tide'. Similarly his 'sliding Foot' is suspended (temporarily comes to a stop) against the roots of trees. In 'The Garden', too, Marvell employs the term 'sliding foot' about the stream issuing out of the fountain.

The concluding homage to Mary Fairfax underlines the basic idea of the poem by presenting her as a true reflection of purity and innocence. She is herself the archetypal pattern of beauty responsible for each separate manifestation of beauty in her own environment. As the exponent of peace, beauty, and innocence, she serves as the great counterfoil to 'bloody *Thestylis*' (line 401), the cruel goddess of war, *sanguinea Bellona*. D. C. Allen associates Mary Fairfax with heavenly wisdom, with the goddess Athena as explained by Plato, and with the heroine of the Christian poem, *Sophia Salomonos*. As the former she represents what Plato calls 'the mind of God', an interpretation which fits nicely into the context which I have tried to establish. As the latter, in the words of D. C. Allen, she is an emanation rather than a creation of God. She is 'the vapor of the power of God', a 'reflection of eternal light', a 'spotless mirror'.[25]

If the purpose of man's quest be the subjugation of the body to the mind in a spiritual baptism resulting in purification and illumination, then what could be more suitable than a concluding apostrophe to that wisdom which issues from the mind of God?

This reading of Marvell's poem has revealed an undoubted unity of theme and purpose. As in 'The Garden', literal description is made the vehicle of insights into various kinds of truth. Various levels of meaning merge at all important points. The mowers are actual labourers, at the same time that they stand for soldiers engaged in a bitter and devastating civil war. On a third level – as Israelites crossing the Red Sea – they symbolise the ancient quest for purification through baptism. This baptism is then achieved through an *imitatio Christi*, that is, by a crucifixion of all carnal desires so that the divine principle in man, his mind, may regain its ancient purity and supremacy. Just as the fallen state implies the dominion of body over mind (a state of affairs which leads to war both in the body politic and in the microcosmos of man), the regenerated state is marked by a supremacy of mind over body (a state reflected in the relationship between Fairfax and his house), and by mutual love not only between mind and body, but also between man and the *res creatae*, and man and God. This is the ultimate truth revealed by Marvell's poem, and one which Fairfax was likely to interpret as an acknowledgement of his own professional concern with the theological exposition of the Hermetic *corpus*. Writing for such a patron, Marvell could safely include philosophical or theological allusions beyond the range of the *profanum vulgus*. In this circumstance lies perhaps his subtlest compliment to his noble employer.

SOURCE: *The Happy Man*, revised 2nd ed. (1962). This essay was revised again for this volume in 1969.

NOTES

1. See H. Flanders Dunbar, *Symbolism in Medieval Thought* (New Haven, 1929) pp. 19 ff.

2. This historical approach is discussed by E. Katherine Dunn in her study 'The Medieval "Cycle" as History Play: an approach to the Wakefield Plays', in *Studies in the Renaissance*, VII (1960) 76–89. The main purpose of universal history is to unfold God's plan for His chosen people, and it was often believed during the years of the civil war and the Protectorate that England had assumed this role. St Augustine's *City of God* is the *locus classicus* for the Christian view of history as a cosmic 'week' consisting of seven 'days' or periods marked by the following events: the Creation (or the Fall), the covenant with Noah, the covenant with Abraham, the exodus, the reign of David, the Babylonian captivity, the incarnation of Christ and the second coming. In such a history questions of chronology would be irrelevant if one is concerned primarily with the typological import of events singled out for their relevance to the scheme of redemption.

3. Don Cameron Allen, *Image and Meaning: metaphoric traditions in renaissance poetry* (Baltimore, 1960) pp. 115–53.

4. Thus he comments on the fact that Noah's stay in the Ark for forty days is a type of Christ's retreat into the wilderness for forty days in order to contemplate his mission. If Marvell intended his allusion to the former event to provoke associations with the latter (if, in other words, he views Noah as a type of Christ), his re-enactment of Christ's passion in stanzas LXXVII and LXXVIII has been carefully prepared for. See also Allen's interpretation of Mary Fairfax as a personification of divine wisdom.

5. This study provides interesting information about the various avenues through which certain typological significances had become sufficiently familiar for poets to be able to draw upon them for the sake of their generally accepted symbolic value.

6. Quotations in this paragraph are from Jean Daniélou, S. J., *From Shadows to Reality* (1960) pp. 11, 19, 83.

7. Compare lines 285–8 and 349–50 with the following excerpt from the prefatory poem ('Pneumato-Sarco-Machia: or Theophila's Spiritual Warfare'):

> Then be sure
> That all thy outworks stand secure . . .
> Design
> With constant care a watch o'er every part;
> Ev'n at thy Cinque-ports, and thy heart
> Set sentinels. Let Faith be captain o'er
> The life-guard, standing at the door
> Of thy well-warded breast . . .

Quoted from *The Caroline Poets*, ed. G. Saintsbury, I (Oxford, 1905) p. 322.

8. It is possible that Du Bartas, as translated by Sylvester, may have prompted Marvell to associate the massacring mowers with Moses and the punishment he inflicted on the erring Israelites for their adoration of the golden calf. Du Bartas had compared the furious onslaught of the 'zealous Prophet' to that of a group of reapers:

> each where [he] strowes his way
> With blood and slaughter, horror and dismay:
> As half a score of Reapers nimbly-neat,
> With cheerful ey choosing a plot of Wheat,
> Reap it at pleasure, and of *Ceres* locks
> Make *hand*-fulls sheaves, and of their sheaves
> make shocks;
> And through the Field from end to end do run,
> Working a-vie, til all be down and don.

Du Bartas His Diuine Weekes And Workes (1621) p. 372. The passage occurs in the Second Week, the Third Day and the Third Part ('The Lawe').

9. Allen, op. cit. p. 118, refers in this context to the 'homo perfectissimus' of Renaissance painting.

10. Benlowes gives fine expression to this traditional idea in a prose passage prefaced to his epic: 'The life of a true Christian is a continual conflict . . . our blessed Saviour coming like a Man of War, commands in Chief, under the Father . . . When He offers Himself to us, He then invades us . . . He binds when He embraceth us. In the cords of love He leads us captives; and he kills us into life, when He crucifies the old, and quickens in us the new man. So then here is no death, but of inbred corruptions: no slaughter but of carnal affections, which being mortified the soul becomes a living sacrifice, holy and acceptable unto God.' *The Caroline Poets*, ed. Saintsbury, I 321.

11. To 'plant' ordnance meant to put or place ordnance in position for discharging. The *Oxford English Dictionary* quotes the following example from 1650: 'Plantying your ordenaunce here and there on your walles and Bulwarkes . . .'

12. See Joan Grundy, 'Marvell's Grasshoppers', in *Notes and Queries*, CCII (April 1957) 142, [Editor's note: also P. Legouis in *Notes and Queries*, CCIII (March 1968) 108–9] and Allen, op. cit. p. 134.

13. *Early English Text Society* (1866), Original Series, no. 16.

14. Isabel Gamble MacCaffrey, *Paradise Lost as 'Myth'* (Cambridge, Mass., 1959) p. 167.

15. Daniélou, op. cit. pp. 69–72.

16. Quoted ibid. p. 91.

17. See the Latin argument prefixed to Canto XII, part of which may be translated as follows: 'This grove is a temple; the open boughs are the panelled ceiling, each trunk forms the pillar (or column) of the sacred house, the passable forest is the open door . . . I praise God with my voice, and the choristers fall in (harmonise) of their free will . . . the echo acts as clerk and says Amen.'

18. See Maren-Sofie Røstvig, *The Happy Man*, 2nd ed. (Oslo, 1962) p. 171.

19. Daniélou, op. cit. p. 13.

20. Allen, op. cit. p. 146.

21. The Authorized Version uses the word 'encamping': 'But the Egyptians pursued after them, all the horses and chariots of Pharaoh, and his horsemen, and his army, and overtook them [the Israelites] encamping by the sea . . .' Exodus 14:9.

22. See note 12.

23. *Theophila* IX 81 and IX 91.

24. Thus Ficino writes: 'Ergo qui Solis est lumen? Umbra Dei: Ergo quid Deus est? Sol Solis est Deus, Solis lumen est Deus in corpore mundi.' Ficino, *Opera Omnia* (Paris, 1641) I 596. The 1495 edition of Ficino's *Epistola* (book I, page 2 verso) provides a more reliable text in that it reads 'Ergo quid Solis est Lumen?'

25. See Allen, op. cit. pp. 148–53.

[Editor's note.] Fuller notes appear in the original publication of this essay.

JOHN E. HARDY

Andrew Marvell's 'The Coronet': the frame of curiosity (1962)

When for the Thorns with which I long, too long,
   With many a piercing wound,
   My Saviour's head have crown'd,
I seek with Garlands to redress that Wrong:
   Through every Garden, every Mead,   5
I gather flow'rs (my fruits are only flow'rs)
   Dismantling all the fragrant Towers
That once adorn'd my Shepherdesses head:
And now when I have summ'd up all my store,
   Thinking (so I my self deceive)   10
   So rich a Chaplet thence to weave
As never yet the king of Glory wore:
   Alas I find the Serpent old,
   That, twining in his speckled breast,
About the flow'rs disguis'd, does fold,   15
   With wreaths of Fame and Interest.
Ah, foolish Man, that would'st debase with them
And mortal Glory, Heavens Diadem!
But Thou who only could'st the Serpent tame,
   Either his slipp'ry knots at once untie,   20
And disintangle all his winding Snare;
Or shatter too with him my curious frame:
And let these wither, so that he may die,
Though set with Skill, and chosen out with Care.
That they, while Thou on both their Spoils dost tread, 25
May crown thy Feet, that could not crown thy Head.

This short poem of Andrew Marvell's has much thematically in common with 'Lycidas', the work of his great contemporary Milton. It is in many respects, other than its length, a smaller poem than 'Lycidas'.

And yet, in some sense by virtue of its very compactness, it finally achieves on at least one theme a largeness of implication that is denied to the longer poem. But it will be best to leave until the end of the essay any attempt explicitly to define that theme.

Marvell expresses here the basic paradox of all religious poetry, that the honor paid to God by the mortal poet, the 'crown', or 'garland', of the poem which celebrates Him, can never add anything to His immortal glory. Indeed, the love of Him enjoining first of all humility, the more carefully the poet works at constructing his tribute, the more 'pride' he takes in his work, the more must it seem worthless to adorn Christ. Thus, in the final resolution of his conceit, Marvell pictures the flowers – the beauties of poetic expression – with which he had first intended to crown the Saviour's head, as worthy now only to be crushed under His feet.

But the 'frame' of line 22, at least in one respect, is the poem itself – with its winding together of various images, various rhetorical and rhythmic effects, upon the one central theme, like so many flowers in the banded circle of a garland. It is a 'curious' frame, in that it is intricately, cunningly wrought, and also, as its composition is a species of inquiry, in that it embodies intellectual 'curiosity', about which there is inevitably a sense of overweening pride, when the object of the inquiry is as here a religious mystery. And, in order that the poet's final humility, his offering the frame to be 'shattered', may be really effective – since the greater the apparent reason for pride the greater is humility's virtue – we must examine the structure of the poem to see just *how* curiously it is contrived.

The poet symbolizes his own sins, his offense against Christ, as adding more 'thorns' to the crown which was put upon His head before the crucifixion – His acceptance of that original mockery, of course, having signified His assumption of the guilt of mankind. Marvell proposes now to replace the thorns, at least the ones that he has contributed, with flowers. He would make up for, 'redress' the wrong he has done to Christ, with a tribute of poetic praise. But we have to go no further than this before encountering the first 'curious' construction – the ambiguity of the word 'redress'.

Its primary meaning – or what, so to speak, the poet first intends or hopes it should mean – is as we have observed 'to make up for', offset, the wrong of his sins. But the *wrong*, '*that* wrong', is, in the metaphoric context, either the thorns themselves, or the wounds they make. And in this connection, 're*dress*' carries suggestions of more literal significance. Again hopefully, the poet may seem to propose that the wounds will be 'dressed' with the flowers, bandaged, with a view to healing them. But on the other hand, perhaps the garlands will only re-dress the thorns, in the sense of covering them up, to conceal and disguise their still remaining hurtfulness. In a sense, the garlands themselves threaten to become a kind of thorns, a further offense against Christ – of presumption.

And if we examine closely, we can see, well before his dismay is embodied in the image of the discovery of the serpent, the grounds for the poet's misgivings. In the passage (lines 5 through 8) that describes his going out to gather the materials for his handiwork, we begin to suspect how the garland might be taken as an insult to Christ. He says, parenthetically, '(my fruits are only flow'rs)'; and, recalling as it does the symbolism of Christ's parables, His warning of what happens to those who are barren branches of the mystical Vine, who do not 'bear fruit', this phrase betrays a latent anxiety, a fear that the gift is necessarily unworthy. But, through line 7, it would seem that the flowers, although they are '*only* flowers', will at least be fresh ones. He seeks them in the 'garden', and the 'mead'. And, the sense of this clause being grammatically complete before the 'that . . .' modifier of line 8, the 'fragrant Towers' could be taken simply as a striking, visual image of tall, flowering plants which he 'dismantles', strips of their covering, in the sense of picking the blossoms off them. Indeed, the phrase, 'that once adorn'd my Shepherdesses head' could be interpreted as only continuing this meaning – the 'towers', the plants, 'once furnished adornment (flowers), for my Shepherdesses head.'

But then, if we learn that 'tower' had in the seventeenth century the specific meaning of a kind of high, elaborate headdress for women, constructed sometimes of wire and pasteboard heavily covered with flowers, we realize that the 'Tower' here must be, not living plants, but just this flowered millinery. The 'garden', after all, is only the dusty properties room of pastoral poetry. The poet is proposing to 'honor' Christ with a garland made up of whatever faded blossoms he can salvage from the discarded costumes of some Phyllis or Chloe whose wardrobe he has formerly furnished.

The proposal is an insult, not because the poetic convention represented by this frumpery derives from the pagan, classical tradition. The practice of merging Christian and classical themes is well established by Marvell's time, and often serves as a way distinctly of glorifying the Christian figures, with Christ Himself becoming, for example, a kind of superior Hercules, whom the classical hero only dimly foreshadows. Nor is it, unqualifiedly, insulting that the particular, derivative mode here should be the pastoral, which from the first was regarded by the classical writers as an inferior mode. For, regardless of this ancient opinion, the pastoral is inevitably a major Christian mode, from the clear dictate of Biblical usage. From Genesis on into the New Testament, the basic metaphorical materials, of fruits and flowers, the serpent, for that matter, among the flowers, the teacher as shepherd, with Christ Himself pre-eminent in that role, simply are as much the properties of the basic Hebrew–Christian writings as they are of Virgil and his Greek predecessors. Moreover, the Biblical writings may be taken (as they are by Milton, for example) essentially to dignify, on their own independent authority, the pastoral mode, and, combining it as they do with an heroic mode, ultimately to disqualify the harsh judgement that was imposed upon Midas and to reconcile, again pre-eminently in the figure of Christ, the conflicting claims of Pan and Apollo. This attitude once established, its grace can be secondarily extended to the classical pastoralists themselves, somewhat to redeem their apparent follies.

But the trouble with Marvell's usage here, at least temporarily is, that no such attitude, whereby the dignity of the classical mode is *dependent* upon the grace of Christ, has been established. At the moment he is not saying in effect that some things in the classical tradition of pastoral faintly foreshadow the Christian truth, but rather that there is something about the Christian which, as it were, reminds him of the classical. Or, actually, it is not even classical, except in the most remotely derivative sense. This garden-party Shepherdess with her fantastic headdress represents the all too modern, now merely non-Christian and faddish pastoral, in no sense genuinely mythic, at the stage of its final decadence. And to trick Christ out, not even as a secondhand Pan, not even as male, but in ornaments borrowed from the finery of this recherché bawd, is indeed the crowning insult.

But we have already observed that this is only a momentary effect. The assumption of the mask of pastoral decadence is only a part of the larger, dramatic design of the poem. The very ingenuity of the design – the compressed richness of this particular passage in itself, as well as the way it is integrated in the poem as a whole, just the degree of the poet's *awareness* of the shameful decline of the pastoral – redeems to a great extent the tawdriness of that to which he alludes. The faded flowers are, after all, freshened and revived in the replanting.

To the extent that the parenthesis '(my fruits are only flow'rs)' is an expression of modesty, like that of the 'forc'd fingers rude' passage in Milton's 'Lycidas', it is an apology only for the immaturity of this and the poet's former work, which has so far produced only blossoms and not yet anything more substantial, any fruit. Good or bad – and there is no implication that he does consider them, as flowers go, in any way inferior – they are finally at least *his* flowers, although taken from the convention yet growing anew in the ground of the poem's own context. And if the apology does, for a moment, seem to extend to the whole flower-kind of poetry, the pastoral – an identification which, in fact, it would be difficult to make, since the 'fruit' is pastoral too – it can be only for a moment, in view of the status which the mode has in the Christian tradition.

In other words, what the poet ultimately fears, in his anxiety about fashioning a proper tribute to Christ, is not that there is anything wrong with gathering one's materials from garden or mead, nor yet that he has, in a sense, left the garden altogether now and is picking his flowers off old costumes. Even these did at first come from the garden, and as we have seen can be revived. Rather, what he fears is that the whole world of poetry, of all modes, is a ruined garden. Or is it not, indeed, the whole world, not simply of poetry but of man's work in general? Marvell does not suggest that the poet, in his special offices, offends Christ, but that he does so as spokesman for all men. In line 17, it is not 'Ah, foolish Poet', but 'Ah, foolish Man'. It is still here, in the midst of this garden – ultimately, the world as one great, spoiled Eden – still in the pastoral scene, and making a battleground *of* the garden, that Marvell finally shows us Christ in a version of that traditional characterization which I have mentioned, as a superior Hercules – in His heroic role, subduing the serpent.

Marvell, then, is sufficiently proud of his own role as poet, and of his performance in the part. To pick up the argument now in the third section (lines 9 through 16), it is clear that the 'sum' of his 'store' is considerable. All this that he has set aside and now sorts and counts up, to see with what he may weave the chaplet – the total of all his knowledge of poetic conventions, and of Biblical lore, his skill in forming images, and intricate conceits out of the various meanings of words, everything that he has gathered from other sources and also built out of his own imagination – he values highly. The word 'store' itself, in addition to the other meanings, has an evaluative sense. He will weave a 'rich' fabric with it. His thinking that the chaplet will be, however rich, the finest that Christ ever had – such 'as never yet the king of Glory wore' – is, of course, a delusion; '(so I my self deceive)'. And his calling Christ 'king of Glory' incidentally enforces the ironic disparagement of the chaplet's beauty also in a visual way. A 'glory' is a nimbus, or halo; the projected light of Christ's own grace, such is the implication, provides for Him the perfect 'chaplet', or crown, which the poet's can only obscure. But that the construction of the tribute can advance Marvell's own 'Fame and Interest' as an artist, there is no doubt.

For, if he were convinced from the start that his work was merely trifling, if he had not so high an opinion of his prowess, and hence some real hope of making his reputation and fortune, then the problem which is the theme of the poem could not exist; there would be no serpent among the flowers. His pride *is* the serpent. The serpent's coils, in line 16, are precisely 'wreaths of Fame and Interest'.

And yet it is 'the Serpent old' that he discovers. The problem as such, of man's noblest enterprise being mocked and betrayed by his pride in it, of his finding the aspiration to do the work apparently hopelessly entangled with the temptation to turn it to his personal glory and advantage, is not a problem that Marvell is the first to face. It is as old as man himself. Further, the serpent is 'old', of course, in being identified with that one, Satan, who tempted Eve – which is just another way of stating what I have said about the antiquity of the problem itself that he represents, but which does define it as a more specifically religious problem, as that of the *sin* of intellectual pride.

And it is in this sense of the extreme age, the universality of it, that we with Marvell at once detect the true dimensions of his theme, the 'problem' of it, and first catch sight of a possible way out. In the first place, merely the recognition that the danger is not entirely to oneself, but is shared with all men, is in itself humbling, and so begins to defeat pride. And further, in the specifically religious context, one is reminded by the age of the serpent as identifying him with Satan, the original tempter, that he is therefore the adversary of Christ, whose redemption is also universal. 'As old as man himself', we have said; but Satan is even older than that. Just by identifying his own sin with original, universal sin, as he is implicitly doing here, Marvell has started already to shift the burden of it to Christ, to Him 'who only could'st the Serpent tame'.

But before we leave this third section of the poem, the point I have been trying to make – that the dismay of the 'Alas!' is not despair, that almost from the very moment of this exclamation, when he discovers the serpent among the flowers and shrinks back from his work, the poet is beginning to see the way out of his self-deception – is a point which can be reinforced by consideration of the imagery of these lines. The image of the snake coiled hidden among the flowers, who is 'twining', insinuating, his breast both 'in' and at the same time, his 'breast' being of course the whole under-length of his sinuous body, 'about' the 'flowers disguis'd' – the imitative cunning of the lines' movement is secured principally in the use of the verbals and pre-positions – is a figure that picks up again the motif of masking, con-cealment, which we saw briefly stated in the implications of the word 'redress' in the fourth line. Further, although the snake's breast is 'speckled' in the sense of its representing sinfulness, the condition of being spotted, maculate – "not-innocent", "touched" – there is also here a literal representation of the protective coloring which enables him so easily to merge his 'wreaths' with the wreathed blossoms. Not only is it hard to distinguish his twisted shape from that of the thickly braided garland itself, but his mottled skin closely resembles the parti-colored petals of the flowers among which he hides. And yet, the point is that despite all the ingenuity of his 'disguise' (the syntax of the lines permits 'disguis'd' to be taken as modifying both 'flowers' and 'breast'), the serpent has now been 'found' – 'Alas! I find the Serpent old.' If the disguise has not been quite penetrated, cannot be immediately stripped away, at least it has been recognized *as* a disguise. What was only a possible implication in the ambiguities of the word 'redress', a sense of misgiving in the apologetic tone of the second section, where the poet is gathering his flowers, is now beyond question. Now he knows that the serpent is there; he has seen him. And once the problem has been recognized, the repressed anxiety openly admitted, the weight of sin consciously felt, he has already begun to relieve his perplexity.

Thus, there is a certain calmness of disillusionment about the quieter exclamation that opens the final section of the poem. The 'Ah' ex-presses now a kind of sadly chastened *acceptance*, of the truth which in the first shock of discovery had provoked the dismayed 'Alas'. And after, in these two lines – 'Ah, foolish Man, that would'st debase with

them / And mortal Glory, Heaven's Diadem!' – making full admission
of the folly of his efforts, the poet proceeds without further hesitation
through firmly balanced verses to the end, wholly resigning to the
discretion of Christ's will the question of what is to be done about the
serpent. But if there is no continuation of the mood of perplexity –
the tone, reflecting the emotional attitude of the speaker, remains fairly
constant, or at any rate is steadily intensified toward the climactic
resignation, with no more uncertain shiftings – still there are in the
statement many curious involvements, of diction, syntax, and imagery,
which we shall have to explore more fully.

'Diadem' here is the last of a series of words, beginning with 'coronet'
in the title, which Marvell has used in referring to ornaments for the
head, and which in their variety express something of the essential
irony of his attitude in the poem. Now, the nearest referent for 'them',
in the preceding line, is 'wreaths of Fame and Interest', or just 'Fame
and Interest'; but these being, as we have seen, inextricable from the
other elements of the work, 'them' must refer also to the 'flowers'.
It is the entire structure – the interwoven wreaths, of flowers, *and* of
Fame and Interest – that would 'debase' the 'Diadem'. And it is, in this
connection, easy enough to see one significance of the fact that all the
words used specifically for the ornaments which the poet would present
to Christ – *coronet*, or 'little crown', *garland, chaplet* – carry a sense of the
diminutive, of something light and insubstantial. By comparison to the
great crown, the Diadem of the eternal kingdom (the word 'diadem' is
normally reserved for the emblem of absolute sovereignty), anything
made of corruptible, earthly substances is of small value and significance. It is, therefore, quite appropriate that the crown composed of the
ephemeral flowers, even before the serpent is found among them,
should be named as it is – and foolish, indeed, that the poet should ever
have thought it could in any way please or honor Christ to have this
flimsy contrivance as it were flung over the crown of His own glory,
only to obscure that radiance.

And yet, while all along using the diminutive to name it, he *has* for a
time thought it might be acceptable. And, curiously enough, the very
smallness of the thing might be seen as the quality that seemed so to
recommend it. For, what is merely the *biggest* piece of headgear mentioned in the poem is the 'Tower' of the Shepherdess's costume, the
very outlandish size of which is the principal mark of decadence in the
usages the Shepherdess represents, the gross and corrupted elegance

which it is offensive to have associated in any way with the poet's purpose of expressing his love of Christ. Thus, although as we have seen he is not able finally to purge his work entirely of the taint of decay that the borrowed flowers bear, yet the poet's tearing down the 'Towers',[1] and making the smaller, less pretentious chaplet from the remnants, tends as far as it goes in the proper direction of compliment to Christ.

That is, the use of the flowers in this way has, first, a certain basic artistic honesty about it; the work does not deny the nature of the materials. The structure is not so elaborate; but it is, unlike the 'Tower' with its hidden framework of wire and pasteboard, self-supporting. Further, the chaplet does, in its comparative weightlessness and fragility, actually in a way imitate the 'Diadem'. For, of course, the value of the sovereign crown is not in its superior size or heaviness, but in what it signifies – precisely, the sovereignty. And the point can be put in still another way. We might at first think of the 'diadem' as being a large, heavy crown of gold, made of enduring metal as opposed to the fragile substance of the flowers – having that genuine magnificence of which the exaggerated artificiality of the 'Towers' is a mockery – and perhaps see in 'debase' an implicit metaphor of the *debasement* of metals. Actually, however, 'diadem' will support a quite different interpretation. The word has the literal meaning of something 'bound over, or around', the head. It originally referred to the kind of simple crown, a headband, or fillet, that was so worn, rather than to the larger, more hatlike contrivances that sit upon and cover the top of the head. Its shape and size, then, and the manner in which the original 'diadem' is worn, make it in fact very similar to the garland. Moreover, the first 'diadems' were not made of metal, but of cloth.

What the usage finally tends to suggest is that to represent the majesty of Christ, that most assured sovereignty, what one needs is the nearest thing to no crown at all. Recalling the previous reference to Christ as 'king of Glory', and the significance of the word 'glory' as 'halo', we see 'Heaven's Diadem', if it can be visually represented at all, just as this weightless radiance of inner sanctity. And in the way of 'mortal Glory', the near-weightless crown of 'flowers', the wreath of poetic praise, wreath of words, becomes the closest imitation of that circle of pure light.

Of course, the poet as 'Man' is 'foolish'. But his foolishness is that of an over-subtle intelligence, overly fond of its own ingenuity; it is not simplemindedness. He knows, from the start, enough about the nature of Christ, and of man's proper relationship to Him, to realize that any conceivably acceptable gift must have some semblance of humility about it. What we have called the 'basic artistic honesty' of his reducing the 'Towers' to a 'chaplet' is that initial semblance of humility; and in a measure, the measure of man's capacity for truth, which is the measure of his ability to own his foolishness, it is a semblance that holds good, or rather is restored and renewed, even in the light of this comparison to 'Heaven's Diadem'.

For the poet's error, after all, has been just his forgetting, in his fascination with the work itself, that it *is* a semblance that he constructs, an image. And once he has corrected this error, remembered that the crown of thorns has long since, without the need of his assistance, been replaced by the heavenly glory, to which divine original he can merely compare his tribute – once he has, to put the matter another way, simply recalled the nature of humility, that it is a disposition of the mind *towards* something, or someone, and so must seek its perfection outside itself – then he has already to a great extent recovered that humility. He has, just in recognizing that the poem cannot *take the place* of 'Heaven's Diadem', or alloy that purity with its unpurged grossness, realized for the first time how closely it can, in fact, *imitate* that glory.

Thus humbled, the poet aspires then no longer to any closer view of Heaven itself, but instead urgently implores Christ as it were to come down again to his assistance. Since the serpent Satan appears here as 'Fame and Interest', as pride, Christ is his supreme enemy, the one 'who only could'st the Serpent tame', primarily by virtue of His perfect humility. In His grace, His own entire freedom from the motives of 'Fame and Interest', He is the only one who can see through and follow up to untie them the intricate and ever-changing convolutions of the writhing serpent without risk of involving Himself, and being caught in their 'winding snare'. The knots, it should be observed, are 'slipp'ry knots', constantly altering their position and configuration, rather than remaining hard and fast so as to make them easier to release. The poet, with the power of mere words, themselves 'slipp'ry', unstable, their meaning changing always with time and syntax, can never wholly extricate the pure design, the pure formal intention, of his garland from the toils of his confused motives; but Christ, who is the Word, could if He so willed it 'at once' set all aright.

But having once presumed upon his own strength, and seen his error in that, the poet is careful now not to presume still more foolishly upon God's grace. Christ could, *if* it were His will, disentangle the serpent, and leave the garland of flowers intact; but there can be no attempt to dictate His choice. As the final test of his humility, the poet must admit, and accept without complaint, the possibility that He will elect to destroy both garland and serpent together.

In other words, Marvell admits the possibility that man is utterly incapable of 'framing' a pure intention of praise, that all his words, no matter with what care 'chosen out' and with what skill 'set' in context, are basically corrupt, from the corruption of his intelligence itself. In the complex system of reference among the pronouns – 'these' in line 23 referring indefinitely to the flowers that make up the 'frame' in the preceding line, but also serving as the antecedent of 'they' in line 25, which in the possessive 'their' obviously becomes inclusive of the serpent ('he' in the second half of line 23) as well as the flowers, so that ultimately 'these' must refer back to 'them' in line 17, which as we have noted primarily means the 'wreaths' of 'Fame and Interest', of the serpent – he suggests that the 'frame' of the poem's formal statement of intention and the 'Serpent', prideful motives, have become almost entirely, almost 'substantially', indistinguishable. It seems to me, further, that 'my curious frame' clearly means not only the form of the poem but the form of his, man's own being. It is the order or condition in which man's own parts physical and spiritual are joined in this life ('this mortal frame'), that image of Himself which God has made, and which Satan and man himself together have corrupted. Thus, the basic impurity of man's work, the poem, is implicitly attributed to the impurity of man's fallen nature, which would itself have to be changed if the work is to be purged and the wreaths of the serpent distinguished and separated from the wreath of flowers. So long as man remains what he is, corrupt and corruptible, destined for destruction, it cannot be otherwise with his work.

To the eye of God, of course, the serpent and the flowers are distinguishable. Christ, as we have observed, *could* untie them. He can, and it is promised that He will, redeem man's nature. But – if Marvell does not here dictate Christ's choice, between untying the knots at once ('at once' meaning both 'all together' and 'without delay') or crushing serpent and 'frame' together, if in fact he does not demand anything, but only pleads that either be done – still, there is a distinct suggestion that the latter alternative is the more likely. The final redemption, according to the traditional interpretation of the promise, can come only after man in his present nature has suffered much pain of mind and body, and finally death.

And yet, is not the matter of ultimate importance just that the redemption is promised, and will be, whether soon or late? If as I see it 'my curious frame' does mean both poem and man, Marvell is saying that he accepts the destruction of his work exactly on the same terms that, as a Christian, he accepts the necessity for his own death. And this is a considerable qualification of what might seem at first sight mere abandonment of the poem's purpose.

Christ's conflict with 'the Serpent old' is prior even to the cause of man's salvation; the poet implicitly recognizes and accepts this. But what man purchases with his death in Christ, in willing submission to the exigencies of His mortal combat with Satan, is the renewal and perfection of life. And if man and his work are indeed inseparable, then the work shares in this compact, is also assured of immortality. As man images forth the mind of God, and in Christ's redemption is restored to perfect semblance of his original, so too the poem, that images man's mind, is perfected.

The poem seeks its own destruction. The image of His 'shattering' the frame, and 'treading' upon the 'spoils'[2] of the mingled wreaths, of the dead serpent and the withered flowers – the tone here contrasting strongly with that of the opening sections, where the poet goes out in eager delight to gather his flowers – presents Christ in his role of martial hero. The garden, as we have put the matter before, is turned into a battlefield. In this connection, the implicit reference in the metaphor of the ruined wreaths' becoming a kind of 'crown' for His feet, is to the practice of dressing the victorious warrior in the spoils, parts of the captured armour, of his fallen enemy. But the self-destruction, the 'suicide', of the poem is that of martyrdom. It is as if the garland of flowers were used to *hold* the serpent for the blow of Christ's heel – 'And let these wither / So *that* he may die.' The humility is more, after all, than mere submission to the cause of Christ's justice. It is active co-operation with that cause. The poem shares actively in the glory of the triumph over itself.

And if there is a tendency here to contradict what we observed earlier about the complex reference of the pronouns, if even to make such a distinction between the active and passive involvement of the flowers and the serpent in furnishing the sign of Christ's triumph is not quite possible – the two remaining grammatically still inseparable, the corruption of the image, the poem, remaining still unredeemed at the end – yet, it must be remembered that this entire passage is only a vision, of Christ's *final* triumph over Satan. What Marvell is suggesting, in a sense, is precisely that nothing in the complex problem of man's relationship to his work is resolved yet, nor can be, until that of his relationship to God is settled. And this gives the poem (I think we have already sufficiently established the fact that Marvell considers this particular poem as worthy as any) claim at least to temporal 'immortality'. Although imperfect it will last as long as man lasts, in the state of *his* imperfection.

Or, to come now at last to what is perhaps the central structural irony, this whole poem is in a way only a projection of intentions. The 'chaplet' which the poet was *'thinking . . . to weave'* before he discovered the serpent among the flowers, seems never really to have been completed. The rest of the poem, beyond this point, becomes a kind of consideration of what *would* be the state of affairs ('Ah, foolish Man, that *would'st* debase with them . . .'), *if* such a project were attempted to completion. The poem has never actually committed itself to be judged as anything more than a statement, a declaration and rather hasty retraction, of ambitious intent. We can, therefore, make a distinction between this poem, finally, and that other, the 'garland', 'chaplet', etc., which so to speak it 'imagines'.

And in these terms – the terms of this poem's *imagery* – with the destruction of the chaplet's 'frame', its being shattered and broken, knocked out of round and placed under Christ's feet, rather than upon His head, the frame of the poem proper is brought full circle, put into round. There is a curious suggestion, in these last lines, of an image of the uncompleted and broken garland – that 'crowns', does not perhaps simply lie beneath, but again is bound over and around His feet – as a kind of snare for Christ: as if to say, that although He cannot be held by presumptions to honor Him, yet by humility, by man's admission that to add anything to the glory of which He is already possessed is impossible, He can be captured. And if the remaining entanglement of the flowers with the coils of the dead or dying serpent, as though *that* 'snare' too still held His feet, makes such an interpretation of the metaphor finally intolerable – if there is no way yet perfected to catch Christ – assuredly the poem as a whole catches the reader. Its circle remains entire.

Once our interest is engaged, for whatever initial reason, there is no way out of the problems raised – as, for example, what devotion to Christ might have to do with compliments to a shepherdess – except farther in. There is no ultimately effective appeal to the history of poetic convention, or to mythography, or even to theology, as such. If an 'answer' lies anywhere, not of course to how man is to know Christ, but simply to the meaning or 'intent' of the poem, it is only in the total relationship between the image here, of the dismantled towers, and other images of *this* poem – or, further, between the imagery as a whole and the tonal structure, between these two together and the syntax, and so on. The critical emphasis must be, not upon what materials Marvell has used, and where he got them – out of what orders of knowledge and inquiry, what sciences, in which poet and critic both are inevitably amateurs (although the word may be taken to make them *lovers* of such studies) – but upon what he has, here, wrought with them. We bear down critically, not upon the admittedly flimsy structure of his intention to praise God, an effort in which man, whether poet or not, is always an amateur, but upon the vital structure only of his *statement* of that intention.

And yet, if this should seem after all to devalue the subject of the statement, to make it seem that the poem is merely rhetorical contrivance, I would insist finally that it *is* about man and Christ, that it has real reference to something outside itself. Perhaps the best way to put this point, of its meaningfulness, and at the same time the idea of how one finally 'escapes' the poem only by going farther in, would be to pick up again the image of the 'flower'.

In discussing the imagery, we have for the most part accepted it, so to speak, at face value. We *know* that there is no tangible wreath of flowers, no tangible snake among the flowers, etc. But we go along with the metaphor, and work out the details of its inner harmony, in some sense just because we know that the poet is not trying to deceive us with it.

Thus, the 'flow'rs disguised' of line 14, as we have seen, are both disguised and disguising. Serpent and flowers disguise each other. But if we should at this point suddenly insist upon being literal-minded, and realize that the whole thing is a 'disguise', that 'serpent-and-flowers' as a unit must be a mask for still some other entity, we might ask what the *nearest* real referent for the imagery is. We should have to see that it is language itself.

The matter has been mentioned, in passing, before. I have spoken of the 'wreath of words', and of how words themselves are 'slipp'ry', unstable, and of the corruptibility of language as reflective of the corruption of man's intelligence through sin. But language in itself is the true, central, 'hidden' theme of the entire poem. It is the one, 'external' frame of reference in which all elements of the metaphoric statement dependably cohere. (I should be careful to point out that I do *not* mean 'poetic language'. Once more, the speaker of the poem identifies himself as 'Man', not 'Poet'.) Man's intelligence is corrupt, but we know this most specifically *as* the corruption of his language. It is when the Serpent *speaks* to Eve, speaks from the form of the dumb beast, and she answers, that the loss of innocence occurs.

It is then that man becomes 'double-tongued', like the serpent, and can no longer keep clear the true distinctions between himself and God, himself and external nature (the plants and beasts), and hence can no longer truly commune with either. (Myths like that of Orpheus express our desire to reverse this process, and to have the beasts and the trees 'truly' speak to us.) There is no way in which he can express his thoughts except in speech; it is the medium in which he must frame all his intention and his 'curiosity', his inquiring and communing intelligence; but it is also the curious frame that binds and represses him, that will not *let* him say ever exactly what he means. It is this fundamental duplicity of all language – not, as rational conceptualists would like to think, only 'poetic language', but all language – its basic, ineradicable ambiguousness that defies all efforts at purification, which is exemplified by Marvell in the specific and deliberate ambiguities of the poem.

And it is thus, once we see it, in referring its own perplexity most immediately to the perplexity of language itself, that the little poem achieves in one sense the ultimate dimensions of poetry, and begins to break out of the frame in which it has trapped itself and us. Christ comes to the world as Logos, as the Word incarnate. Here, in admitting at last, at the very center of the 'conceit' or formal preoccupation, the frailness of their own intentional order, of their contextual or syntactical frame – in willingly 'falling apart', the words begin to move toward the Word, to seek that final unity which they cannot find in any of the sciences of man.

SOURCE: *The Curious Frame: seven poems in text and context* (1962).

NOTES

1. Perhaps it is not too curious to see Marvell's Shepherdesse as a mock-heroic version of 'towered Cybele', the goddess of cities and fortifications, who is commonly represented in art with the attribute of an immense headdress designed to show the character of her patronage. 'Dismantling' would reinforce this literal reading of 'towers'. And the usage would serve ironically to justify the true heroic mode of the final section.

2. There is, perhaps, some reference here to the 'spoiling' (rotting, withering) of vegetable matter, appropriate to the flower imagery. But *N.E.D.* does not, in fact, give an instance of the use of the word, even as a verb, in this sense, before the end of the seventeenth century.

E. W. TAYLER

Marvell's Garden of the Mind (1964)

THE significance of Andrew Marvell's experiments in the pastoral genre must be carefully assessed if we are to understand the emotional and intellectual concerns that give purpose and weight to his finest lyrics. For Marvell was not much given to direct statement, his considerable virtues being of an ironic, allusive kind. As a consequence his poems, taken singly and without regard for the conventions of their genre, are more open to appreciation than analysis,

> Annihilating all that's made
> To a green Thought in a green Shade.

Although the body of his lyric verse is small, attempts to discern continuity and regularity, to define basic assumptions and deep commitments, have been frustrated by his reliance on a semi-private vocabulary, by his attitude of urbane detachment, and by a group of brilliant but apparently random poetic experiments. In his pastoral poems, however, Marvell for once explored the possibilities in a particular genre and developed the implications of a single theme: it is here, revealed by his modifications of the pastoral *kind* and by his personal response to the paired terms of Nature and Art, that we possess the clearest indication of attitudes elsewhere concealed by ironic wit.

Marvell wrote a number of poems that are clearly a part of the pastoral tradition, and there is considerable variation in his treatment of them within the genre. Variety has always been characteristic of the genre itself; despite – perhaps even because of – its stereotyped conventions, the form has lent itself to a remarkably wide range of poetic and other intentions. Marvell's use of the genre is no exception, although some of his experiments, such as 'Two Songs at the Marriage of the

Lord Fauconberg and the Lady Mary Cromwell', remain comparatively uninteresting, not only because of their occasional nature, but also because the simple Hobbinols and rustic Thomalins are vehicles for little more than courtly compliment.

Marvell's best pastorals, however, depart radically from such relatively unambitious themes and purposes: situations are no longer simple, man is no longer artless, and feelings become quite complicated. The traditional lover of pastoral is replaced by the Mower, a figure at once cheerfully ingenuous and darkly mysterious, whose relationship to Nature seems complex and ambiguous and who suffers strangely at the hands of an unusual shepherdess. In short, Marvell's intentions become much more ambitious, growing in both scope and intensity, but the pastoral *kind* remains to provide a form in which the maturer interests may be expressed.

'Ametas and Thestylis making Hay Ropes' and 'Daphnis and Chloe' are possibly among the first of Marvell's pastoral experiments; at least they show no hint of his more serious concerns. Possibly among the first . . . There is no way of determining exactly when most of the *Miscellaneous Poems* were written.[1] In any case, precise knowledge of chronological order would have absolute value only if we could depend on a poet to exhibit straight-line progress toward a particular goal. But success may be lost as well as found, and poets, like other men, commit themselves to a variety of ends, sometimes returning with new understanding to an old problem only after a number of years, so that later work may bear the sediment of early efforts. If 'Ametas and Thestylis' and 'Daphnis and Chloe' are not chronologically early, they are nevertheless experiments that did not lead to additional poems of the same type. They are poems of the fashionable world in the tradition of the love-debate *pastourelle*. Marvell adopts the ethics of this tradition, probably influenced by the French *libertins* of the seventeenth century, and attempts to make the pastoral form sustain some fairly sophisticated arguments about love.

In 'Ametas and Thestylis' the witty debate closes quickly with the usual gesture:

> Then let's both lay by our Rope,
> And go kiss within the Hay.

In 'Daphnis and Chloe', where a similar theme is attenuated through approximately eight times as many lines, Marvell may have realized that he had extended himself in this direction about as far as he could go. Although there is no doubt that the shepherdess this time remains virtuous, the last stanzas show that the two poems exhibit essentially the same attitude:

> But hence Virgins all beware.
> Last night he with *Phlogis* slept;
> This night for *Dorinda* kept;
> And but rid to take the Air.

> Yet he does himself excuse;
> Nor indeed without a Cause.
> For, according to the Lawes,
> Why did *Chloe* once refuse?

These are obviously poems addressed to something very like Court society, perhaps the small circle of literati at Appleton House, who might be relied upon to appreciate both the wit and the delicious excitement of the naturalistic ethics. To Marvell at this time, as to Tasso in *Aminta*, it seems that 'what pleased was proper', according 'to the Lawes' of *libertin* naturalism.

'Clorinda and Damon' and 'A Dialogue between Thyrsis and Dorinda' may be viewed as transitional poems. Although Marvell's most central and characteristic preoccupations do not yet appear, the poems imply movements in the direction of the best pastorals through their explicit rejection of 'naturalistic' or *libertin* ethics. What pleases is no longer necessarily proper; Marvell even begins to use the pastoral form to discuss religious matters. Such a use was of course not at all uncommon, either in the Middle Ages or in the Renaissance. We have seen that it had behind it the putative foreshadowing of Christ in Vergil's Fourth or Messianic Eclogue, the mystical glosses on the pastoral Song of Songs, the shepherds of the Gospels, the medieval uses of the genre, and numerous Renaissance 'imitations', so that Sidney could assert confidently in his *Apologie for Poetrie* that the genre, 'under the prettie tales of Wolves and Sheepe, can include the whole considerations of wrong dooing'.[2] Puttenham similarly emphasizes that the genre does not simply attempt to 'represent the rusticall manner of loues and communication: but vnder the vaile of homely persons, and in rude speeches to insinuate and glaunce at greater matters'.[3] But the poetical and critical traditions notwithstanding, Marvell apparently at first found it hard to 'insinuate and glaunce at greater matters'.

Marvell's problem was one of technique: How is it possible to write on complex, civilized themes while still retaining all the baggage of traditional pastoral? The answer lies in the allegorical potentialities of the form. Puttenham alludes to this solution with the words 'insinuate and glaunce', but Marvell in 'Thyrsis and Dorinda' attempts to discuss 'greater matters' more or less directly. The speakers are therefore so ingenuous in relation to the subject-matter that even rustic charm cannot save the piece. Although Dorinda has reservations about Death, being unsure where she will 'go', Thyrsis assures her it merely means a new home in Elizium. Dorinda remains only partially satisfied, and presents her swain with a question he could not hope to answer directly and still retain his rustic character:

> But in Elizium how do they
> Pass Eternity away?

Thyrsis' rejoinder conflates planetary music, English sheep dogs, and allusions to the Golden Age in an attempt to reassure the shepherd lass:

> Oh, ther's, neither hope nor fear
> Ther's no Wolf, no Fox, nor Bear.
> No need of Dog to fetch our stray,
> Our Lightfoot we may give away;
> No Oat-pipe's needfull, there thine Ears
> May feast with Musick of the Spheres.

This answer so intrigues Dorinda that she persuades her swain to share 'poppies' with her, thus 'smoothly pass away in sleep', and arrive in Elizium ahead of schedule.

Is the poem a religious allegory? Perhaps. Elizium is a land of 'Everlasting day', the inevitable resting place of the 'Chast Soul': 'Heaven's the Center of the Soul'. But these religious allusions do not form a consistent pattern, nor are they meaningful additions to the dramatic situation of this dialogue between a shepherd and his lass. The subject seems to be, ultimately, the attractiveness of heaven, but if the pastoral is Christian in this sense, its message – that one may anticipate the joys of heaven with a suicidal 'poppy' – is distinctly un-Christian. If the poem is allegorical, its dark conceit leaves a reader in obscurity. Since Marvell was a sophisticated man, an urban wit, he could not have found the convention – admittedly often broken – of rustic speakers and rude diction entirely to his taste; and he had apparently not yet learned to use the pastoral form successfully to hint at complicated notions, to 'insinuate and glaunce at greater matters'.

Marvell himself wrote a kind of poetic commentary on the difficulty of expressing complex matters through the simple diction of unsophisticated shepherds and shepherdesses. 'Clorinda and Damon' resembles 'Thyrsis and Dorinda' in its concern with Christian rather than 'naturalistic' values, but in 'Clorinda and Damon' the rejection of *libertin* ethics has become the main dramatic issue of the poem. It is more successful poetry than 'Thyrsis and Dorinda', mainly because its religious burden nowhere conflicts with the pastoral situation and vocabulary; the pastoral form has become a vehicle for 'greater matters' that deepen without distorting the literal meaning of the pastoral dialogue. Clorinda represents the *libertine* shepherdess, dedicated to natural pleasure on the nearest 'grassy Scutcheon', but Damon, mysteriously armed against her Marlovian blandishments, declines to live with her and be her love:

> C. Seize the short Joyes then, ere they vade.
>   Seest thou that unfrequented Cave?
> D. That den? C. Loves Shrine. D. But Virtue's Grave.
> C. In whose cool bosome we may lye
>   Safe from the Sun. D. not Heaven's Eye.
> C. Near this, a Fountaines liquid Bell
>   Tinkles within the concave Shell.
> D. Might a Soul bath there and be clean,
>   Or slake its Drought?

Damon explains that 'Pastures, Caves, and Springs' no longer entice him, for the 'other day' he encountered Pan:

> C. What did great *Pan* say?
> D. Words that transcend poor Shepherds skill,
>   But He ere since my Songs does fill.

Not the Pan of woodland and stream, of riggish dance and goatish desire, but the Great Pan of *The Shepheardes Calender* and 'The Nativitie Ode' whose ethics and words indeed 'transcend poor Shepherds skill'. This Pan is Christ, and thus what began as a relatively slight pastoral lyric has become the vehicle for a weighty event in scriptural history:

the impact of Christ's Revelation on natural man. And Marvell has
been notably successful in communicating these 'greater matters'
without using 'Words that transcend poor Shepherds skill'.

Presumably a man of Marvell's ironic disposition would find
techniques of indirection and allusion particularly congenial, but there
are obvious dangers in the use of such methods. Most obviously, there
is the possibility that readers may misinterpret, or even entirely over-
look, the significance of a reference such as that to 'great Pan'. The
word, after all, is the same; it is the meaning that has changed. Less
obviously, and perhaps for that reason more common, there is the
danger of misunderstanding what the poet intends to accomplish
through the use of a particular allusion at a particular time: a single
allusion, however suggestive, does not invariably mean that the poem is
a detailed allegory. It is this last danger that seems to have complicated
exegesis of 'The Nymph complaining for the death of Her Faun'
where the Faun – to mention only one of the controversial figures –
may be presumed to represent everything from Christ to the Church
of England.[4]

'The Nymph complaining' is admittedly thick with classical and
Christian allusions, and they lend an effect of depth and solidity to a
work that could otherwise have been maudlin and melodramatic in
tone. But it will not do to mistake the function of these allusions.

The Nymph's Garden can hardly fail to suggest the Garden of Eden,
and the Faun itself – 'Lillies without, Roses within' – clearly stands for a
kind of Edenic harmony with Nature, the original purity and innocence. Difficulties appear, however, when the reader tries to anchor
such symbolic overtones to a detailed, inclusive interpretation. Consider the lines in which the Nymph accuses the 'wanton Troopers' of
their crime:

> Though they should wash their guilty hands
> In this warm life-blood, which doth part
> From thine, and wound me to the Heart,
> Yet could they not be clean: their Stain
> Is dy'd in such a Purple Grain.

I think it is safe to say that Marvell nowhere wrote a sentimental line,
but there is in the Nymph's words an emotional excess that lies just
this side of the maudlin – until suddenly in the following two lines it is

channeled into a spiritual context in which such language is entirely appropriate to its object, the Crucifixion:

> There is not such another in
> The World, to offer for their Sin.

If we now felt inclined, we might possibly see the poem in the following way: the Faun is Christ, the Nymph is the Virgin Mary, Sylvio is the God alienated by the Fall, the Garden is Eden, and what is really a very fine poem has become absurd. There is no doubt that this exegetical activity 'enriches' one's experience of the poem, but surely it does the work a disservice to see a simple equation in such consciously oblique references. We are not dealing with one-to-one allegory but a technique of allusion almost random in nature:

> O help! O help! I see it faint:
> And dye as calmely as a Saint.
> See how it weeps. The Tears do come
> Sad, slowly dropping like a Gumme.
> So weeps the wounded Balsome: so
> The holy Frankincense doth flow.
> The brotherless *Heliades*
> Melt in such Amber Tears as these.

By establishing connections, at strategic points, between the simple dramatic situation and scriptural or other history, Marvell has transformed the traditional pastoral epicedium into an intense experience; and although its intensity cannot be adequately accounted for in terms of the death of a faun, it seems equally clear that the poem is not to be read as a detailed allegory.

For the moment, however, reading 'The Nymph complaining' is perhaps less interesting than the difficulties in reading it. Marvell was to make use of this technique of allusion in his most unusual group of poems, those concerned with that strange figure the Mower. Reminiscences of classical and Christian literature everywhere deepen the texture of these poems, yet the function of Marvell's oblique references remains obscure. And their obscurity assumes greater importance in connection with the Mower, for the poems in which he appears offer problems even on the literal level, problems that seem to require an allegorical solution. In the Mower episode of 'Upon Appleton House,

to my Lord Fairfax' the reader finds himself beset by difficulties
resembling those in 'The Nymph complaining'. There is, however,
this difference: the literal action, the basic dramatic situation, of the
Mower episode seems completely intelligible only through reference to
another level of meaning.

In the Mower episode[5] the traditional shepherd is replaced by the
Mower, a figure who reflects something of the pastoral convention and
something of what his name suggests. On the one hand, the Mowers
exhibit the usual idyllic charm of rural life; from their sea of 'unfathomable Grass' they 'bring up Flow'rs', and their dances illustrate their
simple, close relationship with Nature:

> Where every Mowers wholesome Heat
> Smells like an *Alexanders sweat*.
> Their Females fragrant as the Mead
> Which they in *Fairy Circles* tread:
> When at their Dances End they kiss,
> Their new-made Hay not sweeter is.   (427–32)

Yet their idyllic harmony with Nature may be shattered with incredible
rapidity:

> With whistling Sithe, and Elbow strong,
> These Massacre the Grass along:
> While one, unknowing, carves the *Rail*,
> Whose yet unfeather'd Quils her fail.
> The Edge all bloody from its Breast
> He draws, and does his stroke detest;
> Fearing the Flesh untimely mow'd
> To him a Fate as black forebode.   (393–400)

Viewed against the usual sentiments of the pastoral tradition, the
incident is quite extraordinary: the moment of violence suddenly
obliterates the mood of pastoral calm.

Thestylis, conventionally the simple shepherdess (often the simple
shepherd!), is referred to as 'bloody', her actions vulture-like: 'Greedy
as Kites has trust it up.' 'Death-Trumpets creak' in the throats of the
parent birds, and the meadows suddenly become a 'Camp of Battail',
'quilted ore with Bodies slain'. The entire incident has occupied only
four stanzas (L–LIII), but the reader acquainted with pastoral conventions will want to know why it is there at all. What are we to make of

it? The language is too forceful and violent to be dismissed as a fanciful conceit provoked by the sight of a few hayricks: the accident of the 'bloody . . . stroke' seems to possess some significance above and beyond the literal level of the action. Unlike 'The Nymph complaining', however, this episode does not seem to allude to an area of experience in which the appropriateness of the violent language may be appreciated.

Of course, there are in the episode, as elsewhere in Marvell, many literary and historical allusions, and yet they seem to illuminate only the passage at hand and not the accident of the 'bloody . . . stroke'. But perhaps the pun on 'Levellers' represents a covert allusion to the Puritans, so that 'the Field' is the field of Civil War, the Mower is Cromwell, and the 'Rail' is Charles? Or maybe the Mower is Fairfax . . . This kind of reading, though variations of it have appeared persuasively in print, seems to me to depend primarily on rare ingenuity and a real ability to confuse vehicle and tenor; it also requires a reader to attend to one system of allusions while resolutely refusing to think about others. What does one do with the references to 'Roman Camps', 'Desert Memphis Sand', 'Pyramids', 'Manna', 'Marriners', and 'Israalites'? Is Marvell warning his countrymen against the menace of Israeli seamen operating out of Egypt? Note what happens when we actually *pursue* an allusion – those 'Levellers', for example. In Stanza LVI the 'levell'd space' after the harvest is described in a highly suggestive conceit:

> The World when first created sure
> Was such a Table rase and pure.

But if we are disposed to view this comparison as an attempt to make the meadows symbolize the world at a certain moment in history, we are quickly disabused in the next two lines where Marvell draws on his knowledge of bullfighting to find a more apt simile:

> Or rather such is the *Toril*
> Ere the Bulls enter at Madril.

Like the Nymph's Faun the Mower reveals a capacity for harmony with nature, but as always in Marvell the relationship of man and Nature is precarious, liable to be lost in a moment. This double attitude will be familiar to readers of 'The Picture of little T.C. in a Prospect of

Flowers', where the Nymph 'reforms' the 'errours of the Spring',
but is warned that an offense against course of *kind* will shatter the
idyllic relationship:

> But O young beauty of the Woods,
> Whom Nature courts with fruits and flow'rs,
> Gather the Flow'rs, but spare the Buds;
> Lest *Flora* angry at thy crime,
> To kill her Infants in their prime,
> Do quickly make th' Example Yours;
>   And, ere we see,
> Nip in the blossome all our hopes and Thee.

Such hints as this of darker depths in Nature are focused in the Mower,
where they form a strong contrast to the more conventional tone of
traditional pastoral.

Although the allusions in 'Upon Appleton House' offer perhaps
even more difficulties than those of 'The Nymph complaining', it at
least seems clear that the accident of the 'bloody . . . stroke' possesses
considerable emotional significance for Marvell. Indeed, in 'Damon
the Mower' the 'bloody' interlude is repeated, this time within the
convention of the pastoral love complaint. Damon, pining for the love
of Juliana, reflects on his harmony with nature:

> And, if at Noon my toil me heat,
> The Sun himself licks off my Sweat.
> While, going home, the Ev'ning sweet
> In cowslip-water bathes my feet.

But Juliana is the source of 'unusual Heats', all Nature wilts, and the
'Massacre' of 'Upon Appleton House' reappears with more serious
consequences. Again all grass is flesh:

> While thus he threw his Elbow round,
> Depopulating all the Ground,
> And, with his whistling Sythe, does cut
> Each stroke between the Earth and Root,
> The edged Stele by careless chance
> Did into his own Ankle glance;
> And there among the Grass fell down,
> By his own Sythe, the Mower mown.

Again the reader of 'decorative' pastoral is unprepared for the sharply detailed, realistic moment of violence, and again he does not quite know what to make of it. Although the commonplaces of pastoral hyperbole have become strangely serious, there is no real explanation for the darker implications of the piece, suggested but undefined:

> Only for him no Cure is found,
> Whom *Julianas* Eyes do wound.
> 'Tis death alone that this must do:
> For Death thou art a Mower too.

Surely the significance of the Mower would have been clear to Fairfax's circle at Appleton House, but to the modern reader there may seem to be a lack of awareness on Marvell's part that in the Mower he has created an ambiguous figure. At least, in contrast to 'The Nymph conplaining', there is no technique to show the reader, more or less precisely, what the ambiguity means. Although it is evident that the Mower possesses considerable emotional meaning for Marvell, above and beyond the figure's literal significance, there is no context in which the 'bloody' incidents are seen as purposeful excess, in which the force of the language is justified, or in which the capacity of the Mower for both harmony and conflict with Nature is resolved. The central tenet of pastoral verse, the idyllic correspondence between man and Nature known as the pathetic fallacy, has apparently been deliberately violated, and yet there is no overt explanation of why Marvell departed so radically from the pattern of traditional pastoral. The significance of these departures can be appreciated fully only in the context of the other Mower poems, only as we compare context with context in order to make private meanings public.

'The Mower to the Glo-Worms' is a pretty little lyric that has no obscurities for someone not overcurious about the last stanza. The first three stanzas invoke the Glo-Worms, whose function it is to guide the 'wandring Mowers'. In the fourth and last stanza the 'unusual' Juliana reappears, the Mower's harmony with Nature is again lost, and the whole affair is given an intellectual emphasis oddly at variance with the conventions of pastoral love lyrics:

> Your courteous Lights in vain you wast,
> Since *Juliana* here is come,
> For She my Mind hath so displac'd
> That I shall never find my home.

By ignoring the other Mower poems we could probably find a place for this lyric in the tradition of the pastoral love complaint – even though love is not explicitly mentioned in the poem. Certainly this 'displacement' of the mind seems to be far less serious than the accident of the 'bloody . . . stroke'. And yet another poem in the series, 'The Mower's Song', suggests that Marvell's use of the word 'Mind' was anything but casual.

'The Mower's Song' also concerns Juliana and the mind, and again Marvell adventures from the pastoral theme of harmony with Nature:

> My Mind was once the true survey
> Of all these Medows fresh and gay;
> And in the greenness of the Grass
> Did see its Hopes as in a Glass;
> When *Juliana* came, and She
> What I do to the Grass, does to my Thoughts and Me.

The pastoral harmony between the Mower and Nature no longer exists; the correspondence is in the past tense. As in 'The Mower to the Glo-Worms', moreover, Marvell sees the lost harmony, the 'true survey', as having had its basis in a particular condition of the mind, now lost with the coming of Juliana. Her presence – the word 'love' is again absent from the poem – has dark implications for the Mower. The refrain,

> When *Juliana* came, and She
> What I do to the Grass, does to my Thoughts and Me,

recalls the violence of the 'bloody . . . stroke' and once again demonstrates an imaginative refashioning of Isaiah's proposition: for the Mower all flesh is grass, all grass flesh.

Stanza II emphasizes the Mower's alienation from Nature and explicitly jettisons the convention of attributing human emotions to Nature by exactly reversing the terms of the pathetic fallacy:

> But these, while I with Sorrow pine,
> Grew more luxuriant still and fine;
> That not one Blade of Grass you spy'd,
> But had a Flower on either side.

The word 'luxuriant', because of the ambiguous antecedent of 'these', may be read as a significant pun: if the antecedent of 'these' is taken to be 'Medows', as the context requires, then 'luxuriant' simply denotes exuberant growth; if, however, 'these' is taken to refer to 'Thoughts', its immediate grammatical antecedent, 'luxuriant', then includes a pun on its old meaning of 'lascivious'. For it will presently appear that this poem and also the next to be considered – 'The Mower against Gardens', beginning 'Luxurious Man, to bring his Vice in use' – are about how man gets and employs his lascivious thoughts.

In Stanza III the Mower reproaches the 'Unthankful Medows' that could a 'fellowship so true forego', and then, in the next stanza, he turns to threats of 'luxuriant' proportions:

> But what you in Compassion ought,
> Shall now by my Revenge be wrought:
> And Flow'rs, and Grass, and I and all,
> Will in one common Ruine fall.
> For *Juliana* comes, and She
> What I do to the Grass, does to my Thoughts and Me.

Ostensibly, the Mower's motive for revenge is the betrayal of the meadows that meet in their 'gawdy May-games' while he and his 'Thoughts' suffer from Juliana.

Although such an explanation seems more satisfactory than any derived from the literal action of 'Upon Appleton House' or 'Damon the Mower', it still fails to account for the darker undertones of the whole poem or the emotional metre and diction of this stanza, especially in the refrain, and in the third and fourth lines whose three commas and repeated connectives accentuate the slow, impressive movement of a heroic style. Granted that the intensity of such threats is common, if not to real lovers, then at least to their literary counterparts, it remains difficult to find a place for the Mower's threat in the pastoral tradition. Not only has the original correspondence between the Mower and Nature been lost, but now the Mower seems determined to contribute to his own alienation from the 'true survey'. Pastoral harmony has become pastoral discord.

But if we pause for a moment to examine the poem in more abstract terms, the situation may be summed up in such a way as to explain Marvell's modifications of the pastoral *kind* and to provide some answers to the questions I have been raising throughout. Man once existed in an ideal correspondence and harmony with Nature: the appearance of woman resulted in the loss of the ideal state, in the awareness of mortality, in the inclination to sin. This is, of course, the Christian story of the Fall of Man from the pastoral harmony of Eden.

The Mower, to be sure, is not Adam nor is Juliana Eve; the poem must be read with at least as much literary tact as is required by 'The Nymph complaining'. It is not accurate to say that 'The Mower's Song' is an allegory of the Fall of Man, but neither is it sufficient to plead that this is a very complex poem that new critics (from Putten-ham on) should be assiduous to read on a minimum of two levels. The reader has been led to consider a pastoral love complaint in relation to an event in scriptural history, but the exact poise or balance that Mar-vell has achieved remains hard to state explicitly: genre becomes trope.

In 'The Mower's Song' Marvell has avoided the limitations of con-ventional pastoral almost entirely, and avoided them successfully, despite the fact that he is perhaps most oblique and indirect here. Since the poem is more subtle and carefully articulated than the Mower episode of 'Upon Appleton House' or 'Damon the Mower', a reader appreciates the significance of another area of experience, one that 'transcend[s] poor Shepherds skill', without being confused by sug-gestive but irrelevant, or only momentarily relevant, terms; that is, by allusions and comparisons which, while they may throw light on the passage at hand, yet fail to form a consistent group amongst themselves.

There is in 'The Mower's Song' a simultaneous blending of kinds of experience as Marvell accommodates the literary technique of pastoral to scriptural history. With the exception of one key word – 'fall' – he does not even use terms ambiguously suggestive of scriptural events. Instead, he has made the plot or action of the poem significant in itself; the organization of the action and the relationship of the Mower to Nature are in themselves expressive of the Fall of Man. Even though the Fall is barely suggested by the plot, the diffuse connection estab-lished in the reader's mind is enough to provide an explanation of the characterization of Juliana and to reveal the basis for the Mower's ambiguous relationship with Nature. Genre has merged with scrip-tural history, as indeed it often had before during the Middle Ages and Renaissance. The genre that had always described *an* Eden here describes *the* Eden, the theological 'home' of 'The Mower to the Glo-Worms', from which man lapsed with the coming of woman: 'For She my Mind hath so displac'd. . . .' As Golding's Ovid has it,

> Moreouer by the golden age what other thing is ment,
> Than Adams tyme in Paradyse.[6]

Which is not to imply that Marvell is 'traditional' in any restricted sense; he draws on earlier pastoral, but he is not indistinguishable from the tradition. By manipulating the traditional form of the pastoral, Marvell has managed to make it an adequate vehicle for his own attitudes toward Christian history, for clearly he has not limited himself to a simple retelling of the story of the Fall.

Marvell sees the Fall primarily as a change that occurred in the mind of man, as a change in the way man looks at or thinks about Nature, because he carefully distinguishes between 'Thoughts and Me' and takes pains to emphasize the role of the mind: 'My Mind was once the true survey. . . .' The fifth and last stanza of 'The Mower's Song' illustrates the attitude:

> And thus, ye Meadows, which have been
> Companions of my thoughts more green,
> Shall now the Heraldry become
> With which I shall adorn my Tomb;
> For *Juliana* comes, and She
> What I do to the Grass, does to my Thoughts and Me.

The grammatical structure of the refrain refuses to let the reader regard man's experience with Nature and man's experience of himself and his 'Thoughts' as separate or unconnected. The Fall is seen as a change in the response of the mind to Nature: 'Companions of my thoughts more green'. Man's present spiritual condition is a tomb with Nature figuring as its decorative heraldry. Thus man's inability to think 'thoughts more green' corresponds to his alienation from the 'true survey' of Nature that he formerly enjoyed, from the Edenlike state of mind that allowed him to exist in harmony with a 'companionable' and 'compassionate' Nature.

The remaining poem in this group, 'The Mower against Gardens', reinforces the conclusions derived from 'The Mower's Song', and provides even more explicit statements of Marvell's attitude toward the mind of man, the Fall, and Nature – all of which permit us to see that Marvell was engaged in the traditional Nature–Art controversy.[7] The lapsed, corrupted mind of man is the subject of the poem, the theological time is post-Fall:

> Luxurious Man, to bring his Vice in use,
> Did after him the World seduce.

Although the poem bristles with horticultural puns and theological allusions, the main theme is clear: Man, through the activities of his 'double . . . Mind', corrupts the meadows – 'Where Nature was most plain and pure' – and fulfils the threat of 'The Mower's Song' ('Will in one common Ruine fall'). Theologically speaking, the fallen mind possesses for most religious thinkers some knowledge of good as well as evil, but here Marvell restricts himself to man in his knowledge of evil. He is represented as having overreached his natural limits and succumbed to the medieval vice of *curiositas*:

> And yet these Rarities might be allow'd,
> To Man, that sov'raign thing and proud;
> Had he not dealt between the Bark and Tree,
> Forbidden mixtures there to see.

Marvell communicates his theme by developing a contrast between the natural, untouched meadows and the artificial garden. The meadows are 'sweet Fields' where Nature is free to impart a 'wild and fragrant Innocence'.[8] On the other hand, the activities involved in making the garden – that 'dead and standing pool of Air' – are expressed in witty vice-metaphors: the bastard plant no longer knows the 'Stock from which it came'; grafting produces an 'uncertain and adult'rate fruit'; the emasculated cherry (stoneless) is induced to 'procreate without a Sex' – for this 'green Seraglio has its Eunuchs too'. Thus two worlds are presented in opposition: one, the world created by man, expressed in metaphors of 'luxuriant' illegitimacy; the other, a world of fauns and gods, is the preferred state, where 'presence' rather than 'skill' is the ideal agent.

Man's emphasis on 'skill' has led to a corresponding neglect of the innocence to be had from the 'sweet Fields' of Nature. Nature, then, when not deformed by 'Forbidden mixtures', still preserves something of the intercourse between heaven and earth that man forfeited through the Fall. Man's 'double . . . Mind', on the other hand, has attempted to recreate, out of its knowledge of evil, the Garden of Eden – and the result is Acrasia's Bower.[9] Art has corrupted Nature.

I have been trying to define some of Marvell's fundamental commitments by pointing out a development in his thought and literary technique from the highly derivative and naturalistic pastorals of the fashionable world, to a criticism, especially in 'Clorinda and Damon', of *libertin* ethics, and finally to the use of the pastoral form as a vehicle for the expression of his more mature concerns. Marvell was not of course unique in using the pastoral form for Christian ends; in fact, our historical perspective makes such a use seem almost inevitable. Given the 'Christianization' of Vergil's Fourth Eclogue, the shepherds of the Gospels, the mystical glosses on the Canticles, and the medieval and Renaissance tendency toward allegory, it is hard to see how readers and writers could fail to identify a conception like that of the Golden Age, where a bountiful, beneficent Nature literally dropped food into men's laps, with the Christian idea of the Garden of Eden. Nor was Marvell unique in using pastoral as a way of responding to the division between Nature and Art. Given our knowledge of the tradition, such a use, again, seems almost inevitable. But if Marvell's use of pastoral is not unusual, his particular modifications of the tradition are, and it is here that the poet reveals himself and his philosophy of man most clearly.

The way Marvell manipulates the most venerable pastoral convention, that of man in idyllic sympathy with Nature, leaves no doubt that he was deeply preoccupied with man's double estate – his capacity both for harmony with, and alienation from, Nature. This attitude towards man in relation to Nature is, moreover, not simply a matter of temperament; it has a firm, precise theological basis in the scriptural fact of the Fall from Eden and the consequences that may be supposed to have proceeded from it.

Thus three main traditions are necessary for an understanding of Marvell's poetry: the literary tradition of pastoral; the philosophical tradition of Nature and Art that has always been associated with pastoral; and the Christian tradition, which gives a particular shape and meaning to the other two. In the more poetic (and private) terms with which I have been working, Marvell sees the Fall as having produced a 'double . . . Mind', one that possesses both the Mower's capacity for the harmony of the 'true survey' and the alienation of the 'bloody . . . stroke'; for Innocence and Vice; for Nature and Art.

Art or 'skill' is the immoral activity of a 'double . . . Mind' as it deals in 'Forbidden mixtures'. Marvell makes the matter most explicit in 'Upon Appleton House', where the activities of 'Man unrul'd' contrast unfavorably with the instinctively good behavior of birds and

beasts (stanza II). Stated in the conceptual terms with which we are
familiar:

> But Nature here hath been so free
> As if she said leave this to me.
> Art would more neatly have defac'd
> What she had laid so sweetly wast;
> In fragrant Gardens, shaddy Woods,
> Deep Meadows, and transparent Floods.   (st. x)

Nature, 'orderly and near' (IV), produces Fairfax's garden, which is not
artful but nevertheless 'in order grows' (XXXIX). For Marvell the *locus
amoenus* is, like Milton's Eden, the result not of 'nice Art' but 'Nature
boon'. Art is, in short, a principle of corruption, of false rather than true
order, the instrument of man's further alienation from Nature and
hence from God, whose Book of the Creatures human Art has
deformed.

The Mower in these terms becomes a much more comprehensible
figure. Clearly he is Marvell's symbol of fallen man, the lowest of the
angels and the highest of the beasts, made in the image of his God and
yet capable of the depths of depravity. The Bible notes that God made
man upright, but he has sought out many devices, like Marvell's
'Luxurious Man' who, 'to bring his Vice in use,/ Did after him the
World seduce'. The result is the Mower, the natural man who displays
a faculty for both harmony and alienation, a faculty possibly shared by
all men in all times in relation to Nature. And yet Marvell's Nature is
not Wordsworth's, because the one is ordered where the other is
spontaneous. Similarly, the Mower is symbolic but not Symbolist,
for the meanings clustered around Marvell's mysterious figure, while in
the last analysis indefinable, are in an important sense neither vague nor
illimitable but retain by association something of the firm outline
characteristic of their theological formulation. Nor is the Mower's
ambiguous relationship with Nature in any way Empsonian; the ambiguity is limited, defined, by scriptural history, and it may finally be
resolved through reference to the theological fact of the Fall.

The themes of harmony and alienation, most clearly articulated in
connection with the Mower figure, appear to be similarly, though less
obviously, present in the ironic wit of most of Marvell's best lyrics,
lending these deceptively casual verses the weight and precision derived
from a specific view of man and the universe. There seems to be little

doubt, for example, that 'The Picture of little T.C.' would be an extremely slight effort if it were not for the last stanza, where the dark moral undercuts the courtly posturings of the preceding lines. The same is true of the concluding lines of 'A Dialogue between the Soul and Body':

> What but a Soul could have the wit
> To build me up for Sin so fit?
> So Architects do square and hew,
> Green Trees that in the Forest grew.

Here a knowledge of Marvell's general attitude toward Nature and Art permits us to appreciate the full force of the Body's wry comparison; the Soul is like the architect not only in its amoral capacity to 'build' but also in its immoral capacity to use Art to deface 'green' Nature. Marvell's language, perhaps to a greater degree than that of most poets, reveals its full resonance only in relation to the entire body of his lyric verse, which is the reason that T. S. Eliot has done the poet a disservice in suggesting that the critical task in the 'case' of Marvell is 'to squeeze the drops of the essence of two or three poems': 'The fact that of all Marvell's verse, which is itself not a great quantity, the really valuable part consists of a very few poems indicates that the [distinguishing] quality of [his verse] is probably a literary rather than a personal quality.'[10] It has seemed to me, rather, that the literary quality of this individual talent is, despite its traditional elements, highly personal.

Even the more explicitly religious poems are difficult to appreciate in isolation. 'The Coronet', for example, may appear at first glance to be a purely religious meditation, but it is to be read as a pastoral. The 'I' of the poem speaks of his 'Shepherdess', and a whole dimension of the poem vanishes if we are inattentive to what is involved when Marvell represents his 'I' as a singer-shepherd. The poem is a paradigm of conversion, a dramatization, like Herbert's 'The Collar', of the need for Grace through the deliberate cultivation and then rejection of blasphemous or religiously mistaken thoughts. Marvell's shepherd begins by announcing his intention to reform, to replace his Saviour's crown of 'Thorns' with a 'Chaplet' of flowers (his 'fruits are only flow'rs'):[11]

> Dismantling all the fragrant Towers
> That once adorn'd my Shepherdesses head.

But he is forced to reject these thoughts, for he finds that pride, the 'Serpent old', has become part of the 'Chaplet' with 'wreaths of Fame and Interest'. (Chaplet means prayer as well as wreath, and therefore also refers to the song of the shepherd.) The ascent, as St Bernard says, is through humility rather than pride; and thus the shepherd begs God to 'disintangle' the 'winding Snare' of Satan 'Or shatter too with him my curious frame',

> Though set with Skill and chosen out with Care.
> That they, while Thou on both their Spoils dost tread,
> May crown thy Feet, that could not crown thy Head.

The little Augustinian drama is complete, the progress from sinner to saved that so absorbed the seventeenth century ('The Collar', Walton's life of Donne, or Donne's 'If poisonous minerals . . .') has been re-enacted in the poem with great concentration of meaning. A good example of the concentration possible in this kind of pastoral may be found in the 'curious frame' of line twenty-two: it refers first to the artful chaplet (poem and prayer and wreath) that is 'set with Skill', the 'skill' or Art that deformed the 'Meadows' in 'The Mower against Gardens'; but it also refers to the human being, that overly curious creature whose Art may obscure the divine Nature within; and finally it refers to the poem itself, an object of curious Art that must be 'disintangled' from human 'Fame and Interest' in order to become a pure chaplet or psalm in praise of the 'king of Glory'. By the end of the poem the sinner has been saved, and the pagan shepherd-poet has become a David, that shepherd-poet who danced before the Ark of God.

Even in the poems of human love the theme of alienation from Nature through Art gives Marvell's tone a distinctive toughness, setting such a lyric as 'To his Coy Mistress' clearly apart from others of its kind. Whereas the lovers of Donne's 'The Sunne Rising' are identified, in half-ironic hyperbole, with the universe, the sun being advised to

> Shine here to us, and thou art every where;
> This bed thy center is, these walls, thy sphere,

Marvell's 'am'rous birds of prey' gain our attention through their isolation, their defiant opposition to the world:

> And tear our Pleasures with rough strife,
> Thorough the Iron gates of Life.
> Thus, though we cannot make our Sun
> Stand still, yet we will make him run.

This attitude of ironic defiance, the tough determination to live with one's nature though it is somehow out of joint with the world, has been much admired. Yet we have seen that Marvell's attitude is only superficially admirable in modern terms, for it stems not from the metaphysical disillusionment of the twentieth century, but from the theological conviction that man fell from the ideal harmony of the Garden of Eden. In contrast to that of the Underground Man, Marvell's malaise has a cure within the terms of the system that defines the nature of his illness.

The fact is that Marvell, unlike most of his modern readers, thought it possible to recover the lost harmony with Nature, which before the Fall man had possessed in the Garden. There is more than a hint of the possibility in the ordered innocence of the Fairfax garden of 'Upon Appleton House', where the recovery is linked to contemplative retirement. In the 'Horatian Ode' Cromwell leaves his 'private Gardens' and joins 'wiser Art' to 'Nature', so becoming the union of active and contemplative or the 'Man . . . that does both act and know'. But the clearest illustration appears in the contemplative lesson of 'The Garden', probably Marvell's most famous and variously read poem. The themes of alienation and harmony, of Art and Nature, are present in 'The Garden', and probably it could be demonstrated that they are as sure a guide to the total attitude of the poem as any of the numerous influences already brought to bear on its richly suggestive verses. But here my purpose is only to round out this discussion of Marvell's pastoral experiments, to sketch the workings of man's 'double . . . Mind' in its knowledge of good rather than evil. It is in this sense that 'The Garden' offers a solution to the desperate condition of man implied by 'The Mower against Gardens' and 'The Mower's Song'.

The speaker of the poem withdraws from the 'busie Companies of Men' into the solitude and innocence of the garden, finding there what the reader of pastoral will recognize as an elegant condensation of the 'soft' primitivism associated with the Golden Age:

> What wond'rous Life in this I lead!
> Ripe Apples drop about my head;

> The Luscious Clusters of the Vine
> Upon my Mouth do crush their Wine.

Doubtless these lines are sensuous, but sexual, hence sensual, connotations are more easily kept where they belong, in the background, if we remember that this is an account of what Nature really *was* during the Golden Age, animated in Marvell by a Christian Neoplatonism that saw the landscape tremulous with divinity. This garden is neither the Acrasia's Bower of 'The Mower against Gardens' nor the spiritual tomb of 'The Mower's Song'. There Nature had been corrupted by the overcurious Art of man's 'double . . . Mind', but here the intimacy of the speaker with Nature is meant to recall the harmony of the Garden of Eden. Here intimacy precedes the purification of the mind:

> Mean while the Mind, from pleasure less,
> Withdraws into its happiness:
> The Mind, that Ocean where each kind
> Does streight its own resemblance find;
> Yet it creates, transcending these,
> Far other Worlds, and other Seas;
> Annihilating all that's made
> To a green Thought in a green Shade.

The withdrawal of the mind, creating an inner world of Nature and annihilating the outer world corrupted by Art, precedes the illumination of the soul in the next stanza; thus for a moment the poet, translating physical into spiritual geography, recovers the 'true survey' of 'The Mower's Song'.

Through the process of 'annihilation' the speaker has managed to think 'thoughts more green' in a world seduced by the Art of 'Luxurious Man'. Art, or 'all that's made' by the mind of man, has been transformed into Nature, or the 'green Thought in a green Shade'. Within himself the speaker has formed a garden, a paradise notably free of dainty devices: this is the *hortus conclusus* of the mind, established within not by Art but by the other impulse of that 'double . . . Mind', by 'Annihilating all that's made/ To a green Thought in a green Shade'. The Mower has, after all, found his 'home', the spiritual residence of Adam's sons located in the dark backward and abysm of theological time, and his return has fulfilled the promise of Milton's angel:

> then wilt thou not be loth
> To leave this Paradise, but shalt possess
> A Paradise within thee, happier far.

To us Marvell's attitude toward Nature and Art perhaps seems primitivist, even rigidly anti-intellectual, and yet his intention probably extended no farther than the effort of the moralist to put matters in proper perspective: so that salvation might be attained, so that the lost pastoral innocence, the paradisiacal integrity of Nature, might be reconstituted with the aid alone of literary Art in the garden of the mind.

SOURCE: *Nature and Art in Renaissance Literature* (1964).

NOTES

1. It is possible to use external or direct internal evidence to date a number of Marvell's poems, especially the satires and those few published before 1650. But by far the greater part of his lyric poetry appeared only posthumously in 1681. One may speculate, and speculate quite reasonably, that much of the pastoral verse must have been written in the early 1650s at Nun Appleton, when Marvell was tutor to Mary Fairfax: an earlier Fairfax had translated Tasso; the house and grounds favored contemplation; an audience educated in the subtleties of pastoral literature remained at hand; the pastorals reveal technical accomplishments lacking in the poems before 1650 and show few overt affinities with the later satires; and the long 'Upon Appleton House' betrays many similarities with the short pastoral pieces. But in the absence of further evidence these speculations remain speculations.

2. *Elizabethan Critical Essays*, ed. G. Gregory Smith (Oxford, 1904) I 175.

3. *The Arte of English Poesie*, ed. G. D. Willcock and Alice Walker (Cambridge, 1936) p. 38. Both Sidney and Puttenham refer to the 'allegorical' rather than the 'decorative' tradition of pastoral. John Fletcher's definition, on the other hand, refers to the latter tradition: 'Understand, therefore, a pastoral to be a representation of shepherds and shepherdesses with their actions and passions, which must be such as may agree with their natures, at least not exceeding former fictions and vulgar traditions; they are not to be adorned with any art, but such improper ones as nature is said to bestow as singing, and poetry; or such as experience may teach them, as the virtues of herbs and fountains, the ordinary course of the sun, moon, and stars, and such like.' 'To the Reader', *The Faithful Shepherdess*, in *The Works of Francis Beaumont & John Fletcher*, ed. W. W. Greg 1908 III 18.

4. M. C. Bradbrook and M. G. Lloyd Thomas, *Andrew Marvell* (Cambridge, 1940) pp. 49–50, tend to identify the faun with Agnus Dei and see the 'love of the girl for her fawn' as a 'reflection of the love of the Church for Christ'. Everett H. Emerson, 'Andrew Marvell's "The Nymph complaining for the death of her Faun"', in *Études anglaises*, VIII (April–June 1955) 107–10, argues that while the poem is not an 'allegory', it nevertheless embodies Marvell's emotional response to the Church of England in the 1640s. This poem, like the 'Horatian Ode', has become the occasion for numerous articles; it is an academic *cause célèbre*, plunder in the running battle between Historical Scholar and New Critic. My own feeling is that the poem is best read as a pastoral epicedium on the loss of

love, but I do not hazard a full-scale interpretation here because it would not be entirely pertinent to the rest of my argument and because my purpose is not polemical.

5. Only some 64 (stanzas XLIX–LVI) of the 776 lines of 'Upon Appleton House' are devoted to the Mowers as the poet, oscillating between physical and spiritual topography, moves in verse from house to garden to meadow to wood. Courtly compliment to Lord Fairfax is a major theme of this extraordinary work, but Marvell also explores the relation of man to nature and a variety of other important themes. The informing principle of the entire poem lies in an ideal of conduct embodying 'measure' and 'proportion' in the 'vast and all-comprehending Dominions of Nature and Art'.

6. *The .xv. Bookes of P. Ovidius Naso, entytuled Metamorphosis, translated oute of Latin into English meeter* (1575), sig. A7ʳ. Cf *The Shepheardes Calender*, 'June', lines 9–10, *The Complete Poetical Works of Spenser*, ed. R. E. Neil Dodge (Cambridge, Mass., 1936) p. 29.

7. Frank Kermode, whose sensitive, learned criticism is useful in any reading of Marvell, locates the poem within the established terms of the Nature–Art controversy and cites a number of relevant documents outside Marvell; see 'Two Notes on Marvell', in *Notes and Queries*, CXXVII (March 1952), 136–8, and 'The Argument of Marvell's "Garden"', in *Essays in Criticism*, II (July 1952) 225–41, the latter reprinted in this volume pp. 125–40. A more general view of Marvell in relation to Nature may be found in J. H. Summers, 'Marvell's "Nature"', in *Journal of English Literary History*, XX (June 1953) 121–35, reprinted in this volume pp. 141–54; Summers chooses to emphasize only one aspect of the Mower: 'He symbolizes man's alienation from nature.'

8. Like John Rea, who maintains that a 'green Medow is a more delightful object' than the 'Gardens of the new model' because 'there Nature alone, without the aid of Art, spreads her verdant Carpets, spontaneously imbroydered with many pretty plants and pleasing Flowers, far more inviting than such an immured Nothing' – *Flora: seu, De florum cultura. Or, a Complete Florilege* (1665) p. 1.

9. The literary and philosophical contrast between two kinds of gardens is an important theme in medieval and Renaissance literature. Readers of the *Romance of the Rose* will be familiar with the theme, but of course the famous example occurs in Spenser, where the Garden of Adonis in which Art complements Nature is contrasted with the Bower of Bliss in which Art usurps the proper functions of Nature.

10. 'Andrew Marvell', in *Selected Essays*, 3rd ed. (1951) p. 292. [See also this volume, p. 45]

11. The allusion to Matthew 7:20 ('Wherefore by their fruits ye shall know them') implies the entire poem: flowers must become fruits through the Grace of God.

[Editor's note.] Fuller notes appear in the original publication of this essay.

EARL MINER

The Death of Innocence in Marvell's 'Nymph Complaining for the Death of her Faun' (1967)

INTERPRETATIONS of this poem run a very wide range from literal to allegorical, classical to Christian, pastoral to historical; large numbers of classical, medieval, and Renaissance writers have been adduced for sources and analogues.[1] With all this learning, critical analysis, and even common sense brought into play, it might be thought that the poem had become sufficiently clear. Of course the opposite is true; so various are the types of interpretation that it is necessary to choose from all the proffered help. Moreover, it appears to me that the poem deals with a theme insufficiently discussed, the death of innocence, which I hope to discuss with the evidence provided by the poem and to set into the context of earlier studies. If this essay were an attempt at exhaustive analysis, it would also concern itself with the very characteristic wit of the poem – its glances and hesitations, its suggestions and withholdings. The wit provides for the maximum inclusiveness of experience in small compass and for the minimum pressure of the weight of any specifiable detail. It would be difficult to accept any reading of the poem that did not recognize, at least implicitly, the importance and difficulty of its wit.

There is general agreement that 'The Nymph complaining for the death of her Faun' is a version of pastoral complaint, and that into the pastoral, idealized world have come the 'wanton Troopers' who threaten to destroy it. Although it is not clear that there is general agreement about the plot of the poem, that is probably only because it has seemed too simple a matter to deserve comment. Since anything simple in the poem provides a useful starting point, we may begin by considering the events of the poem, not in the sequence in which they are narrated, but in the sequence in which they are imagined to have occurred. There are four actions or episodes that can be described with considerable assurance.

Episode I: lines 25–36. The Nymph and her 'Huntsman' Sylvio had been in love. While still not found to be 'counterfeit', he gave her the Faun. The love did not last long, however, because Sylvio 'soon' 'beguil'd' the Nymph, who was left with 'his Faun' where before she had had (in the familiar love trope) his 'Heart', with the obvious pun.

Episode II: lines 37–92. 'Thenceforth I set my self to play / My solitary time away' – with the Faun. The long middle section of the poem recounts her loving care, the beauty and good nature of the sportive Faun, and its purity.

Episode III: lines 1–24. The 'wanton Troopers' shoot the Faun, which lies bleeding to death before the Nymph as she questions the nature of such men and the heinousness of their act.

Episode IV: lines 93–122. The Faun languishes and dies. The Nymph resolves to have cut, as a memorial, a marble statue of her weeping self and, at its foot, an alabaster image of the Faun.

Now our questions must begin. The one most relevant to the summary of the plot is surely that of the relation between the characters – the Troopers, the Faun, Sylvio, and the Nymph. To begin with the Faun, it is contrasted with Sylvio and the Troopers.

> Thy love was far more better then
> The love of false and cruel men.   (53–4)

If the applicability of the couplet is not clear enough, Sylvio had been described as 'false' three lines before, and in the opening lines of the poem the Troopers were revealed to be cruel. They are described as 'wanton' (line 1) and 'ungentle' (line 3). What is not clear is the reason why Marvell has the Nymph say to the Faun in that couplet that its love is much better than that of the Troopers. Is it merely hypothetical, or is she in a state of mind only to reject men categorically, or have there been passages between the Troopers and her? The questions are not directly answered, but there is a kind of solution in the relation between Sylvio and the Troopers. He is not a usual pastoral shepherd of the kind that one expects to discover in the world inhabited by seventeenth-century nymphs. He is a self-styled 'Huntsman' (line 31). What the couplet does, then, is thematically relate Sylvio's betrayal – his 'counterfeit', 'false' behavior toward the Nymph – to the Troopers and their slaying of the Faun. What this implies, and requires for logical consistency, is a thematic relation of the Nymph to the Faun, and this is precisely the most extensively worked out relation of the poem. The couplet quoted is followed (in lines 54–62) by a comparison of the Faun's beauties with those of the Nymph and even with those of 'any Ladies of the Land' (line 62). In the next passage (lines 63–70) the Faun's speed is compared to that the Nymph can boast of. After a lengthy comparison (lines 71–92) of the Faun to the 'flaxen Lillies' of the Nymph's garden, and after the death scene (lines 93–110), the poem concludes with its description of the memorial statues. The last two lines imply a final comparison.

> For I would have thine Image be
> White as I can, though not as Thee.

Ostensibly the lines say that the Nymph cannot provide an alabaster as white as the Faun. But the obvious point is the metaphorical one made explicit earlier in the poem (lines 55–62); the Nymph herself is not as 'white', as pure as the Faun.

Not as white as the Faun, the Nymph is whiter than Sylvio or the Troopers. We take her word for the one and her manner for evidence of the other. But it requires the utmost care to describe just how 'white' the Nymph herself is and to say on what evidence one has measured her whiteness. Marvell does not permit us to ask anything so 'ungentle' as whether the Nymph has lost her chastity, but he does provide a pastoral love plot and comparisons between the Nymph and the Faun. It is the animal that is said to have 'pure Virgin Limbs' (line 89). Sylvio is 'Unconstant' (line 25), 'counterfeit' (line 26), 'wild' (line 34), and 'false' (lines 50, 54). He 'beguil'd' (line 33) the trusting Nymph. Neither these details nor the strong force of the tradition of the woman's love-complaint makes it necessary that our Nymph had yielded to Sylvio before he proved untrue. Marvell himself is gallant enough not to make an issue of it. But what is implied by the parallel suggested earlier (between the Troopers' slaying of the Faun and Sylvio's betrayal) is the destruction of innocence. Or, to put it differently, the Faun grew up knowing the Nymph, whereas the Nymph grows up in another sense knowing Sylvio and the Troopers. She is the

superior in experience and sophistication, both of them attributes that
are inimical to innocence.

In deciding how far we may go in relating the loss of innocence to the
love plot of the poem, the only passage that might be thought to be
useful to us is, in the event, a complicating factor. Towards the end of
the poem, the Nymph speaks of making an offering of tears at 'Diana's
shrine' (line 104). In view of all the recondite tradition that has been
discovered to be related to the poem, one hesitates to come out with
any remark so obvious as that Diana is goddess of chastity, but this is at
least of demonstrable relevance to the poem. The problem is: how is it
relevant? Diana is also goddess of the hunt, commonly pictured in
statues and paintings as the Nymph imagines her marble and the Faun's
alabaster statues to be grouped. But we cannot allow an identification
of the Nymph with Diana: the Nymph would not shoot a deer, she
would not destroy the innocence represented by the animal. The mani-
fest dissonance of this aspect of 'Diana's shrine' with its traditional
trophies of the hunt very greatly qualifies any possible inference that
might be drawn about the chaste innocence of the Nymph. Moreover,
what is offered is tears. The Nymph takes the 'two crystal Tears' (line
102) shed by the Faun as it dies and, using them as a kind of essence,
fills up the 'golden Vial' (line 101) with her own tears. Under what
conditions are tears the appropriate offering to Diana, goddess of
chastity and the hunt? Each reader must answer, and answer with care.
The Faun goes to a suitably classical Elysium to join 'Swans and
Turtles', 'milk-white Lambs' and 'Ermins pure' (lines 106–8). The
Nymph does not speculate about where she will spend eternity.

It is useful to say what there is that can be shown from the poem itself.
There is, so to speak, a two-part plot; the related episodes of the shooting and the death of a Faun are separated by the recollection of a love
story anterior to the shooting. Parallelisms between the characters in
the two plots show that the poem is a love-complaint as well as a complaint for the death of a pet. Such parallelisms demonstrate further that
the death of the Faun is relevant not just in itself as the death of an
innocent but also as an analogue for the damaged innocence of the
Nymph. The two wounds or, in a very tenuous metaphorical sense,
the two deaths of the Faun and the Nymph establish the theme of the
poem as that of the death of innocence. The Faun dies through the
sudden intrusion of the 'wanton Troopers' upon a pastoral world, and
the Nymph is wounded by her 'counterfeit' 'Huntsman' friend, Sylvio.

In the one case, the action is decisive, and the innocent dies, while Innocence remains as a principle. In the other case, there is a betrayal leading to experience and knowledge, the loss of Innocence as a principle except in recollection. The Nymph is aware of the difference, and one major function of the Faun in the poem is to provide her with the psychological satisfaction of nursing an innocent when she has become experienced. This maternal, or if that is too strong, this feminine prizing of a substitute for innocence, is related to the other surrogate role played by the Faun, the *surrogatus amantis*, of which more subsequently. What, above all, the wit of the poem suggests is that the death of the Nymph's innocence is but partial. She is only guilty by comparison with a symbol of complete, ideal innocence, not by comparison with the Troopers. But at the same time the wit insists that her participating awareness is as much involved as the actions of Sylvio.

Thus far I have treated matters which, the wit apart, seem to me demonstrable from the poem, and the wit itself is palpably there as well, although different people might assess its functions and significance differently. There are other elements that are felt by readers, but that are, like the wit, difficult of assessment. The poem has not proved the less attractive for the tenuousness of these other matters. Quite the contrary. But the problems are such that the evidence for further interpretation is so fine and the sources so increasingly external to the poem that hesitation like Marvell's own wit is equally called for and difficult to sustain. I suggested earlier one further kind of interpretation, the psychological. Pierre Legouis has given a double psychological interpretation, one feature of it being the general situation in which the Nymph finds herself grieving, the other the relevance to Marvell's own experience.[2] The former would be difficult to fault; the latter is open to disagreement because Marvell's personality itself is so variously interpreted. Another interpretation that is in practice psychological, although presented in learned exposition of the traditions, *topoi*, and tropes of the poem, is that of D. C. Allen, who argued (with much else) that the Faun is a *surrogatus amoris* for the Nymph.[3] He adduced many classical, medieval, and Renaissance precursors. But the precursors are really not needed, since we can all sense from the Nymph's detailed account of her care of the Faun, play with it, and love for it, that she has turned upon the Faun the affection rebuffed by Sylvio. Indeed, although one feels that the German translator of the poem, Werner Vorfriede,[4] goes altogether too far in describing the situation

as 'eine bacchantisch-erotische Szene zwischen Nymphen und Faunen',
he is right to the extent that, psychologically at least, the Faun is less
a *surrogatus amoris* than a *surrogatus amantis*. It was only after Sylvio
had proved untrue that the Nymph turned for consolation to the Faun.

> Thenceforth I set myself to play
> My solitary time away,
> With this . . .   (37–9)

But beyond this sort of obvious taking consolation in one creature and
devoting to it the affection she had once devoted to another, human,
creature, it is difficult to see what kind of detailed analysis is possible.
The difficulty with psychological readings is that the poem requires
that they be made with the greatest tact, lest hints be taken as avowals
and hesitations as refusals or, in contrary fashion, what is simple and
obvious be rendered altogether complex and abstruse.

Those who have sought to explore the even less conclusive thematic
significances of the poem have worked from what have been presumed the sources of the poem. One of the first of the thematic
interpretations was the religious interpretation advanced by M. C.
Bradbrook and M. G. Lloyd Thomas,[5] who argued that although the
poem opens 'with straightforward and charming naturalism', it ends 'by
drawing largely on The Song of Solomon and its identification of the
fawn with Christ', or that 'the love of the girl for her fawn is taken to
be a reflection of the love of the Church for Christ'. Although they
were far from arguing a thoroughgoing allegory for the poem, Miss
Bradbrook and Miss Thomas did succeed in drawing attention to the
religious suggestiveness of the Garden passage (lines 71–92). Strenu-
ously objected to by some more recent criticism,[6] the religious interpretation has been severely modified. Most people would be willing to
compromise to the extent that, although they would deny a religious
allegory, they would agree that the Garden passage does use religious
language and that, in effect, there are religious 'overtones'.[7] The
difficulty with the religious reading is that its full validity requires a
thoroughgoing allegory that hardly sorts with the love plot of the
poem. (The Faun is hardly at once Christ and a *surrogatus amoris* or
amantis.) It seems possible to conclude, however, that Marvell sought
in the Garden passage a glancing, witty, but serious parody of The
Song of Songs that reveals more about the innocence lost by the

Nymph and more about her solemnity concerning the Faun than any patterning of the Nymph upon the Church and the Faun upon Christ.

The other 'sources' of the poem have not been so fully followed through, primarily because it is not wholly certain that most of them are in fact sources, or analogues, call them what one will. The most widely known of the proposed sources is that given currency by H. M. Margoliouth in his edition of Marvell,[8] William Browne's story of Fida's Hind in *Britannia's Pastorals* (I iii–iv). This source has the advantage over almost all the works brought forward by Allen in that Marvell can be believed to have read it. Moreover, it does have a parallel action, beginning with a pastoral love story and going on to the slaying of the Hind by an outside force, Riot, and ending with larger thematic suggestions. But if Marvell was indebted to this story, his version is a very different reaction colored by a wit unknown to the solemn Browne of Tavistock. The story of Fida and her Hind remains a possible source which is of relevance to the outlines of Marvell's poem but of little pertinence to the handling. Much the same thing may be said of the story of the stag of Cyparissus treated by Ovid in *Metamorphoses* X 106–42. In itself, the story is far less close to Marvell's than is Browne's, since it involves the homosexual love of Apollo for a male protagonist; a killing, albeit an accidental one, of the stag by Cyparissus himself; and indeed little except a young person, a deer, and a slaying of the deer that is in common with Marvell's poem. Le Comte has, however, in effect claimed a debt to the kind of story Ovid tells by stressing the possibility of similar metamorphosis in Marvell's poem (lines 91–2), and even more the analogue of the weeping Nymph to Niobe.[9] If Marvell recalled Ovid's story, he changed it with great freedom.

The final 'source' is one that seems to me capable of more exploration than it has received in the past, both because it is in a work that Marvell certainly knew and because of intrinsic resemblances with both this poem and with other poems by Marvell. It is the story, first identified by Kenneth Muir, as an 'echo'[10] – the death of Silvia's pet deer at the hands of Ascanius in the seventh *Aeneid* (lines 475–509). The passage tells how the furious Allecto puts the hounds of the Trojan huntsman Iülus on the scent of the stag of Silvia, who had tended it with her own loving hands; how Ascanius himself shoots the stag with an arrow; and how the action rouses the Latins to battle against the Trojans. What is closest to Marvell's poem in this story is Silvia's tending the animal by hand, the mortal wounding by an outsider, and the dying of the animal before the mourning girl. What seems farthest from the poem is Virgil's context and import. The episode is the third and climactic action of Allecto to stir up the Latins to war against the Trojans. The war is an obstacle to the founding of the new Troy, Rome, and the story of Silvia is a tragic idyl amid the larger workings of fate in the epic of the formation of a new nation.

What I wish to propose as a possibility (the evidence admits no higher degree of probability) is that the death of Marvell's Faun has a historical or political significance dependent upon a parallelism with this passage from the *Aeneid*. What the parallel connects with in the poem is what first meets our eye there, the 'wanton Troopers' of the opening line. Le Comte observed that 'Troopers' was first applied to the Covenanting army of 1640, and Muir suggested that the poem might possibly be based upon an episode of the Civil War.[11] In exploring such hypotheses, we may begin with the question posed by J. B. Leishman's book, *The Art of Marvell's Poetry* (1966): 'Is it not likely [in spite of earlier poems on the death of pets], however, that Marvell's untraditional particularisation of this traditional topic, the slaughter of a child's pet by foraging (and presumably Parliamentary) troopers, was suggested to him by the sort of thing that was going on all around him, and had been going on all over England since the beginning of the Civil War . . . ?' (p. 156). It must be admitted that such an interpretation, applied to the Virgilian context, does not allow for the love plot of Marvell's poem. Although such a consideration prevents our considering the passage from the *Aeneid* as a full parallel, we may grant as much and then go on to where the parallel does take us.

What it leads us to is a qualification, typical of Marvell, of the Nymph's view of what has happened. She feels that she is wholly misused by Sylvio and that the death of the Faun is an unqualifiedly wanton tragedy. Virgil's episode, however, treats the action as a highly pathetic and unfortunate one in the desirable course of the establishment of a new and greater nation. It is wholly possible that Marvell used his story as a similar, though (in view of the tone of the poem) yet more regrettable episode in the reshaping of England into a new commonwealth. The suggestion of a parallel with Virgil implies that Marvell felt the new order as inevitable as that represented by Aeneas, *fato profugus*, but nonetheless tragic in its by-actions. An older, more ideal world of pastoral sanctity is invaded and its prime representative destroyed by the invasion. (I cannot, however, discern a thorough-going historical parallel, with the Faun representing Charles I and the Nymph England.) Such destruction suits with the theme of the death of innocence that I believe unquestionable in the poem. As with three concentric circles, then, we have the Nymph's fall from innocence to experience; the destruction of innocence in its most perfect embodiment, the Faun; and the loss of national innocence in the tragedy of a war overturning an ancestral order. It need hardly be said that such a *tone* is to be found in Virgil's episode. And I think that Marvell's attitude in the 'Horatian Ode' and in 'Upon Appleton House' is sufficiently mixed to allow for an *a priori* acceptance of this third concentric of meaning, as is Marvell's well-known statement that, 'upon considering all, I think that the [Parliamentary] cause was too good to have been fought for. Men ought to have trusted God; they ought and might have trusted the King with that whole matter.'[12]

'Upon Appleton House' makes a similar, although more explicit and demonstrable, allusion to military and political matters in the description of Fairfax's gardens as a fort (sts XXXVI–XLVI) and in the preceding narration of the elder Fairfax's dispossessing (line 272) of the nunnery of 'the blooming Virgin *Thwates*' (sts XI–XXXV). These two passages alone provide a provocative topical gloss upon 'The Nymph complaining for the death of her Faun', showing how love, innocence, experience, pastoral, and war can be made to exist in the same poem. The two passages very considerably strengthen the possibility that the similar pastoral overtones and immured innocence of the world of the Nymph have a topical significance like that discerned by many readers in the wanton Troopers. 'An Horatian Ode upon Cromwel's Return from Ireland' weighs similar elements of 'ancient Rights' of 'the Kingdome old' which Cromwell with his 'forced Pow'r' was establishing 'Into another Mold' (lines 38, 35, 66, 36). Similarly, there is Charles I, 'the Royal Actor' on 'The tragick Scaffold' (lines 53, 54). Again, we discover an order that may be considered in some sense ideal yielding to force from the outside. Of course in the 'Horatian Ode' the balance is favorable to Cromwell and 'the forced Pow'r' rather than to the old order. What these two poems suggest is that the situation of the Nymph is one in which innocence is caught and destroyed by an outside force and by its own intrinsic weakness and that this innocence, like that of Silvia's affection for her deer in the *Aeneid*, is connected with a political tradition yielding to the superior strength of a new order. The love the

Nymph felt for Sylvio is like the desire of the 'Virgin *Thwates*' to enter
the nunnery of 'Upon Appleton House' in that the innocence of both
holds the roots of experience. The political significance discernible in
the situation of the Nymph is indeed closer to the treatment of such
issues in 'Upon Appleton House' than that in the 'Horatian Ode'. But
all three poems possess complexities of tone that make them by no
means easy to sort out.

Marvell's poem about the Nymph and her Faun is truly 'enigmatic'.[13]
The Civil War saw a rebirth of the enigmatic poetry of the Renaissance,
in which emblem, parallelism, beast fable, pastoral, parallel, or allegory
– 'darke' conceits of various kinds – were employed to convey a hidden
meaning for those who shared knowledge and assumptions with the
author but not for others. In the middle decades of the seventeenth
century, the enigmatic mode was commonly employed to support
the Royalist cause (the parliamentary victors could speak more plainly)
and also by men like Marvell with divided feelings. Lovelace's poem
'The Grasse-hopper' is a notable instance of this kind, and it is highly
likely that another poem by him, 'The Falcon', possesses a similar
significance. In such poems the styles of various poets in the first half
of the century are blended into semi-opaque dark conceits dealing with
events of the realm. What is typical of such poems is the suggestion –
through allusion, emblem, or traditional tropes – of historical implications along with a simultaneous withdrawing, a reluctance to follow
through with the metaphorical vehicle to a fully established tenor.
Such a glancing technique well suited Marvell's wit and division of
mind, providing the basis of two of his finest poems, 'Upon Appleton
House' and the 'Horatian Ode'. It is true that the political presence in
those poems is more heavily felt than in the true enigmatic mode of
'The Grasse-hopper' or even of Spenser's 'November' eclogue. But the
complexity of tone retains much of the enigmatic character in the
absence of obscure political tropes and figures. A historical reading of
'The Nymph complaining for the death of her Faun' suggests, on the
other hand, that although the meaning ultimately arrived at is clearer
than that of the 'Horatian Ode', the poem obscures that meaning with
the usual opacities of the enigmatic mode. Ruth Wallerstein allowed
room for such significances, without saying exactly what they were,
when she described the poem as 'a pastoral lyric of the symbolic parallels
of which Marvell was deeply aware, so that they pressed upon his
imagination, without, however, ever verging into actual allegory'.[14]

In this poem the 'symbolic parallels' are, I have argued, those involving the death of innocence in the betrayed love of the Nymph, the death of her pure Faun, and the death of an old order. Along with this death there is the birth of experience in the Nymph's increased understanding of herself and Sylvio, as also of her awareness that the Faun is purer than herself. And her pastoral tragedy suggests a national epic in which a pastoral 'Garden' world of the 'ancient Rights' of the 'Horatian Ode' are destroyed by the incursion of 'wanton Troopers', who, however, while reminding the Nymph of her faithless Sylvio, also remind Marvell of Ascanius and the birth of a new nation.[15]

SOURCE: *Modern Philology* LXV (1967).

NOTES

1. In lieu of the usual initial review of existing scholarship, I shall first attempt to establish critically what the poem says and only thereafter go to other possibilities, in the discussion of which most of the scholarly and critical studies of the poem will be introduced.

2. See Legouis, *Andrew Marvell: poet, puritan, patriot* (Oxford, 1965), especially pp. 56–7, substantially the same interpretation as in the earlier, French version of this standard study, but in respect to Marvell himself somewhat qualified in his brief article, 'Marvell's "Nymph complaining for the death of her Faun": A *mise au point*', in *Modern Language Quarterly*, XXI (March 1960) 30–2.

3. Allen, 'Marvell's "Nymph" ', in *Journal of English Literary History*, XXIII (June 1956) 93–111. The article is something of a *tour de force* vitiated by one's doubt that the poet possessed the learning of the scholar in the Fathers and such worthies as the Venerable Bede. Allen's sceptical *panache* involves, among other things, the introduction of learning explicitly irrelevant and he scorns anyone with the 'undergraduate' temerity to say 'that the poem is about lost chastity'. The epithet apart, I think it equally simple-minded to suppose that to the seventeenth century chastity was a simple undeflowered state or that innocence cannot be lost in other ways.

4. Vorfriede, 'Ein Gedicht von Andrew Marvell', in *Neue Rundschau*, LXXII (1961) 868–79.

5. Bradbrook and Thomas, *Andrew Marvell* (Cambridge, 1940) pp. 47–50.

6. See Edward S. Le Comte, 'Marvell's "The Nymph complaining for the death of her Faun" ' in *Modern Philology*, L (Nov 1952) 97–100. Allen has his objections, too, in the article cited in note 3, above.

7. See Karen Williamson, 'Marvell's "The Nymph complaining for the death of her Faun": A Reply' [to Le Comte], in *Modern Philology*, LI (May 1954) 268–71.

8. *The Poems and Letters of Andrew Marvell*, 2 vols. (Oxford, 1952) I 222.

9. See Le Comte's essay, cited in note 6, above.

10. Muir, 'A Virgilian Echo in Marvell', in *Notes and Queries*, CXCVI (March 1951) 115. Le Comte, Allen, and I myself have all apparently come upon the 'echo' before reading Muir's anticipation.

11. Le Comte, p. 100; Muir, p. 115. E. H. Emerson in 'Andrew Marvell's "The Nymph complaining for the death of her Faun" ', in *Études anglaises*, VIII (April–June 1955) 107–10, suggested that the poem embodies 'Marvell's emotional reaction to the fate of the Church

of England in the 1640s'. In his trenchant 'Réponse à E. H. Emerson in *Études anglaises*, VIII (April–June 1955) 111–12, Pierre Legouis called such a reaction 'impossible', 'contraire à la logique'. As Emerson was aware, his interpretation depends upon a date for the poem in the early 1640s, and as Legouis remarked, the hypothesis that the poem concerns the Anglican Church, that Marvell was a supporter of the Church in the 1640s, and that the poem therefore dated from the 1640s is a hypothesis with circular logic. It will be evident that I think Emerson wrong in the particulars of his topical significance.

12. From *The Rehearsal Transpros'd* (1672) in *The Complete Works in Verse and Prose of Andrew Marvell, M.P.*, ed. Alexander B. Grosart, 4 vols (1872–75) III 212.

13. Harold E. Toliver, *Marvell's Ironic Vision* (New Haven and London, 1965) p. 129. Toliver discusses the poem in terms of what he calls the pastoral and history, but he weighs 'history' more as I mean 'experience' than as history as it is usually meant.

14. Wallerstein, *Studies in Seventeenth Century Poetic* (Madison, Wis., 1950) p. 336.

15. [Editor's note.] To the scholarly and critical studies introduced by Professor Miner (see note 1) may be added: Ruel E. Foster, 'A Tonal Study: Marvell's "Nymph . . ." ', in *University of Kansas City Review*, XXI (1954) 73–8; Leo Spitzer, 'Marvell's "Nymph . . . ": sources *versus* meaning', in *Modern Language Quarterly*, XXI (Sept 1958) 231–43, reprinted in *Seventeenth Century English Poetry*, ed. W. R. Keast (New York, 1962) pp. 305–20; Jack E. Reese, 'Marvell's "Nymph" in a New Light', in *Études anglaises*, XVIII (Oct–Dec 1965) 398–401, and the reply by Pierre Legouis, ibid, 402–3; Geoffrey H. Hartman, ' "The Nymph . . . ": a brief allegory', in *Essays in Criticism*, XVIII (April 1968) 113–35.

Select Bibliography

BIBLIOGRAPHY

Theodore Spencer and Mark van Doren, *Studies in Metaphysical Poetry 1912–38* (Columbia U.P., 1939).

Lloyd E. Berry, *A Bibliography of Studies in Metaphysical Poetry 1939–60* (U. of Wisconsin P., 1964).

There is a comprehensive, annotated bibliography to 1926 in Pierre Legouis, *André Marvell* (1928). Both Hofmann and Toliver contain lengthy bibliographies.

CRITICISM: BOOKS AND MONOGRAPHS

Andrew Marvell 1621–78; tercentenary tributes, ed. W. H. Bagguley Oxford U.P., 1922; Russell & Russell, 1965).

Andrew Marvell, ed. G. de F. Lord (Prentice-Hall, 1968).

M. C. Bradbrook and M. G. Lloyd Thomas, *Andrew Marvell* (Cambridge U.P., 1940).

Dennis Davison, *Marvell's Poems* (Arnold, 1964; Barron, 1964).

Klaus Hofmann, *Das Bild in Andrew Marvells lyrischen Gedichten* (Carl Winter, 1967).

Lawrence W. Hyman, *Andrew Marvell* (Twayne, 1964).

Pierre Legouis, *André Marvell: poète, puritain, patriote, 1621–78* (Didier, 1928; Russell & Russell, 1965).

——*Andrew Marvell: poet, puritan, patriot* (Clarendon, 1965; rev. 2nd ed. 1968).

J. B. Leishman, *The Art of Marvell's Poetry* (Hutchinson, 1966; Minerva Press, 1968).

John Press, *Andrew Marvell* (Longmans, 1958).

Victoria Sackville-West, *Andrew Marvell* (Faber, 1929).

Harold E. Toliver, *Marvell's Ironic Vision* (Yale U.P., 1965).

John M. Wallace, *Destiny His Choice* (Cambridge U.P., 1968).

CRITICISM: ARTICLES AND ESSAYS

D. C. Allen, 'Marvell's Nymph', in *Journal of English Literary History*,
XXIII (June 1956) 93–111; reprinted, with 'Upon Appleton House'
in Allen, *Image and Meaning: metaphoric traditions in renaissance
poetry* (Johns Hopkins P., 1960) pp. 93–114, 115–53.

Carl E. Bain, 'The Latin Poetry of Andrew Marvell', in *Philological
Quarterly*, XXXVIII (Oct 1959) 436–49.

Joan Bennett, *Five Metaphysical Poets* (Cambridge U.P., 1964).

Francis Berry, *Poet's Grammar* (Routledge, 1958; Hillary House, 1958).

Ann Evans Berthoff, 'The Allegorical Metaphor: Marvell's "The Definition of Love"', in *Review of English Studies*, XVII (Feb 1966) 16–29.

—— 'The Voice of Allegory: Marvell's "The Unfortunate Lover"',
in *Modern Language Quarterly*, XXVII (March 1966) 41–50.

James F. Carens, 'Andrew Marvell's Cromwell Poems', in *Bucknell
Review*, VII (May 1957) 41–70.

Paola Colaiacomo, 'Alcuni Aspetti della Poesia di Andrew Marvell',
in *English Miscellany*, XI (1960) 75–111.

Rosalie L. Colie, 'Marvell's "Bermudas" and the Puritan Paradise', in
Renaissance News, X (Summer 1957) 75–9.

John S. Coolidge, 'Marvell and Horace', in *Modern Philology*, LXIII
(Nov 1965) 111–20.

Patrick Cruttwell, 'The War's and Fortune's Son' in *Essays in Criticism*,
II (Jan 1952) 24–37; adapted and incorporated in Cruttwell, *The
Shakespearean Moment* (Chatto, 1954; Columbia U.P., 1955).

Dennis Davison, 'Marvell's "Definition of Love"', in *Review of English
Studies*, VI (April 1955) 141–6. (And see F. Kermode in *RES* VII
(April 1956) 183–5; D. M. Schmitter and Pierre Legouis, in
RES XII (Feb 1961) 49–51, 51–4.)

Barbara Everett, 'Marvell's "The Mower's Song"', in *Critical Quarterly*,
IV (Autumn 1962) 219–24.

S. L. Goldberg, 'Marvell: Self and Art', in *Critical Review*, Melbourne-
Sydney, VIII (1965) 32–44.

Joan Hartwig, 'The Principle of Measure in "To his Coy Mistress"', in
College English, XXV (May 1964) 572–5.

G. R. Hibbard, 'The Country House Poem of the Seventeenth Century', in *Journal of the Warburg and Courtauld Institute*, XIX (Jan-
June 1956) 159–74.

John Hollander, *The Untuning of the Sky: ideas of music in English
poetry, 1500–1700* (Princeton U.P., 1961).

Lawrence W. Hyman, 'Marvell's "Garden"', in *Journal of English Literary History*, XXV (March 1958) 13–22.

—— 'Politics and Poetry in Andrew Marvell', in *PMLA*, LXXIII (Dec 1958) 475–9.

G. de Forest Lord, 'From Contemplation to Action: Marvell's poetic career', in *Philological Quarterly*, XLVI (April 1967) 207–24.

Isabel MacCaffrey, 'Some Notes on Marvell's Poetry Suggested by a Reading of his Prose', in *Modern Philology*, LXI (May 1964) 261–9. (And see Kitty Datta, in *MP* LXIII (May 1966) 319–21.)

William A. McQueen, 'The Missing Stanzas in Marvell's *Hortus*', in *Philological Quarterly*, XLIV (April 1965) 173–9.

Joseph A. Mazzeo, *Renaissance and Seventeenth Century Studies* (Columbia U.P., 1962; Routledge, 1962); includes 'Cromwell as Machiavellian Prince', from *Journal of the History of Ideas*, XXI (Jan–March 1960) 1–17, and 'Cromwell as Davidic King', from *Reason and Imagination*, ed. J. A. Mazzeo (Columbia U.P., 1962; Routledge, 1962) pp. 29–55.

Earl Miner, 'The "Poetic Picture, Painted Poetry" of "The Last Instructions to a Painter"', in *Modern Philology*, LXIII (May 1966) 288–94.

Kenneth Muir, 'Andrew Marvell', in *University of Leeds Review*, III (Dec 1952) 128–35.

Ruth Nevo, *The Dial of Virtue* (Princeton U.P., 1963).

—— 'Marvell's "Songs of Innocence and Experience"', in *Studies in English Literature*, V (Winter 1965) 1–22.

S. Gorley Putt, 'Mosaiques of the Air', in *English*, II (Autumn 1939) 366–75.

Maren-Sofie Røstvig, 'Andrew Marvell's "The Garden": A Hermetic Poem', in *English Studies*, XL (April 1959) 65–76; adapted and incorporated in Røstvig, *The Happy Man*, 2nd ed. (Norwegian Universities P., 1962).

J. E. Saveson, 'Marvell's "On a Drop of Dew"', in *Notes and Queries*, V NS (July 1958) 289–90.

Kitty Scoular, *Natural Magic: studies in the presentation of Nature in English poetry from Spenser to Marvell* (Oxford U.P., 1965).

Donal Smith, 'The Political Beliefs of Andrew Marvell', in *University of Toronto Quarterly*, XXXVI (Oct 1966) 55–67.

Daniel Stempel, '"The Garden": Marvell's Cartesian ecstasy', in *Journal of the History of Ideas*, XXVIII (Jan–March 1967) 99–114.

Stanley Stewart, *The Enclosed Garden* (U. of Wisconsin P., 1966).

James R. Sutherland, 'A Note on the Satirical Poetry of Andrew Marvell', in *Philological Quarterly*, XLV (Jan 1966) 46–53.

H. R. Swardson, *Poetry and the Fountain of Light* (U. of Missouri P., 1962; Allen & Unwin, 1962).

R. H. Syfret, 'Marvell's "Horatian Ode" ', in *Review of English Studies*, XII (May 1961) 160–72.

E. M. W. Tillyard, *Poetry Direct and Oblique* (Chatto, 1934; Macmillan 1934).

Leonard Unger, *The Man in the Name* (U. of Minneapolis P., 1956).

Ruth Wallerstein, *Studies in Seventeenth Century Poetic* (U. of Wisconsin P., 1950).

Frank J. Warnke, 'Play and Metamorphosis in Marvell's Poetry', in *Studies in English Literature*, V (Winter 1965) 23–30.

C. V. Wedgwood, *Poetry and Politics Under the Stuarts* (Cambridge U.P., 1960).

John Wheatcroft, 'Andrew Marvell and the Winged Chariot', in *Bucknell Review*, VI (Dec 1956) 22–53.

George Williamson, 'The Context of Marvell's *Hortus* and "Garden" ', in *Modern Language Notes*, LXXVI (Nov 1961) 590–8; reprinted with 'Bias in Marvell's "Horatian Ode" ', in Williamson, *Milton and Others* (U. of Chicago P., 1965; Faber, 1965).

Notes on Contributors

A. ALVAREZ is a freelance writer and reviewer in England. His books include *The School of Donne*, *The Shaping Spirit*, *Beyond All this Fiddle* and *Under Pressure*.

F. W. BATESON was a fellow of Corpus Christi College and lecturer in English at the University of Oxford. He is the author of *English Comic Drama 1700–1750*, *English Poetry and the English Language*, *English Poetry*, *Wordsworth*, and *A Guide to English Literature*. He is founder and co-editor of *Essays in Criticism*.

CLEANTH BROOKS is Gray Professor of Rhetoric at Yale University. He is author of *The Hidden God*, *The Well Wrought Urn*, *Modern Poetry and the Tradition* and *William Faulkner: the Yoknapatawpha Country*. He collaborated with Robert Penn Warren on *Understanding Poetry*.

DOUGLAS BUSH is Gurney Professor of English at Harvard University. He is author of *The Renaissance Tradition in English Poetry*, *Classical Influences in Renaissance Literature*, *Science and English Poetry*, *Paradise Lost in Our Time*, and *English Literature in the Earlier Seventeenth Century*.

J. V. CUNNINGHAM is Professor of English at Brandeis University. He is author of *Woe and Wonder: the emotional effects of Shakespearean Tragedy*, and *Tradition and Poetic Structure*.

T. S. ELIOT, who died in 1965, was one of the most distinguished poets of the twentieth century and is well known for his *Prufrock*, *The Waste Land*, and *Four Quartets*. His plays include *Murder in the Cathedral* and *The Cocktail Party*. He was an original and immensely influential critic, and his essays are collected in *Selected Essays, On Poetry and Poets* and other volumes.

WILLIAM EMPSON is Professor of English Literature at the University of Sheffield. His critical studies include *Seven Types of Ambiguity. Some Versions of Pastoral* (in U.S.A.: *English Pastoral Poetry*), *The Structure of Complex Words* and *Milton's God*. His *Collected Poems* appeared in 1955.

JOHN EDWARD HARDY is Professor of English at the University of South Alabama. He is author of *Man in the Modern Novel* and *The Curious Frame*. He collaborated with Cleanth Brooks on *Poems of Mr John Milton*.

CHRISTOPHER HILL is Master of Balliol College, Oxford. An historian, his works include *The English Revolution 1640, The Century of Revolution* and *The Intellectual Origins of the English Revolution*.

FRANK KERMODE is Lord Northcliffe Professor of Modern English Literature at University College, London. He is author of *The Romantic Image, Wallace Stevens, Puzzles and Epiphanies* and *The Sense of an Ending*. He has edited *English Pastoral Poetry from the Beginnings to Marvell* and *Selected Poems of Andrew Marvell*.

F. R. LEAVIS was a fellow of Downing College, Cambridge, and has been Visiting Professor in English Literature at the University of York. He was an editor of *Scrutiny*. He is author of *New Bearings in English Poetry, Revaluation, The Common Pursuit, The Great Tradition* and '*Anna Karenina*' *and Other Essays*.

J. B. LEISHMAN, who died in 1963, was a senior lecturer in English Literature in the University of Oxford and fellow of St John's College. He was author of *The Art of Marvell's Poetry, The Metaphysical Poets, The Monarch of Wit, Translating Horace* and *Themes and Variations in Shakespeare's Sonnets*. He was a translator of Rilke and Hölderlin.

EARL W. MINER is Professor of English at the University of California at Los Angeles. He is author of *Dryden's Poetry* and *The Japanese Tradition in British and American Literature*.

MAREN-SOFIE RØSTVIG teaches English at the University of Oslo. She is author of *The Happy Man* and *The Hidden Sense*.

J. H. SUMMERS is Professor of English at Washington University, St Louis. He has edited the Dell edition of *Andrew Marvell: Poems* and is author of *George Herbert* and *The Muse's Method*, a study of *Paradise Lost*.

E. W. TAYLER is an assistant professor in English Literature at Columbia University. He is author of *Nature and Art in Renaissance Literature*.

MICHAEL WILDING is a senior lecturer in English Literature at the University of Sydney. He is author of *Milton's 'Paradise Lost'*.

Index

Addison, Joseph 15, 22; *Spectator* 13

Aikin, John 22; *General Biography* 18

Airy, Osmund 30

Aitken, G. A. 31

Allen, Don Cameron 216–17, 222, 225, 229, 277, 279; *Image and Meaning* 230n, 231n, 232n, 286; 'Marvell's "Nymph"' 283n

Alvarez, A. 182–93, 289

Ambrose, St 218

'AMETAS AND THESTYLIS' 14, 16, 28, 86, 250

Anacreon 205

Anderson, Robert (*Poets of Great Britain*) 17

Andrewes, Lancelot (*XCVI Sermons*) 92n

'APPLETON HOUSE' 17, 19–20, 23, 27, 30–1, 34–5, 42, 49, 72, 74, 76, 79–83, 86, 90n, 111, 132, 134, 142–147, 150, 182, 196, 210–12, 215–32, 255–8, 261–2, 265–6, 269, 271n, 272n, 281–2

Arnold, Matthew 26–7 and n

Asclepiades 208, 213n

Aubrey, John 10; *Brief Lives* 10n, 91n

Auden, W. H. 160

Augustine, St 225; *City of God* 230n

Ayloffe, John 13; *Marvell's Ghost* 12

Bacon, Francis 75

Baroni, Leonora 201

Bartas, Du 231n

Bateson, F. W. 39, 165–81, 289; *English Poetry* 90n, 289

Baudelaire, Charles 46, 49

Baxter, Richard 66–7; *A Holy Commonwealth* 90n

Bayley, Lewis ('A Divine Colloquy between the Soul and her Saviour') 91–2n

Beardsley, M. C. *see* Wimsatt

Beeching, H. C. 32

'BELLIPOTENS VIRGO' 14, 17

Belloc, Hilaire 102

Benlowes, Edward 91n, 218, 226–7, 231n; *Theophila* 216, 232n

Benson, A. C. 31

Berkeley, George 167

'BERMUDAS' 17, 19, 21, 23–6, 28, 30, 35, 81, 84, 146, 149, 185, 196

'BILL-BOROW, UPON THE HILL AND GROVE AT' 17, 42, 83–4, 143, 196, 210

Bird, Otto 163n

Birrell, Augustine (*Andrew Marvell*) 31n, 32

'BLAKE'S VICTORY, ON' 14, 42, 88–9

'BLOOD'S STEALING THE CROWN, ON' 14–16, 43

Blundeville, Thomas (*Exercises*) 202n

Book of Quinte Essence 222

Bowles, William Lisle 17

Bradbrook, M. C. 38, 70, 90, 127; 'Marvell and the Poetry of Rural Solitude' 139n; and Thomas, M.G. Lloyd (*Andrew Marvell*) 90n–92n, 139 and n, 271n, 278, 283n

Brant, R. L. 35n

'BRITANNIA AND RAWLEIGH' 17

Brittin, Norman A. 33n

Broadbent, J. B. (*Poetic Love*) 37

Brooks, Cleanth 38–9, 93–113, 114–124, 289

Brown, John (*John Bunyan*) 91n

Brown, Stuart Gerry *see* Thomas, Wright

Browne, William (*Britannia's Pastorals*) 279

Browning, Robert 56

Bruno, Giordano 129, 216

Buckingham, 2nd Duke of 42, 90n

Bunyan, John 91n

Burke, Edmund 16; *Correspondence* 16n

Burnet, Bishop (*History of My Own Time*) 11

Bush, Douglas 39, 114–24, 289; *English Literature in the Earlier Seventeenth Century* 14n, 163n

Butler, Samuel 19; *Hudibras* 16

Butt, John 40

Campbell, Thomas (*Specimens of the British Poets*) 17

Campion, Thomas 141

Carew, T. 134, 182, 214n; *Poems* 194; 'Rapture' 130, 133

Carler, Edmund (*History of the University of Cambridge*) 15

Carlisle, Earl of 43

Carlyle, Thomas 30

Carroll, Lewis 187

Castiglione, Balthazar of 137; *The Book of the Courtier* 140n

Catullus 47–9, 205–7, 209

Chalmers, Alexander (*English Poets*) 17

Chambers, E. K. 31–2, 36

Chapman, George 138

'CHARACTER OF HOLLAND' 19–20, 30, 42–3

Charles I 46, 96, 98, 100–1, 103–4, 106, 109, 113, 121

Chaucer, Geoffrey 58

Christie, W. D. 29

Churchill, Charles ('The Author') 11

Clare, John 22

Clarendon, Earl of 110–11

'CLARINDON'S HOUSE-WARMING' 43

Cleveland, John 59, 160, 182, 186, 188 210–11; *Poems* 163n, 194; 'To the State of Love' 210; 'Upon Phillis Walking' 160, 210

Clifford, Thomas 43

'CLIMB AT COURT' 14, 20, 35

'CLORINDA AND DAMON' 83, 146, 251, 253, 265

Coleridge, Hartley 30; *Biographia Borealis* 22

Coleridge, Samuel Taylor 21, 36, 50, 53; *Notebooks* 21n

Collins, William 49, 54

Conceit(s) 26–9, 31–2, 36, 55, 58, 63n, 68, 159, 162, 186–8, 193, 200, 282

Cooke, Thomas 14–16

'CORONET, THE' 17, 27, 78, 154, 182, 233-48, 267-8

Cowley, Abraham 17-18, 22, 46, 48, 54-5, 69, 129-30, 132, 182-3, 191, 207, 209; 'Anacreontics' 46; 'My Dyet' 205; *The Mistress* 194, 201, 205; 'The Muse' 136; *Verses lately written upon several Occasions* 213n

'COY MISTRESS, TO HIS' 13-14, 19, 23-4, 26, 28, 30, 39, 46, 50, 73-74, 87, 91n, 92n, 150, 155-64, 182, 190, 196, 203-10, 268

Craik, G. L. (*Sketches of the History of Literature and Learning in England*) 24-5

Crashaw, Richard 68, 182, 183, 195, 197; *Epigrammata Sacra* 198; *Steps to the Temple* 194; 'The Weeper' 198

Cromwell, Oliver 11, 67, 69, 79, 85-86, 89, 90n, 92n, 93-112, 114-24, 184. See also 'DEATH OF O. C'; 'FIRST ANNIVERSARY'; 'HORATIAN ODE'

Cummings, R. M. 40

Cunningham, J. V. 155-64, 289

'DAMON THE MOWER' 14, 73-4, 76, 146, 148, 258, 261-2

Daniélou, Jean (*From Shadows to Reality*) 217, 230n, 231n, 232n

Dante 52-3, 58-9

'DAPHNIS AND CHLOE' 14, 17, 74, 250

Datta, Kitty 287

Davenant, Sir William (*Gondibert*) 194

Davies, H. Neville 40

Davies, Sir John (*Nosce Teipsum*) 139n

'DEATH OF LORD HASTINGS' 94

'DEATH OF O. C., ON' 36, 42, 88, 118

'DEFINITION OF LOVE' 38, 69-70, 76, 182, 189-90, 195-6, 201-4, 209

Defoe, Daniel 23; *Review* 12

Dennis, John 26-7; *Heroes of Literature* 28n; *Studies in English Literature* 28n

'DIALOGUE BETWEEN THE RESOLVED SOUL AND CREATED PLEASURE' 71-2, 149, 182

'DIALOGUE BETWEEN THE SOUL AND BODY' 20, 39, 71-2, 148, 165-81, 210, 267

'DIALOGUE BETWEEN THE TWO HORSES' 12, 14, 43

Dickinson, Emily 35

Dombras, T. T. ('Poetical Miscellanies') 14n

Donne, John 28, 68, 125-6, 141, 160, 182, 184, 186, 188, 190, 192-3, 195, 197, 200-3, 205, 209-10, 212, 268; 'Extasie' 60; *Songs and Sonets* 201, 203-4; 'The Sunne Rising' 268; 'Valediction' 201-2; 'The Will' 203

Doren, Mark van *see* Spencer

Dove, John (*The Life of Andrew Marvell, the Celebrated Patriot*) 22-3

Doughty, Oswald (*A Victorian Romantic*) 30n

Downing, Sir George 43

Drayton, Michael (*Second Nimphall*) 92n

'DROP OF DEW, ON A' 21, 27, 32, 86, 143, 182, 195, 197

Dryden, John 46, 53-4, 67, 69, 89, 182, 184; 'Epistle to the Whigs' 12; *Fables* 13; 'McFlecknoe' 16; *Miscellany Poems* 14; *Religio Laici* 12

Dunbar, H. Flanders (*Symbolism in Medieval Thought*) 230

Dunbar, William ('Lament for the Makaris') 163

Duncan, J. E. 32, 37; *The Revival of Metaphysical Poetry* 32n, 40

Duncan-Jones, E. E. 16n, 35n, 40

Dunn, E. Katharine 230n

Dutton, William 42, 196

'ELEGY UPON THE DEATH OF MY LORD FRANCIS VILLIERS' 94

Eliot, T. S. 36–8, 45–59, 91n, 141, 158–61, 163n, 182, 186, 191, 194, 267, 289–90; *Old Possum* 186

Ellis, George (*Specimens of English Poetry*) 17

Ellrodt, Robert 200; *Les Poètes métaphysiques anglais* 213n

Emblem books 129, 131, 171–2, 176, 179, 213n, 282. See also Freeman, Rosemary; Hawkins (*Partheneia*); Quarles

Emerson, Everett H. 271n, 283n–284n

Emerson, R. W. 33; *Journals* 33n; *Parnassus* 33

Empson, William 60–4, 134, 136, 182, 185, 290; *Seven Types of Ambiguity* 38; *Some Versions of Pastoral* 126

Evelyn, John (*Elysium Britannicum*) 91n

'EYES AND TEARS' 14, 20, 27, 35, 87, 182, 197–8

'FAIR SINGER, THE' 87, 182, 197, 200

Fairfax, Edward 130

Fairfax family 79, 84

Fairfax, Mary 42, 66, 82, 90n, 95, 187–8, 196, 219, 229, 230n, 271n

Fairfax, Thomas, Lord 42–3, 94–5, 187, 196, 215, 217–21, 226–7, 230,

272. See also 'APPLETON HOUSE'

Fane, Mildmay 91n, 127, 130

Fanshawe, Sir Richard (*Selected Parts of Horace*) 112

Ficino, Marsilio 128, 135, 225, 228, 232n

'FIRST ANNIVERSARY' 11, 14, 42, 73–4, 88–90, 117

Firth, Sir Charles Harding 119

Fitzgerald, Edward 30; *Letters and Literary Remains* 30n

Flaubert, Gustave (*Bouvard et Pécuchet*) 49

'FLECKNOE' 16, 18, 20, 28

Fletcher, John ('To the Reader') 271n

Fludd, Robert 216

Foix, François de 215

Foster, Ruel E. 284n

Freeman, Rosemary (*English Emblem Books*) 91n, 213n

'FURTHER ADVICE TO A PAINTER' 43

'GALLERY, THE' 141, 197

'GARDEN, THE' 14, 19–20, 26, 34–35, 39, 60–4, 76–7, 81, 91n, 125–40, 144–5, 196, 210, 218–19, 223, 225, 228–9, 269–70

Gautier, Théophile 46, 49

Gherus, R. (ed. *Deliciae C(entum) Poetarum Gallorum*) 213n

Gibbon, Edward (*Letters*) 15n

'GLO-WORMS, TO THE' see 'MOWER TO THE GLO-WORMS'

Gosse, Edmund (*From Shakespeare to Pope*) 30

Gray, Thomas 16, 49, 54

Greville, Sir Fulke (*Life of Sir Philip Sidney*) 91n

Grierson, Herbert 36; *Metaphysical Lyrics and Poems of the Seventeenth Century* 37

Griswold, R. W. (*Sacred Poets of England and America*) 35

Grosart, Alexander 29, 36; ed. *Works of Andrew Marvell* 90n, 284n

GROWTH OF POPERY 44

Grundy, Joan 231n

Guarini, Battista (*Il Pastor Fido*) 112, 128

Halifax, Marquess of: *Complete Works* 90n; *Letter to a Dissenter* 67

Hall, Bishop Joseph (*Meditations and Vows*) 91n

Hall, S. C. 23; *Book of Gems* 24, 33

Hallam, Henry (*Introduction to the Literature of Europe*) 25

Harding, Walter (*Emerson's Library*) 33n

Hardy, John E. 233–48, 290

Hardy, Thomas 38

Harrington, James 44, 66–7, 90n

Hart, E. F. 14n

Hartman, Geoffrey H. 284n

Hastings, Lord Henry 41

Hawkins, Henry (*Partheneia Sacra*) 131, 138, 139n. *See also* Emblem books

Hawthorne, Nathaniel (*The Scarlet Letter*) 35

Hazlitt, William 18–20, 27; *Complete Works* 19n; *The English Comic Writers* 18; *Lectures on the Age of Elizabeth* 19; *Lectures on the English Poets* 18; *Select British Poets* 17, 19

Herbert, George 143, 147, 182, 193, 195, 200; 'Affliction (I)' 184; 'The Collar' 184, 267–8; 'A Wreath' 154

Hermetic tradition 215–16, 222–3, 225–6, 228, 230. *See also* Bruno, Giordano

Herrick, Robert 162

Hill, Christopher 39, 65–92, 290

'HILL AND GROVE AT BILL-BOROW' *see* 'BILL-BOROW'

Hobbes, Thomas 167; *Leviathan* 82

Hobday, C. H. 92n

Holmes, O. W. 33; *Ralph Waldo Emerson* 33n

Hood, E. P. 27; *Andrew Marvell, the Wit, Statesman and Poet* 25

Hooker, Richard 167

Hookes, Nicholas ('To Amanda walking in the Garden') 91n

Hopkins, Gerard Manley 30; *Correspondence* 30n

Horace 161–2

'HORATIAN ODE, AN' (Cromwell Ode) 20, 22, 26–7, 31, 36, 38–9, 42, 46, 53, 55, 65–6, 69, 81, 84–6, 88, 91n, 93–124, 150, 183–4, 203, 269, 271n, 281–3

Horne, C. J. 26n

Hume, David 156, 167; *Philosophical Works* 163n

Hunt, Leigh 18–20 and n, 27, 30, 36; *Wit and Humour* 19, 24

'INSCRIBENDA LUPARAE' 43

Israeli, Isaac D' 22; *Quarrels of Authors* 21

Jeffrey, Francis 17

Johnson, Samuel: *Dictionary* 16; *Life of Cowley* 50

Jonson, Ben 46, 49, 53, 162, 171, 205–6; 'To the Memory of Sir Lucius Cary and Sir Henry Morison' 143

Keast, W. R. (ed. *Seventeenth Century English Poetry*) 124n, 284n

Keats, John 55–6, 61

Kelley, Maurice (*This Great Argument*) 93

Kermode, Frank 37 and n, 39 and n, 125–40, 272n, 286, 290; 'Two Notes on Marvell' 139n, 272n

King, A. H. 134; 'Some Notes on Marvell's Garden' 139n

King, Bishop 58

King, Bruce 39n

'KINGS VOWS' 43

Klonsky, Milton 125–6, 132

Laforgue, Jules 46, 49

Laing, Gordon J. *see* Shorey

Lamb, Charles 18–21; *Essays of Elia* 19n; *Letters* 19n; *Miscellaneous Prose* 19n

Landor, Walter Savage (*Imaginary Conversations*) 21

Lapide, Cornelius à 215

'LAST INSTRUCTIONS TO A PAINTER' 43

Leavis, F. R. 37 and n, 38–9, 165–81, 182, 290; *Revaluation* 37n, 165, 169–71, 178–9, 290

Le Comte, Edward S. 279–80, 283n

Legouis, Pierre 39 and n, 96, 102, 112, 231n, 277, 284n, 286; *André Marvell/Andrew Marvell* 33n, 35n, 38, 40, 94, 283n

Leigh, Richard 134, 136

Leishman, J. B. 194–214, 290; *The Art of Marvell's Poetry* 40, 280, 290

Lerner, Laurence 38

Letter from Amsterdam to a Friend in England, A (anon.) 10

'LETTER TO DOCTOR INGELO' 92n

'LETTER TO SIR JOHN TROTT' 43

Lewis, Cecil Day 69

Lewis, C. S. (*The Allegory of Love*) 91n

Lipsius 129–30; *De Constantia* 139n

'LITTLE T. C.' 24–6, 92n, 150–3, 182, 196–7, 257–8, 267

Locke, John 167

Love, Christopher 104

Lovelace, Richard 68, 127, 130, 133, 182; 'Against the Love of Great Ones' 133–4; 'Aramantha' 136–137; 'The Falcon' 282; 'The Grasse-hopper' 282; 'Love Made in the First Age' 130; 'Lucasta' 41, 194, 213n. *See also* 'NOBLE FRIEND'

Lowell, James Russell 35

Lowther, Lady Mary 21

'LOYALL SCOT, THE' 43

MacCaffrey, Isabel Gamble (*Paradise Lost as 'Myth'*) 231n

Macdonald, George 27–8

Machiavelli 121

MacLeish, Archibald 141–2

Mallett, David 15

Maniban, Joseph, verses to 17

Margoliouth, H. M. 14n, 94–7, 100, 103, 106–8, 112, 114, 119, 121; ed. *Poems and Letters of Andrew Marvell* 38, 40, 112, 163n, 181n, 213n, 279

Marlowe, Christopher ('Passionate Shepherd') 212

'MARRIAGE OF LORD FAUCONBERG AND LADY MARY CROMWELL' 42, 89, 249–50

Martz, Louis (*The Poetry of Meditation*) 38

Mason, William ('Ode to Independence') 11

Masson, David (*Life of Milton*) 65

'MATCH, THE' 182, 197

May, Tom 94–6; trans. *Pharsalia* 112–13. *See also* 'TOM MAY'S DEATH'

Melville, Herman (*Billy Budd*) 35

Merivale, Herman 27

Metaphysical tradition 36–8, 69, 114, 131, 139, 158, 165–6, 168, 170, 177, 179, 184, 188, 200

Meynell, Alice 31; *The Flower of the Mind* 31n

Meynell, Everard (*Life of Francis Thompson*) 31n

Milgate, Michael 35n

Miller, Bruce E. 164n

Milton, John 11, 41–3, 46–7, 53–5, 64–7, 75–6, 86, 88–9, 122, 128, 194, 236, 270; 'L'Allegro' 49, 212; *Christian Doctrine* 93; *Comus* 46; 'Ad Leonoram Romae canentem' 200; 'Lycidas' 26, 146, 233, 237; *Observations on the Articles of Peace* 123; *Paradise Lost* 93, 134, 227–8 (*see also* 'PARADISE LOST, ON'); 'Il Penseroso' 49, 212

Miner, Earl 273–84, 290

MISCELLANEOUS POEMS 11, 13, 39, 44, 250

Mises, Richard von (*Positivism*) 163n

Mitford, Mary Russell 27; *Recollections of a Literary Life* 25

Momigliano, E. (*Cromwell*) 92n

Montaigne, Michel de 127, 129–30; *Essayes* 139n

Montgomery, Robert (*The Christian Poet*) 17

Moore, Tom ('Canadian Boat Song') 21

Morris, William 51–3; 'Nymph's Song to Hylas' 51–2

Moseley, Humphrey 194

'MOURNING' 197–200

'MOWER AGAINST GARDENS', 74, 76, 129, 145, 261–3, 268–70

'MOWER TO THE GLO-WORMS' 20, 74, 149, 259–60, 262

Mower poems 197, 250, 255–66, 272n

'MOWER'S SONG' 74, 76, 146–7, 260, 262–4, 269–70

Mozart, Wolfgang Amadeus (*Don Giovanni*) 205

Muir, Kenneth 279, 283n

'MUSICKS EMPIRE' 14, 196–7

Nature 84, 125, 127–9, 141–54. *See also* Pastoral tradition

Nelthorpe, Edward 44

Neoplatonism 125–6, 215, 270. *See also* Platonism

Nethercot, A. H. 13n

Newcomb, Thomas (*Bibliotheca . . . a Modern Library*) 12–13

Nichols, John (*Select Collection of Poems*) 13

'NOBLE FRIEND MR RICHARD LOVELACE, TO HIS' 94. *See also* Lovelace

'NYMPH COMPLAINING FOR THE DEATH OF HER FAWN' 14, 17, 20, 24, 26, 28, 30, 33–4, 51–2, 55, 75, 77–8, 182, 185, 254–9, 262, 271n, 273–84

'On His Excellent Friend, Mr Andrew Marvell' (anon.) 11

Origen 218

Ormsby, John 28–9

Ovid 262–3; *Metamorphoses* 272n, 279

Oxenbridge, John 196

Palgrave, F. T. 30; *Golden Treasury* 26, 31, 45; *Landscape in Poetry* 26

Palmer, Mary 44

'PARADISE LOST, ON' 14, 16–17, 19–21, 43. *See also* Milton

Parker, Samue 21, 43, 67; *History of His Own Time* 10–11, 65; *Reproof* 10

Parsons, James (*Human Physiognomy Explained*) 15

Pascal, Blaise (*Lettres provinciales*) 89

Pasquier, Etienne ('On Amœna') 198–9; 'Ad Sabinam' 206–7

Pastoral hyperbole 210, 212, 213n, 259

Pastoral tradition 125, 128–9, 145–6, 196, 235–7, 249–71, 273, 275, 281–283, 284n. *See also* Nature

Paul, St 226

Peacock, J. D. 40

Pécuchet *see* Flaubert

Pepys, Samuel 66, 89

Phillips, J. R. (*Memoirs of the Civil War in Wales and the Marches*) 91n

Phillips, Katharine 130

Philo 218, 226

Pico della Mirandola (*De Imaginatione*) 140n

'PICTURE OF LITTLE T. C.' *see* 'LITTLE T. C.'

Plato 215, 226, 229; *Phaedrus* 224; *Republic* 139n; *Symposium* 128, 139n; *Timaeus* 224

Platonism 125, 127–9, 134–8, 223, 226, 228. *See also* Neoplatonism

Plotinus 125, 135, 137, 274

Poe, Edgar Allan 33–4, 53

POEMS ON AFFAIRS OF STATE 12

Pope, Alexander 46, 58, 168, 171, 177–8, 184; *Dunciad* 165–7, 170, 177–8; 'Windsor Forest' 17

Potts, A. F. (*The Elegiac Mode*) 21n

Prendergast, J. P. (*The Cromwellian Settlement of Ireland*) 91n

Primrose, Dr James (*Popular Errors*) 42

Puttenham, George 131, 135, 251–2,

262; *The Art of English Poesie* 91n, 271n

Quarles, Frances 138, 180–1; *Emblems* 91n, 179–80; *Enchiridion* 91n. *See also* Emblem books

Quiller-Couch, Arthur 32

Ralegh, Sir Walter (*History of the World*) 118

Randolph, Thomas 127, 130–1, 134

Rea, John 272n

Reed, Henry (*Lectures on the British Poets*) 27

Reese, Jack E. 284n

REHEARSAL TRANSPROS'D, THE, 10–11, 43, 181n, 284n

Reid, J. C. (*Francis Thompson Man and Poet*) 31n

'RESOLVED SOUL AND CREATED PLEASURE' 23

Richards, Irving T. 21n

Ridley, Sir Edward 113

Ritson, Joseph (*The English Anthology*) 17

Robbins, Caroline 32n

Rochester, John Wilmot, Earl of ('Tunbridge Wells') 11

Rogers, Henry 23, 35

Romance of the Rose 272n

Ronsard, Pierre 209, 213

Rosenberg, Isaac 36; *Collected Works* 37n

Røstvig, Maren-Sofie 215–32, 287, 291; *The Happy Man* 91n, 232n

Royalism 66, 69, 94, 102, 104, 111–112, 167, 282

Ruskin, John 30

Sackville-West, Victoria 62

Saint-Amant 127; *Jouissance* 130–

133, 135; 'La Métamorphose de Lyrian et de Sylvie' 133

St John, Oliver 42

Sainte-Beuve, C. A. 26–7 and n

Schmitter, D. M. 286

Secundus, Johannes 206, 208–9

Seneca (*Thyestes*) 99

Shakespeare, William 46, 49, 58; *Richard II* 91n

Sharp, R. L. (*From Donne to Dryden*) 13n

Shelley, Percy Bysshe 26, 55–6; 'To a Skylark' 21

Shiels, Robert (*The Lives of the Poets*) 15

Shirley, James ('The Garden') 91n

Shorey, Paul, and Laing, Gordon J. (*Odes and Epodes*) 164n

Sibbes, Richard (*The Soules Conflict*) 90n

Sidney, Philip 271n; *Apologie for Poetrie* 251

Simeone, William 113n

Smart, Christopher 16

MR SMIRKE; OR, THE DIVINE IN MODE 43

Smith, Goldwin 29

Spence, Joseph (*Observations, Anecdotes and Characters of Books and Men*) 12

Spenser, Edmund 272n; *The Faerie Queene* 75, 130; 'Hymns' 128; 'Hymne of Heavenly Beauty' 129, 137; 'November' 282; *Shepheardes Calender, The* 253, 272n

Spingarn, J. E. (*A History of Literary Criticism in the Renaissance*) 163n

Spitzer, Leo 284n

Stanley, Thomas 127, 130, 134–5; 'Apollo and Daphne' 133

'STATUE AT CHARING CROSS' 43

'STATUE IN STOCKS-MARKET' 43

Stevenson, R. L. 30; *Letters* 30n

Strode, William ('On Chloris walking in the Snow') 210, 213n–214n

Suckling, J. 211, 214n

Summers, Joseph H. 141–54, 272n, 291

Swift, Jonathan 23, 46, 90n, 92n; *Tale of a Tub* 11

Sylvester, Joshuah 231n

Symbolism 72, 91n, 129, 133, 137–8, 184–5, 217, 254, 266, 283

Talon, H. (*John Bunyan*) 91n

Tasso, Torquato 130, 210–11, 271n; *Aminta* 128, 208, 251; *Rime* 210, 213n

Tayler, E. W. 249–72, 291

Tennyson, Alfred Lord 26, 30; 'Maud' 30; 'The Princess' 30

Tennyson, Hallam 30; *Life and Works of Tennyson* 30n

Théophile de Viau 127, 131; 'Le Matin' 138

Thomas, M. G. Lloyd 70, 90, 127. *See also* Bradbrook

Thomas, Wright, and Brown, Stuart Gerry (ed. *Reading Poems*) 163n

Thompson, Edward 15–17, 22–3, 27, 29

Thompson, Francis 30–1 and n

Thompson, Richard 44

'THYRSIS AND DORINDA' 14, 41, 196, 251–3

Tibble, John and Anne (*John Clare: his life and poetry*) 22n

Tillotson, K. 26n

Toliver, Harold E. (*Marvell's Ironic Vision*) 284n

'TOM MAY'S DEATH' 42, 94–6, 111. *See also* May

Towne, Frank 164n

Townshend, Aurelian 182

Traherne, Thomas 68

Trench, R. C. (*Household Book of English Poetry*) 27–8

Trott, John 43

Tuckerman, Una Venable 21n

Tupper, F. S. 44

Tuve, Rosemond 169; *Elizabethan and Metaphysical Imagery* 38; *A Reading of George Herbert* 217

'TWO SONGS AT THE MARRIAGE OF LORD FAUCONBERG' *see* MARRIAGE

'UNFORTUNATE LOVER, THE' 35, 71, 76, 197

Vaughan, Henry 68, 91n, 138, 144; 'The Waterfall' 195

Vergil: *Aeneid* 279–81; *Fourth Eclogue* 251, 265

Villon, François 52

Vorfriede, Werner 277–8, 283n

Wain, John (*Interpretations*) 38

Wallace, John H. (*Destiny His Choice*) 39

Waller, Edmund 11, 69, 211, 214n; *Poems* 194, 211

Wallerstein, Ruth 282; *Studies in Seventeenth Century Poetic* 126–7, 284n

Walley, Harold R., and Wilson, J. Harold (*The Anatomy of Literature*) 163n

Walton, Geoffrey 37 and n; *From Metaphysical to Augustan* 37 and n

Warburton, E. (*Memoirs of Prince Rupert and the Cavaliers*) 92n

Ward, T. H. (*English Poets*) 29

Warren, Robert Penn 38, 109; 'Bearded Oaks' 142

Warwick, P. (*Memoirs of the Reign of Charles I*) 92n

Watts, Isaac 15, 187

White, Gilbert 16

Whiting, Nathaniel ('Upon Bellama's Walking in the Garden') 91n

Whitney, Geoffrey (*A Choice of Emblemes and other Devises*) 213n. *See also* Emblem books

Whittier, John Greenleaf 34–5

Wild, Robert ('The Death of Mr Christopher Love') 104

Wilding, Michael 10–40, 291

Wilkins, W. W. (*Political Ballads of the 17th and 18th Centuries*) 27

Williamson, George (*The Donne Tradition*) 37

Williamson, Karen 283n

Wilson, J. Harold *see* Walley

Wilmot, John, Earl of Rochester *see* Rochester

Wimsatt, W. K. and Beardsley, M. C. ('The Intentional Fallacy') 96

Winstanley, Gerrard (*Fire in the Bush*) 91n

Wither, George (*Hallelujah*) 91n

Witty, Doctor 42

Wood, Anthony à 11; *Athenae Oxonienses* 11n

Wordsworth, William 55, 63, 68, 266; *Early Letters* 21n; 'Great Men' 21; 'Intimations of Immortality' 21

Wrangham, Francis (*The British Plutarch*) 17

Yates, F. A. (*The French Academies of the Sixteenth Century*) 139n

'YOUNG LOVE' 14, 17